Prai

STORY INTELLIGENCE

"No matter what it says on your business card, you're in the story business. That's why you need this insightful and actionable book. *Story Intelligence* will equip you with the tools to master storytelling—and the inspiration to use narrative as a force for learning, transformation, and possibility."

—Daniel H. Pink
Author of *New York Times* Best-Selling
When, Drive, and *To Sell Is Human*

"The genius of this book isn't the invention of something new; it's the discovery of a truth we all know intuitively, hidden in plain sight—that story is arguably, in the authors' words, the most powerful force in the nonphysical world. We use it every day. Not only does this book reveal the power of story, but it also identifies the sources of that power and illustrates how to employ it in every aspect of our lives. It has been the most relied upon tool in my career as a speaker and as president of High Point University. We are all stories in motion. Our phenomenal success at HPU has been a function of creating an educational experience that is aligned with the aspirational stories of the best and brightest young women and men in the world and being a catalyst in the achievement of their highest potential. We know our success is a function of our students' success. Thank you, Rick and Scott, for your great insights and making it available to everyone."

—Dr. Nido R. Qubein
President, High Point University

"In recent years, much has been written about the power of stories to shape and give meaning to our lives, but nothing comes near to the encyclopedic treatment given in *Story Intelligence*. It is deep and delightful. Dive in and enjoy yourself."

—Sam Keen
New York Times Best-Selling Author of
Fire in the Belly and *To Love and Be Loved*

"All of us can benefit greatly from seeing the world through a more positive lens. The narratives we adopt in our personal and professional lives, and the social scripts we foster and share with others, when anchored in optimism and meaning, can reinforce our belief that what we think and do matters. It can also propel us forward in challenging times. In *Story Intelligence*, Livengood and Stone make these concepts come to life in a practical way. This book is a valuable read for anyone who wants to make a positive impact with their lives."

—Shawn Achor
New York Times Best-Selling Author of
The Happiness Advantage and *Big Potential*

"Stone and Livengood have written the book of the decade. They offer an original and profound view of why one must discover their latent Story Intelligence and master the art of storytelling to live a life full of meaning, purpose, and salience. This is a visionary, hopeful, and practical book that takes the reader through very tangible steps of realizing the seven powers of story."

—Arvind Singhal
Endowed Professor of Communication,
University of Texas at El Paso
Author of the Award-Winning *Entertainment-Education*

"Richard Stone and Scott Livengood have created the definitive book on storytelling. So much has been written on this in recent years. Not since Joseph Campbell's seminal work on myth have all the disparate elements been brought together in one cohesive whole. Nor has a book emerged as compelling or emotionally rewarding to read. This is it. If you have any interest in storytelling or consider yourself deeply educated, you must read this book. You will be glad you started it from the first page right on through the last. A jewel of a guide filled with practical tips and a plethora of irresistible resources."

—Seth Kahan
Author of *Getting Change Right*

"Why storytelling? Nothing else works. Whether you're trying to make sense of today's world of tumultuous change or influencing how others deal with it, Stone and Livengood's *Story Intelligence* is the comprehensive, practical guide to effective storytelling that you need."

—Stephen Denning
Author of *The Leader's Guide to Storytelling* and *The Age of Agile*

"The ideas in *Story Intelligence* are groundbreaking and revolutionary. The pacing is perfect for both understanding and thoughtful learning, and the authors expand our core human skills so well that you completely buy that you will be far better off with the new capabilities they deliver in these startlingly essential pages. This is the real deal, a mind-expanding tour de force."

—Dan Abelow
Inventor of the Expandiverse
Founder of Everybody Rise

"Twenty-seven years ago, I was teaching an undergraduate class at Vanderbilt University. The topic was symbolism, and one of the prime foci was story. I knew a bit about it but tracked down Richard Stone, who knew a lot. He agreed to be a guest speaker, and my life, as well as the students', would never be the same. He invited the students to share their stories. Trepidation soon melted into laughter, tears, and some awfully good narratives. As the session drew to an end, students wondered how, after several semesters, they had missed crucial aspects of each other. They left with a shared commitment to honor the world of fable and narrative. Since that time, my devotion to fable and fiction has since moved into business, healthcare, education, and the military. Richard Stone and Scott Livengood have produced in *Story Intelligence* the finest and most comprehensive piece of work in the world. It is a delicious blend of theory and story. Reading the book will change your life, enhance your leadership, and bring some new vim and vigor to your organization."

—Terrence Deal
Author of *How Great Leaders Think* and *Leading with Soul*

"Richard Stone and Scott Livengood take their years of listening to stories, years of telling stories, and years of research in the literature to define a new framework that can give insight into the power of storytelling in our lives. What I enjoyed most were the findings and stories they present from the literature as any good storyteller will—and do so to great effect. If you have a question about storytelling, you will find the answer here, told through copious use of stories. How clever!"

—Madelyn Blair
Author of International Best-Seller *unlocked*

"This is a most timely and important book—one that has far-reaching implications at every level: educational, political, economic, and global. Above all, it shows how the most intractable of human conflicts can be resolved once we start to listen to each other's stories!"

—James Roose-Evans
Author of *Older*, *Inner Journey Outer Journey*, and *Finding Silence*

"*Story Intelligence* is a powerful and groundbreaking book. Story and storytelling are as universal to human beings as life itself. When we express our own stories—as *Story Intelligence* teaches us to do—we live far better and more deeply. Captivating, an important read."

—Michael Gurian
New York Times Best-Selling Author of *Saving Our Sons*,
The Minds of Girls, and *Leadership and the Sexes*

"At some level, we all know the power of story to captivate our minds and leave us with precious lessons and colorful memories that often last a lifetime. Very few of us, though, have stopped to explore the nature of stories themselves. These authors have indeed done all of that exploration for us. The research and thought that went into this book is so impressive and lays a strong foundation for anyone who wants to truly understand and better use the power of story in their own work."

—Beverly Kaye
Author of *Up Is Not the Only Way* and *Love 'Em or Lose 'Em*

"As president of Pacific Crest for over thirty years, I have worked with thousands of faculty members and college students. During that time, I have used storytelling as an instrumental tool to produce transformational change. Once I read *Story Intelligence*, I saw so many opportunities to strengthen my abilities using the numerous examples, practical insights, and techniques presented throughout the book. As a result, I have already become more effective, inspiring, and transformational in all of my endeavors."

—Dan Apple
President, Pacific Crest
Author of *The Professional's Guide to Self-Growth* and *Learning to Learn*

"Stories, the ones we tell ourselves and the ones that inspire and inform us, not only shape our lives but our realities. I have learned from experience that among the best stories we can master are those that allow us to see our next steps clearly, to face the future eyes wide open, with courage and dignity. Without these worthy companions, we can easily confront our lesser selves. This book will help us all to be better creators of our own realities through mastering the narratives we hold true."

—Isaac Lidsky
New York Times Best-Selling Author of *Eyes Wide Open*

"While I have been a fan of Gardner's work on emotional intelligence for years, as a leader working on shaping the future through embedding increased levels of positivity in hundreds of major organizations and school districts around the world, I also knew it was only half the story. Social scripts are unwritten rules that dictate how we think and behave together. These are the narratives, good or bad, that determine the collective mindset and rules of engagement inside our organizations—they become institutionalized patterns of thought and behavior. *Story Intelligence* provides that other half. Creating meaningful narratives in our personal and professional lives makes it all possible."

—Greg Ray
Cofounder and CEO, International Thought Leader Network

"I want to thank Scott and Rick for the epiphany this fascinating book has provided me. I love my profession as a surgeon and a researcher in the area of regenerative medicine. I now have a new lens to view the source of satisfaction it gives me. Each of the patients I care for has had their story, at least the one they had anticipated, derailed to a greater or lesser degree. In the context of story, it's my job to restore their story, the life and possibilities that were ahead of them before their health issue. I know anyone who reads *Story Intelligence* will discover a richer landscape and language to interpret their pursuits in life."

—Anthony Atala, MD
G. Link Professor and Director
Wake Forest Institute for Regenerative Medicine,
Wake Forest School of Medicine

STORY
INTELLIGENCE

STORY
INTELLIGENCE

Master Story, Master Life

UNLEASH *the* FULL POTENTIAL
of YOUR IQ *and* EQ
USING *the* 7 POWERS *of* STORY

Richard Stone & Scott Livengood

BOOKLOGIX®
Alpharetta, GA

ISBN: 978-1-61005-980-0 – Paperback
ISBN: 978-1-61005-983-1 – Hardcover
eISBN: 978-1-61005-981-7 – ePub
eISBN: 978-1-61005-982-4 – mobi

Library of Congress Control Number: 2021901755

Printed in the United States of America   0 2 1 8 2 1

⊗This paper meets the requirements of ANSI/NISO Z39.48-1992 (Permanence of Paper)

Richard

To my wife, Elizabeth, who has been by my side for over thirty years now, whose love, wisdom, and grounding in life have been a catalyst for my own growth and learning.

To my father, Leon, who drilled me for hours as a child with vocabulary cards. And my mother, Phyllis, who was an accomplished actress and used to schlep me to the community theater for her rehearsals. I owe them a debt of gratitude for the development of my skills as a writer and communicator. Before he died, my dad encouraged me to write another book, but at the time I wasn't sure I had anything important to say to readers. Thanks for anticipating this book long before I did.

To my Native American teachers, Paula Underwood and Larry Littlebird. Paula's wisdom and insights still resonate in my life to this day and continue to inform much of my thinking about learning and teaching. My good friend Larry Littlebird, who has returned to live on the land at Hamaatsa, has been a constant reminder to listen deeply to the story of the earth that's calling out to all of us to wake up and see.

And to Rabbi Zalman Schachter-Shalomi, may his memory be a blessing, who introduced me to the wisdom tales from the Jewish tradition. And to the twentieth-century philosopher Martin Buber, whose understanding of the sacredness of all relationships has been an essential touchstone for how I think about transformation and healing.

Scott

I am privileged to dedicate this book to the three people who have illuminated my world and my reason for being in it.

First, my love and spiritual partner (and wife), Michelle Livengood, who opened my heart to the depths and expansiveness of what love can and should be. Her kindness and caring are a blessing to me and to all who know her.

Next, to my teacher, mentor, and loving friend, Sam Keen. His prodigious intellect and "keen" insights into how our stories become the mythology that governs our life choices, and consequently, our life experience, whether individually or as a collective body, opened and liberated my mind to a world of possibilities that have enriched my life beyond measure.

And last, while he left the world before I had the chance to know him personally, Joseph Campbell has been my teacher and mentor through his books, recorded interviews, and lectures. He challenged, informed, and enlightened me to follow a path to know the true "me" that is my soul, which has been, to paraphrase him, "the privilege of my lifetime."

To those special people who have been my teachers and soul partners, to all the other souls who have been central to my life story with whom I've shared both joy and pain, and to the souls who will one day participate in my life story, I dedicate this book with equal measures of love and gratitude.

Contents

Note from the Authors

Richard Stone

My first conscious encounter with storytelling occurred in the fall of 1989. However, in retrospect, I now recognize I had been a storyteller for my whole life without assigning the label "storyteller" to my work and play. For as long as I remember, I have enjoyed telling tall tales to friends with the straightest of faces. I unconsciously had joined a centuries-old tradition that was perfected in this country by the likes of Mark Twain, who loved to weave plausible details into whopping lies. It's my way of being playful with friends.

Interestingly, my love for telling stories found its way into developing an award-winning board game called Pitch-A-Story I co-created with a friend in the TV business, Rhett Banning. While we aimed to create an entertaining, fun, and engaging game, we recognized early on that making up and enacting stories is one of the best predictors of children's success in reading and all academic subjects. So, we teamed with an instructional designer and included a guide for teachers.

Early in my advertising career, I relied on stories to engage commercial audiences without overtly describing my writing as storytelling. Years ago, while in prep school in New England, we had a cross-country runner nicknamed "Thunder Thighs" who dominated other regional schools. As I sat down to write a radio commercial for a men's clothing chain in the '80s, suddenly images of Thunder Thighs cresting a hill with his competitors far behind wove their way into an award-winning commercial for jeans.

Long before the brand world discovered the importance of story, story found me.

When I decided to sell my ad agency without any clue what life had in store, I was returning on a backpacking trip on a plane seated next to a couple who were also hikers. What do backpackers do when they first meet? Exchange tales about the trails they have hiked, of course. Somewhere in the conversation, they asked if I had ever been to the National Storytelling Festival. I had never heard of this event, but weeks later joined them on a trip to Jonesborough, Tennessee. I found myself sitting in the audience listening to Michael Cotter, a fourth-generation farmer from Minnesota, as he spoke about the things he witnessed while growing up on the land. I had an epiphany. Turning to my friends, I declared this is what I felt called to do with the rest of my years. Since then, I tell people to be careful whom they sit next to on a plane—it can change your life's trajectory. Three months later, my agency sold, and I embarked on a career in storytelling without any real clue where it would take me. One thing I did know. I wanted to use the power of story to change the world.

Interestingly, my first foray into storytelling was to cowrite a performance piece with my good friend Hedy Schleifer. It was entitled *Schtick and Stone* to raise money for a nonprofit called the Foundation for Mideast Communication. This organization brought together Arabs and Jews to find commonalities when most of the world accentuates their differences. As we'll discuss, listening to the other's story can be transformational. Unfortunately, conflict is fueled often by stories vilifying and dehumanizing our enemies, exalting the truth of our position while degrading the other's stories as misguided lies and misrepresentations of the facts.

In my early career with storytelling, a hospice chaplain generously gave me some suggestions for extending my work to parents and other audiences. In return, I offered to run a professional development session with his staff. The event's success led to my foray into providing story training for hospice professionals and volunteers through a program called Journey into the Healing Power of Story. My goal was to assist patients to tell their story as a means of life review. It turns out our stories of the past often hold the key to finding meaning and context in our lives, a topic we explore further in Chapter 4. One offshoot of that work was the publication of two books. The first was *Stories: The Family Legacy*, which offers readers a wealth of ideas for exploring personal stories and doing life review. Following on its heels was *The Healing Art of Storytelling*. Much of that early work informs the lessons we share with you about the transformative power of story.

In the early 1990s, I was at a stoplight. I looked to my left at a large, flourishing stand of pampas grass. My imagination immediately took off. I was sure if I dug below the surface of the earth, I'd find a creature with grasses growing from his forehead. The result was a children's novel entitled *The Kingdom of Nowt*, delving into the strange world of a race of creatures called Treemungermen, from whose heads grow all of the trees and bushes. We talk more about story and imagination throughout the book. It turns out fiction writing and envisioning future possibilities have a lot in common.

My journey with story also led me to develop various programs for business leaders, informing all I have learned about using storytelling to communicate persuasively and connect with others. One side trip in my career led to working as the StoryAnalytics Master for IDEAS, a former division of the Walt Disney Company. Aside from being the best professional title this side of the Milky Way, I had the chance to be on the team that created StoryCare—an exciting product in the healthcare space to engage professionals to reflect on their practices to improve patient safety. As an educational tool, StoryCare embodies many of the core lessons we'll share in the chapter on enabling learning.

I have made many other side explorations into the practical applications of story. For many years I have worked with the Edyth Bush Institute for Philanthropy and Nonprofit Leadership at Rollins College to teach nonprofit leaders how to use storytelling to more effectively engage audiences with their cause. This work also led me to similar engagements with the Red Cross and the YMCA.

Over the past ten years, I have regularly worked with the Cherokee School for Boys in South Carolina. Their mission is to help middle school boys who have a variety of learning and emotional challenges. Annually, I lead parents in a workshop to discover how they can use the power of story to build stronger ties with their sons. I weave into the fabric of this book many of the lessons I share with these parents.

In the late 1990s and early 2000s, I served on the board of the International Storytelling Center, where I met my co-author, Scott Livengood. At the time, he was the CEO of Krispy Kreme Doughnuts. Through the years, we stayed in touch, and whenever near Winston-Salem, I made a point of visiting. In 2014, we concocted a vision for StoryWork International, dedicated to bringing the transformative power of story to individuals, business leaders, educators, and students. We'll share with you some of the "story technologies" we've been developing.

Throughout my journey with story, one thing has been constant—my growing awareness of story's enduring power to impact all of the ways I see myself and the world. It never ceases to reveal new lessons every time I open myself to its mysterious code. My hope is this book will catalyze a similar journey of discovery for you.

Scott Livengood

I am a storyteller. Not in the way you might imagine. Not a teller of tales in the usual sense, but a storyteller through and through. Discovering the power of story and the insights gained through the lens of story are central to every positive thing that has happened in my life. There is no doubt that well understood and applied, it will have the same significance and value for everyone. That is the foundation of my initiation of a partnership with Richard Stone in StoryWork International and our collaboration on this book. Since an early age, I was obsessed with questions, from "Why do I need to take trigonometry?" to "What is my purpose in life?" I discovered that when I could discern a reason, the issue in question took on more meaning and gained worthiness as an endeavor. For every worthy endeavor, from relationships to business to life, I believe the ultimate question to answer is how to make it the best it can be. The tool I discovered that most illuminated the path to greatest potential was story.

Applying a story model reveals the importance of a decision, a goal, and a vision. Each has an implication, and each sets a trajectory, the highest of which Rick and I have termed one's MasterStory. I didn't realize storytelling was so central to the way I experienced the world until about thirty years ago when, in my thirties, I attended a Sam Keen workshop. Dr. Keen is a best-selling author, speaker, and workshop leader. He led us to understand that each of our lives is a story, and to live an *authentic* life, we had to become the author consciously. The workshop was focused on excavating the source of the stories that were informing our lives. Were they our own or ones we had consciously or unconsciously allowed some other *authority* to encode? And were they limiting us or opening us to our greatest possibilities? It was a seminal moment for me. The more significant epiphany was the realization that not only are our lives a story, but so, too, is every aspect of our lives, including our relationships, our spiritual lives, our careers, and the way we interpret and experience the world.

I was the CEO of Krispy Kreme Doughnuts when I attended that workshop. That epiphany changed the way I approached my role. The brand's positioning and execution became much clearer and easier to interpret and express through the lens of story. Writing our business plan became a storytelling exercise that inspired direction and gave more profound meaning to strategies and intended results. Our shareholders' annual report was a story that picked up from the chapter known as the previous year and set the stage for future chapters. Our public stock offering in 2000, the most successful IPO of the year, and the investor presentations that preceded it were all storytelling.

After a twenty-eight-year career at Krispy Kreme, in 2006, I bought Dewey's Bakery, a small retail bakery with some whole-sale business. The first twelve years were dedicated to building wholesale, primarily through private labels to support the consid-erable investment made in manufacturing plants and equipment. But beginning in 2018, we created the Dewey's Bakery brand of cookies and crackers and launched it nationally to great success. Again, we conceived the flavors and the packaging design through a story process that flowed naturally and authentically from our retail bakery favorites and a ninety-year heritage.

My intersection with pure story and storytelling occurred when I discovered the International Storytelling Center (ISC) in 1999. My wife, Michelle, who is from eastern Tennessee, was showing her North Carolina husband the sights and landmarks from her childhood part of the world. After visiting the birthplace of Davy Crockett (my childhood hero of *King of the Wild Frontier* Disney fame), she took me to Jonesborough. Jonesborough is a treasure. It was the capital of the state of Franklin that ultimately became part of Tennessee when it was established. It's like step-ping way back in time with its well-preserved inns and store-fronts. We happened upon the International Storytelling Center in the heart of the little town. I read the printed material it had made available to passersby like me. To my absolute shock, as I read about the organization's mission and vision, I felt like I had found my organizational soul mate. Within a couple of months, I contacted and met its founder and president and quickly formed a strong bond. We supported the ISC, including building the Krispy Kreme Storytelling Theater on its campus. I went on the board of directors, which I chaired for several years. It was there, through the ISC's National Storytelling Festival and its incredibly talented performance storytellers, that I discovered the pure essence of the power of story. The person I consider the world's most talented storyteller, Donald Davis, became one of my dearest friends to this day. It was there I also met my present-day partner in StoryWork International and coauthor of this book, Rick Stone, who also served on the board.

This book is one of several products that have emerged from a partnership Rick and I established several years ago, which we named StoryWork International (storywork.com). Since then, we have developed programming and workshops in education, healthcare, organizational development, and personal development. Those experiences have deepened our reverence for the power of applied story through witnessing the profound impact it has had on the participants' lives. We have drawn insights from all the work we've done in each of those disciplines. Please read the more detailed description provided about our company.

So why did Rick and I feel moved to write this book? It's simple. We feel compelled to reveal a powerful secret that's been hidden in plain sight for time immemorial . . . a life-changing secret everyone needs to know. With something so universally known as story, how can there be any secrets? Like the "discovery" of emotional intelligence, or EQ, it was always common sense or presumed helpful in life to be socially savvy and adroit. Still, no one had broken it down into its various aspects and studied it. It's the same with story. We hope that the ideas and the application of the material in this book will enrich your life and elevate your potential, prospects, and possibilities.

Preface

If you're looking to improve your life and increase your self-awareness, you'll find in *Story Intelligence* fresh, new approaches to growing your human potential. We also designed *Story Intelligence* to help you develop multiple dimensions of your professional expertise and competence as a storyteller and listener, making whatever work you do more productive, regardless of your occupation or business.

Each chapter is relatively self-contained, although many core ideas thread their way throughout the book, evolving in each successive section. The first chapter, "The Power of Story to Transport," is foundational for everything that follows. We recommend you start there. But if you're an educator or parent, for example, you may be attracted to then jump to a middle chapter, like "The Power of Story to Enable Learning." If you're looking for ways to transform yourself or your business, consider your next step after Chapter 1 to be "The Power of Story to Transform." Or perhaps you're looking to change the future. If so, go to the last chapter on "The Power of Story to Envision Possibilities." Regardless of where you start, you'll find invaluable insights and stories to expand your understanding and enrich your perspective on the topic.

We've divided each chapter into two parts. The first pages elucidate key, underpinning concepts, illustrated with a broad range of exciting research, examples, and stories. The last section of each chapter invites you to journey deeper and lays out concrete, practical tools and methods to expand your story mastery.

We want to forewarn you that we often use the word "story"

in a broad, big-concept fashion that may seem strange at first. You'll find phrases like, "Does story's power to transport us hinge on the truth?" Or, "We need to find ways to use story to change perceptions." Sometimes we'll refer to thought processes or even the future with a phrase like, "change the story." At other times we speak in more familiar terms about the act of orally telling stories or refer to the written tale.

Finally, we're excited to share the culmination of years of work studying and applying the extraordinary power of story. Enjoy!

Introduction

Story Intelligence: A New Paradigm For Becoming Fully Human

Myth is the foundation of life; it is the timeless pattern, the religious formula to which life shapes itself. . . . There is no doubt about it, the moment when the storyteller acquires the mythical way of looking at things, that moment marks a beginning in his life.

—Thomas Mann

Every age has its unique challenges. The one we're currently living through is no exception, leading us to question the status quo on nearly every front. People today have, for the most part, lost touch with the past and are deeply confused about their future. Is it any wonder that a recent survey of Americans found that four in ten of us have not discovered a satisfying life purpose, or that a quarter of us doesn't have a strong sense of what makes our lives meaningful?[1]

If there was ever a proverbial perfect storm, we're living in the middle of it, all of us searching for a clearer path to a better future. Many are questioning the tried and true stories we once used to organize our thinking and lives. Some of these stories have been rendered untrue by escalating events on political and social fronts. At this crossroads, we need to find new stories that uplift us and create the opportunity to discover and pursue new meaning and purpose. We also must unearth within ourselves new capabilities to manage and direct a complicated world that feels most of the time like it's spinning out of control. What we need is a new paradigm for being fully human.

To create this new paradigm, we have turned to the most powerful force we know of in our universe—story. Story determines nearly everything we consciously perceive, feel, and do. What you're doing now, what you'll do next, and what you'll do tomorrow. What you believe in and how you feel about your prospects. Whom you're in a relationship with and how you relate to and interact with others. Where you work, why you're there, and whether you like or dislike your situation. What you think happens when you die. Perhaps most importantly, why you believe you are here on this planet. In this way, story weaves itself into every facet of our being.

To change our paradigm, we must reauthor and reshape the contours of our storied lives and world. To better understand what that means, consider this sentiment from Buckminster Fuller: "You never change things by fighting the existing reality. To change something, build a new model that makes the existing reality obsolete."[2] We suggest a variation on Fuller's words as the central premise of our book: "You never change things by *fighting or clinging* to your existing *story*. To change the *trajectory of your possibilities, construct a new version* that makes your existing *story* obsolete." The capacity to do this is what we call Story Intelligence, or SQ for short. It's an entirely new way of thinking about what it means to be a human being, to be self-aware, and to have agency in the world. If stories are this powerful, doesn't it make sense that we understand their mysterious influence over our lives and learn how to author the best possible story we're creating for ourselves?

Just as we are born with the capacity for language acquisition, we are all born with an abundance of Story Intelligence potential. "Story" is, in a profound sense, every human being's native language. Mastering this language can be enhanced if it's better understood and practiced. It's not reliant on where you come from, whether you're rich or poor, how much you know, or your intellectual development. Now, more than ever, boosting your SQ may be your most important developmental task, indispensable to your personal and professional success, especially in times of crisis.

This capability weaves its way into every aspect of human discourse. Storytelling makes it possible for us to share our experience of the past and paint a picture of our aspirations for the future. It's also crucial to helping us learn, grow, develop, and understand our role in our families, organizations, and society at large. Discovering and making meaning in life is also profoundly reliant on our SQ.

Perhaps most importantly, through shared metanarratives, SQ gives us the capacity to see ourselves as a significant part of an expansive universe stretching beyond the limits of our imagination. These metanarratives helped our ancestors make sense of life's complexities, brought meaning and order to the many puzzles permeating their existence, and helped them have a feeling that they belonged to a welcoming world where good inevitably triumphs over evil. Because we're storytelling creatures, early humans looked at the heavens and were awed, seeing in the sky a panoply of characters, animals, and familiar objects. By creating stories about these celestial bodies, people endowed them with a human dimension, giving the stars a sense of purpose and meaning. In doing so, they incorporated the play of the firmaments into their collective story, allowing them to feel a little less minuscule and insignificant. Without SQ, there would be no Big Dipper, Orion the Hunter, or Virgo. Our lives without these stories would be less interconnected to our world, barren in comparison to the story-filled universe we've created and inhabit. Story Intelligence even imbued humans with the ability to create societies and cultures and collaborate with thousands of others. Amazingly, simple stories manage all of this complexity with ease and elegance.

What's most intriguing is these portrayals of reality live disembodied in our minds. Nearly every aspect of our day-to-day world is borne from our imaginations and sustained through the stories we create, tell, and believe to be inviolably factual. Our imaginations have conjured up religious philosophies and dogma, vehicles of commerce using currencies made of paper or 0s and 1s traversing across telecommunication lines, political systems and nation-states inspiring endless loyalty we're willing to die for, sports teams moving us to celebrate the feats of our stars and vilify competitors as though they are our mortal enemies, and the plans and aspirations we have for a future that does not yet exist. In a fundamental sense, these things are all the stuff of fiction, often fabricated out of thin air with tenuous ties to anything concrete. You see, we humans are story-making creatures endowed with a gift for crafting tales that become, all too willingly, our reality.

SQ is a close progenitor of Emotional Intelligence (EQ), a concept first popularized by Daniel Goleman nearly thirty years ago.[3] But the idea that our ability to discern our own emotions and those of others and act on that knowledge predates Goleman's writing by decades. Joel Davitz and Michael Beldoch[4] first wrote about this issue in 1964, and Howard Gardner, in 1983, set the stage with his groundbreaking work on multiple intelligences.[5] These writers put emotions at the center of our aptitude for living and expanded the definition of what it means to navigate human relationships successfully.

In contrast, the concept of Story Intelligence explicitly puts the power of story at the heart of what it means to be effectual in every realm of our existence, stretching beyond the concepts of intellectual and emotional intelligence. Simultaneously, SQ both undergirds and amplifies our understanding of EQ and IQ, acting as an activator and catalyst for these capacities. It's not enough to simply perceive, understand, use, and manage our emotions. Our ability to function effectively in the twenty-first century depends on our mastering this innate feature of our personal, social, and spiritual existence.

Further, we believe a high SQ has become essential to successfully compete in an increasingly complex, fast-moving, interconnected world. By embracing and understanding the role story plays in every way we interact with ourselves and others, we can actively set the trajectory we'd like our lives to take. Moreover, we can become experts at judiciously managing the stories we're bombarded with daily, developing the necessary know-how to discern the ways they obfuscate fundamental truths and limit our possibilities, as well as unleash our human potential.

While EQ is an accepted precept in education and business today, we forget it wasn't always the case. What prompted Goleman to popularize this new way of thinking about intelligence was the plethora of research emerging in the 1980s and 1990s about the integral role of emotions in human affairs. Brain and cognitive studies strongly suggested there's a whole lot more at play when it comes to successful living than intelligence as a pure function of the intellect. For this reason, Goleman decried how our very name, Homo sapiens, which means "wise man" in Latin, severely obscures our invaluable emotional dimensions.

We are now at the precipice of a similar breakthrough in brain research related to the impactful power of story. New scientific findings highlight the integral narrative structure of our brains, suggesting that it's time for a new name for us—*Homo narrare*—loosely translated as "storytelling human." It's our aptitude as storytellers that distinguishes our species, more defining than our reasoning ability or emotional capacity. In contrast to Descartes' proclamation, "I think; therefore, I am," we believe our new watchword should be, "I story; therefore, I am."

As storied creatures, our weaving the tapestry of our reality has a decidedly dual nature. We're caught in a yin and yang dance, determining nearly every outcome on the human stage.

Wars are started by stories unconsciously or blithely told and retold. Yet we can reach out to our enemies to create peace and a new narrative if we understand how distorted and untrue stories divide us.

Relationships are destroyed by carelessly uttered words filled with lies and false innuendo yet presumed to be true. But we can heal the bitterest conflict by committing to fully listening with our hearts and minds to the other's story, thereby building trust and a new landscape for interaction.

Our politics become polluted when we allow tales of others to limit our capacity to see their perspective and their humanity compassionately. We can also build bridges with those we disagree with by looking for threads of commonality in our shared stories.

Angst and mental illness disrupt our well-being when we allow stories of the past to define us and worries about the future to consume our imaginations. Yet our capacity for storytelling can also help us to become more resilient, opening us to our deepest calling.

In these ways, story is as rudimentary as the elements of fire and water. Stories are capable of warming the heart or burning down instantly what has taken years to build. They can also drown us in despair or quench our spiritual thirst to grow and learn.

One of the invaluable contributions of Goleman's writing was in the arena of education. He provided the springboard for teachers to pivot away from traditional models of instruction and to take into account the whole person. This new perspective added weight and importance to the development of children's emotional capacity. The realms of corporate training and instructional design have readily embraced this transformation.

As the world awakens to the power of story, we envision a similar pivot toward educating youth and adults to the hidden ways story can enliven and enlighten every facet of learning. We anticipate Story Intelligence education becoming the next wave of exciting new curricula starting in early childhood, working its way up to higher education and the corporate boardroom. Our ability to manage the challenges of living in an increasingly complex, technological society depends upon this transformation.

As we have applied many of these story principles in our own lives and professional endeavors over the years, we have identified seven powers of story:

1   To Transport
2   To Communicate
3   To Enable Learning
4   To Create Meaning
5   To Transform
6   To Unite
7   To Envision Possibilities

Developing these seven powers has become urgent, given the world we live in today. We are practically drowning in a multiverse of stories—almost eight billion individual stories and 195 countries with collective stories, not to mention community stories, state stories, and regional stories. What is most troubling is the trend for devolutionary metanarratives in the twenty-first century, which deny the interconnectedness of everything and emphasize that we are all separate. What we end up with is me first, my people first, and our country first. This world view obliterates the needs and suffering of others, and the consequences border on disastrous for the human race. Never before have we experienced so much polarization, both within countries and between countries. And never before have stories so pervasively denied the realities of science or deprecated our deepest values of human respect that undergird the American idea of democracy. How did we get into this situation? We think the reason, assessed through the lens of story, is not difficult to understand.

Let's start with our country. It's not that there has ever been an absence of dissension in the United States. A hallmark of our founding is the freedom of speech, and we've had a long history of disagreement. Where we run into rocky waters is when we have no means to reconcile our differences and divergent values. This leads to deep and widespread polarization and animosity, often stoked by the speech of our elected leaders. What caused this trend?

First, as it relates to values, think about how far science, especially cosmology and physics, has come within the lifetimes of anyone over the age of forty. As famed mythologist Joseph Campbell observed, "Now that we moderns have stripped the earth of its mystery—have made, in Saul Bellow's description, 'a housecleaning of belief'—how are our imaginations to be nourished?"[6] We've replaced our stories of wonder and mystery with facts and equations. We're certainly not saying these incredible advances in knowledge are in any way wrong. They are quite impressive. It's just that we haven't superseded the old stories with new ones that both embrace these discoveries and bring us together at a higher place. Simply said, science is outpacing our stories. This brave new world seems to have had the effect of pushing science and spirituality and religion further apart, each "hunkering down" and translating their beliefs (or non-beliefs) into the political arena, adding to our polarization.

Perhaps the most significant contributor to our polarization is the internet and social media. In earlier times, there was a select, limited number of stories told to us by those with power or position. An explosion of stories in the last fifteen years has shattered that world. Now, each individual has the opportunity to tell their story any way they want to express it. As with stories of old, many of these narratives are a means of advocating, organizing, and creating insular tribes of believers. Each adheres to its own metanarrative, obviating the need for a collective metanarrative to assimilate or infuse disparate stories with a more profound, coherent meaning. Consequently, whereas stories, for the most part, used to connect us, they are now colliding more than ever.

An exacerbator of polarization is the news media. These people are master storytellers, and the combination of the 24-7 news cycle combined with the pursuit of ratings has transformed the news into big business. From TV's beginnings, trustworthy people like "Uncle" Walter Cronkite and Huntley and Brinkley reported the news objectively. But in the early 2000s, objectivity switched to advocacy. Ezra Klein put it this way in his recent book *Why We're Polarized*:

> The old line on local reporting was, "If it bleeds, it leads." For political reporting, the principle is, "If it outrages, it leads." And outrage is deeply connected to identity—we are outraged when members of other groups threaten our group and violate our values. As such, polarized media doesn't emphasize commonalities, it weaponizes differences; it doesn't focus on the best of the other side, it threatens you with the worst.[7]

This combination of universally accessible social media platforms, dedicated news networks competing for viewers, and the resulting twenty-four-hour news cycle has created intractable polarization across the planet. The more profound truth to our current reality is a system that has evolved to promote and propagate stories set up and told in ways to ensure conflict and controversy. It's hard to believe this is the story we would consciously and collectively choose for our country or the world.

Is there a way forward to intentionally choose a foundational story to elevate our collective humanity that serves our best mutual interests? We believe that heightening our awareness that we have a choice to be the authors of both our shared and individual stories is the best and most rewarding path to pursue. But it's a conscious choice that we all must embrace.

To this end, we'll take you into the depths of each of the powers of story, shedding light on the mechanisms undergirding the magic of each. Most importantly, we'll assist you in understanding how to become the master of story in all of its dimensions and show you tools to deploy its power in every phase of your life.

Developing your SQ, you'll learn to communicate with clarity and force to better engage others with your ideas and vision for the future. Developing your Story Intelligence will also fill your life with greater meaning and relevance, strengthening your capacity to fulfill your highest aspirations. Through enhancing their SQ, parents and educators will cultivate a depth of learning and discovery that will improve everything they do to nurture the lives of children. And you'll unearth the skills to transform difficulties, challenges, and wounds into enlivening possibilities. Most importantly, you'll find in these pages story-based tools to assist you in bringing together people divided by conflict and ideological differences.

Finally, we need today more than ever to gather around ritual fires to transcend the old metanarratives and create new stories that are inclusive, just, aspirational, and inspirational. Our world requires now, more than ever, a potent medicine to re-enchant our lives. We must restore and re-story ourselves, consciously building story into our everyday living. By extinguishing the fires of technology, at least temporarily, we can begin again to hear ourselves and the stories the earth is quietly whispering into our ears. Most significantly, we need to start listening more deeply to each other's stories. Hopefully, this book will help the world stoke a new kind of fire, assisting all of us to develop a collective Story Intelligence to illuminate and build a more durable source of meaning and personal fulfillment.

Who would have thought understanding and consciously deploying something as simple as a story could accomplish all of that!

I

The Power of Story to Transport

The ability to take us to a different place and time and empathetically engage us in an alternate emotional reality.

We are, as a species, addicted to story. Even when the body goes to sleep, the mind stays up all night, telling itself stories.

— Jonathan Gottschall

Our journey into Story Intelligence begins with the fundamental Power to Transport. None of the other powers of story would be even remotely possible without it. In fact, without this unique property of stories, humans, as we know them, would also not have been possible. You see, it's difficult to discern which came first, story's capacity to transport us to alternate realities or the way our brain has evolved. While on the surface this is an odd question, it turns out our relationship with story is, if nothing else, a complicated story.

Humans have been telling stories for a long time. Cave drawings celebrating successful hunts and important victories date back tens of thousands of years in Europe, India, South

Africa, and Australia. All are testimony to the human need to capture our experiences for posterity. For our predecessors, these paintings may have been as integral to effective communication as PowerPoint is to us, used as teaching aids to impart invaluable lessons to younger generations. They were critical to a clan's survival, enabling them to virtually transport children beyond the cave to the plains where adults engaged in the dangerous work of killing prey or vanquishing a competing tribe. While we can date these drawings using sophisticated technology, oral storytelling likely predates cave paintings by hundreds of thousands of years.

Something happened early on in Homo sapiens' brains, giving us an evolutionary edge. It enabled us to evolve a form of communication far superior to that of other human species living in the same period. How come Homo sapiens survived, whereas Homo neanderthalensis didn't, even though they had a larger brain than ours? Why were we able to dominate other human species, such as Homo denisova and Homo erectus? Could it be our evolving ability to tell stories was the differentiating factor, which in turn impacted our facility to create cultures supporting much more sophisticated social organizations? Was our secret sauce the fact that narratives have the remarkable power to transport listeners into the vision of the teller? Without that, probably, we'd still be living in small clans eking out a living hunting and gathering. Yuval Harari speculates it's what gave Homo sapiens the ability to dominate and most probably wipe out our cousins.[1] Neanderthals' rudimentary forms of communication no doubt lacked this important transport function that implants an unforgettable picture of possibilities in listeners. It also may be their brains simply weren't wired to hear and synthesize this form of messaging. Regardless, the transport factor may have enabled Homo sapiens to see a more sophisticated mode of organizing themselves for collective, beneficial action.

The act of telling and listening to stories no doubt also affected the path of our brain's development. Consider for a moment storytelling as the first neurorevolution. Yes, the predecessors of Homo sapiens, no doubt, communicated. Still, it was probably not much more evolved than how a band of gorillas converses as it forages for food and seeks shelter and safety. The ability to communicate through stories, though, led to the growth of new and extraordinary mental capacities, enabling us to convey to others enormous amounts of complex, subtle information. In oral cultures, there is significant evidence commoners could remember thousands of stories and tell lengthy sagas taking days to complete. Once these stories were heard and digested, merchants traveling the trade routes took these tales with them and shared them. The fact that diverse cultures tell the same stories all along the Silk Road is testimony to how oral storytelling was the first medium to "go viral." Stories spread like wildfire across the globe. While they didn't circulate at the speeds enabled today by the internet, the relatively short time it took in historical terms was unprecedented.

Contrast this with contemporary cultures more reliant on the second neurotechnological revolution—the printed page. Guttenberg invented the printing press a mere five hundred years ago. It's a drop in the bucket when you consider the eons of time it took to impact the evolution of the brains currently inhabiting our skulls. Even so, there's reason to believe the printed word has diminished our mental capacities in this short time. We once met a Scottish storyteller who knew over three thousand traditional stories and songs by heart, but he no doubt was a member of a dying breed. Since that time, we have not met anyone with such a prodigious memory. By relying on writing in contemporary times, we seem to be severely curtailing or underutilizing this capacity for verbal memory, which raises lots of questions. Has it been extinguished entirely? What facets of our brain are slowly atrophying due to not regularly hearing, learning, and repeating hundreds and thousands of stories? Is it possible to reverse this trend? Or is oral storytelling dead? Could it be that facet of our brains enabling this kind of communication is quickly being deselected as a human trait?

This idea may seem counterintuitive given the fact libraries could suddenly hold more information than one human brain ever could. And this has been eclipsed geometrically by the internet. But as far back as Plato's time, as scribes were capturing the world's wisdom on parchment and hides, there was a growing wariness of what writing was doing to human memory. Plato's *Phaedrus*[2] humorously captures these misgivings in a strange tale of the god Theuth and the king of Egypt, Thamus. Theuth was responsible for the invention of all things dealing with the arts. Thamus served as a sort of clearinghouse for these crafty creations, like the *Good Housekeeping* Seal of Approval. Only with his support could Theuth's handiwork pass muster. One day, Theuth invented writing. He was ecstatic and couldn't contain his enthusiasm. Certainly, this would benefit humankind, improving our memory and making humans wiser. Thamus listened intently to Theuth as he waxed on about writing's many benefits, then stopped Theuth in his tracks, contradicting his suppositions. "My dear Theuth," he said, "this discovery of yours will create forgetfulness in the learners' souls because they will not use their memories; they will trust the external written characters and not remember of themselves. The specific which you have discovered is an aid not to memory, but to reminiscence, and you give your disciples not the truth, but only the semblance of truth; they will be hearers of many things and will have learned nothing; they will appear to be omniscient and will generally know nothing; they will be tiresome company, having the show of wisdom without the reality."[3]

We needn't look far to confirm this insight. As Thamus professed thousands of years ago, I discovered in my work once people write things down, they soon forget them. In a project we did years ago for Walt Disney Imagineering in Orlando, we assessed how the staff shared knowledge throughout the organization. After every major project, the Imagineers had to write a detailed report. The hope was that future generations would learn from all of their successes and mistakes. They stored these tomes in a secure repository on the ninth floor of their offices. When we asked Imagineers if they had ever visited these stacks to read about projects similar to rides or hotels they were currently designing, not one had ever stepped foot on the ninth floor. Why? It turns out, like ancient cultures, Disney's culture is primarily oral when it comes to sharing know-how. If you were designing a new water park and knew I had planned one ten years earlier, you could write me an email and ask me to share my wisdom. If I responded at all, I'd share a relatively cursory account of the project's lessons. There wouldn't be much to be learned.

On the other hand, if you knocked on my door and asked if I had a few minutes to talk, even if we had never met, I would willingly spend hours of my day telling you stories of all of the challenges we faced and everything we gleaned from our errors. Disney discovered that capturing all of that wisdom in an accessible written document was not very useful. They had to find ways to increase the face-to-face connections between the old and new guard if they were going to avoid replicating the costly mistakes of the past.

Fast-forward to today. It would seem our interaction with digital devices may be impacting a new generation of Homo sapiens in unexpected ways. For example, recent research has demonstrated the attention span of heavy multi-screeners has dropped from twelve seconds to eight seconds. That's one second less than the average goldfish![4] When we consider how malleable young minds are, this inability to concentrate may become wired into future generations' brains. Those who rely on smartphones are highly distractible. Brains of heavy digital users are demonstrating patterns found typically among drug addicts. Even worse, extensive digital use severely diminishes our ability to empathize with others.[5] Are we unwittingly reversing the evolution of our storied brains through our technological advances?

Some would argue these devices train our minds and mold our

brains to do many new things, making us more prepared for our contemporary world. The son of a friend was a demon with computer games and translated this skillset to flying planes, becoming a Top Gun in the Air Force. The jury is still out, though. Many parents in Silicon Valley are restricting their children's use of technology.[6] What do they know that we don't?

Can storytelling in all of its richness and applications be just the antidote needed today? Would finding ways to enhance the latent Story Intelligence of our children better prepare them to consciously craft and transmit the best of what our society and culture can offer humankind? How could we teach people to improve their use of a story's unique ability to transport listeners to another place and time to enhance every facet of their lives and work?

In the following pages, you'll see how the extraordinary features of stories achieve remarkable outcomes on almost every level of human interactions and social enterprise. We invite you on a journey into the power of story to transform the way you see yourself and your world, and hopefully, transport you to a new way of being.

The Narrative
Seduction of Our Brains

When someone proceeds to tell us the story of the cow who jumped over the moon, we typically respond after the tale, "Then what happened?" Why is it we're so willing to give our metaphorical hand to the teller of a fanciful story and allow her to transport us into a world where cows can leap into the sky? For sure, this tale defies physics. To our knowledge, cows haven't distinguished themselves to be such good jumpers. Have you ever seen one jump over a fence? A kangaroo jumping over the moon might be a tad more believable. Even then, you'd be stretching credibility. Yet, here we are, sucked into the story as though it's true, asking what happens next. Are we perhaps the most gullible creatures on the face of the earth? Or, is there something more profound and vital happening here when we listen to, read, or see a fictional story about make-believe characters?

The eighteenth-century poet and philosopher Samuel Taylor Coleridge best described how the artifice of stories transports us to imaginary worlds. He called it the "willing suspension of disbelief." Something about stories keys us to abandon all critical judgment. We eagerly dive in headfirst without knowing what awaits us. Is this attributable to some inherent property of the oral storyteller's words or the fiction writer's text? Or does it have more to do with the way our brains are wired?

Jerome Bruner suggests the power of stories to transport us lies in the craft of the telling: "Great storytellers have the artifices of narrative reality construction so well mastered that their telling preempts momentarily the possibility of any but a single interpretation—however bizarre it may be."[7] Aptly, he refers to this as "narrative seduction." How else can we understand why we'd give up all control over our emotions and rational grasp of reality as we sit in a movie theater sobbing uncontrollably when a fictional protagonist meets her untimely end?

On the other hand, Norman Holland[8] suggests this encounter with the world of make-believe is more attributable to our brain's wiring than to the quality of the storyteller's cunning and expertise. When absorbed in a story, our brains change their dominant mode of operation. Typically, when real trouble is brewing, our brains quickly activate all kinds of bodily mechanisms to keep us safe from danger. In contrast, while we're listening to or watching a story, we've learned to quiet the functions in our brain responsible for action and planning. They simply go dormant. Temporarily, our critical minds are anesthetized. We suspend questioning and critique, allowing the facts of the story to go unexamined, no matter how farfetched. Our self-awareness and extended awareness of the outer world comes to a temporary standstill. Also barred from consideration is any drive to survive. When we become embroiled in a dangerous fictional scene, our bodies show all the physiological signs of a real threat. But we don't emit a war cry and reach for our weapons. Nor do we leap from our chair in the theater and charge the screen. Instead, we sit passively. Witnessing all kinds of injustices, touching moments between lovers, and majestic portrayals of heroic deeds evokes nothing more than sweaty palms, tears of sadness or joy, or imperceptible shaking from fear. A suspension of our motor functions accompanies the act of suspending disbelief. When the curtain closes and the lights go on, we get out of our seat and go about our business as though nothing occurred. But the feeling state associated with the story may persist for hours or even days. This phenomenon isn't just a literary axiom. Brain research is elucidating just how impactful stories are on our biological functioning.

Gregory Berns[9] is using fMRI scans to explore the area of the brain in the left temporal cortex associated with language receptivity. He wanted to see if the heightened connectivity while reading a novel in the evenings continued into the next morning, perhaps even persisting for days. If you have ever picked up a book and couldn't put it down or binge-watched five seasons of your favorite TV series, you know what it means when the mood of the book or show colors your experience of everything else you're doing.

It turns out this heightened state of neural functioning does persist. Berns dubbed this "shadow activity," likening it to the muscle memory we develop from performing a motor task like shooting a basketball. This heightened activity also showed up in the sensory-motor region of the brain. Neurons of this region are associated with making representations of sensation for the body, a phenomenon known as "grounded cognition." Just thinking about running, for instance, can activate the neurons associated with the physical act of running. Reading about someone running has a comparable effect. "The neural changes that we found associated with physical sensation and movement systems suggest that reading a novel can transport you into the body of the protagonist," Berns says. "We already knew that good stories can put you in someone else's shoes in a figurative sense. Now we're seeing that something may also be happening biologically."

The jury is out on how long these effects last. But just imagine the impact on the neural connectivity of someone growing up in a culture where reading and listening to stories is a daily activity. Even if you want your kids to excel in STEM, the implications for the role of fiction in education seem to suggest a regular regime can significantly enhance their success and increase their emotional intelligence.

Aristotle wrote in *Poetics* 2,300 years ago: "The plot, then, is the first principle, and, as it were, the soul of a tragedy; Character holds the second place." But maybe he had it all wrong. Perhaps it's our identification with the characters in a story that inclines us to become more engaged with others. Steven Brown found that when presented with short headlines you might typically read in the newspaper, subjects' brains reacted in the same way they would when confronted with real challenges. Using headlines like "Surgeon finds scissors inside of patient" or "Fisherman rescues a boy from freezing lake," subjects' brains were affected "by the character's intentions, motivations, beliefs, emotions, and actions." Brown's research contradicts Aristotle's axiom. "Our brain results show that people approach narrative in a strongly character-centered and psychological manner, focused on the mental states of the protagonist of the story."[10] From this perspective, reading fiction is not merely a pleasurable leisure activity. It's emotionally engaging in extraordinary ways, helping us to be more attuned to others.

When Story Becomes All Too Real

Sometimes these fictions can get us moving and taking action because they are so believable. In 1938, Orson Wells headed up a team of writers for *The Mercury Theatre on Air*, a radio show providing live dramatic readings and a host of musical entertainment. For his live Halloween broadcast, he adapted H. G. Wells' *The War of the Worlds*, written, believe it or not, in 1898.

The program began with its usual musical opening as the announcer told the audience they'd be performing a dramatic adaptation of a novel by H. G. Wells. No doubt, most of the listeners weren't paying much attention. A half-hour into the music, the announcer interrupted the show with a news bulletin proclaiming astronomers had witnessed odd explosions on the surface of Mars. Later in the musical program, the announcer interrupted again, claiming an unusual object had plummeted from the sky onto a farm in New Jersey. A third news flash described a growing crowd surrounding it. Things became dicey when the announcer interrupted the music again to inform the audience Martians emerging from the metal cylinder attacked onlookers with lethal heat-ray guns. One announcement followed another decrying the Martian invasion, describing how the world's capitals were falling. The mighty American military was helpless to do anything about it. The capper came when the announcer reported the Martians had released a poisonous cloud over New York City, killing people by the thousands.

The realistic delivery persuasively seduced most who heard this broadcast. The thin line between reality and fiction evaporated. Perhaps it was because listeners were accustomed to news bulletin interruptions whenever extraordinary events needed reporting. If they had stuck around for the second half of the show, they would have learned the Martians were stopped cold by, of all things, microbes, those invisible little creatures coexisting with your kitchen countertops. And, the evening's drama had been brought to them by one of their favorite advertisers. But many didn't hear this last bit. Wholesale panic broke out. The phone lines to police stations and the military rang off the hook. The next day when people woke to discover it had all been a hoax, a story, there was widespread outrage. Some called for a congressional investigation.

A similar phenomenon occurred nearly one hundred years previously. Charles Dickens published *The Old Curiosity Shop* in weekly serial installments in a London newspaper. As the story unfolded, the orphaned Little Nell lived with her grandfather who ran a curio shop. He desperately wanted to leave Nell better off than her parents, who had died destitute. Foolishly, he gambled away everything he had in a card game, resulting in losing the shop to an evil man.

He and Nell fled to England's midlands, making their way as beggars. As her grandfather lost his mind, Nell suffered from starvation and illness. Things weren't looking good. Readers began to fear the worst. Then, an odd thing occurred. They began writing to Dickens, begging him not to kill off Nell in the novel. They were impassioned and wrote as though they were beseeching a king to pardon some poor servant in real life who had been unjustly charged with a capital crime. There was no question they were reading a piece of fiction. Yet, their growing love for Nell made them cross the thin line between reality and fantasy. Only a story is powerful enough to create this.

Researchers are exploring this phenomenon. Danielle Gunraj[11] was able to demonstrate the hidden mental processes that occur when readers identify with fictional characters. She asked participants to read a vignette about a character who had just moved from New York City to North Dakota. She had to go shopping for several items for her new apartment. When the character in the story remembered a shopping list of fifteen things, the readers in a post-memory test could recall the list as well. It makes you wonder what other capacities and traits we might be imbibing as we explore literature. There are also some thought-provoking hypotheses flowing from this kind of conjecture. If a character in a story suddenly chooses to make more considered, wiser decisions, would we as readers become more prudent?

Today, even pundits and TV psychologists galore advise people how to move through their grief for a fictional character who has died or been ditched by a lover. In one study following serial TV shows running for multiple seasons, researchers discovered the loss viewers felt at the death of a character was not much different from what we feel from actual losses.[12]

Storytellers' ability to magnify the suspension of disbelief uncomfortably reminds us of the immense power of story. In the wrong hands, stories can become potent tools of manipulation. Used ethically, they can be powerful instruments of persuasion and education. People know in some recess of their minds that it's all made up. But they act with emotional zeal. Perhaps Martians brought stories down to our planet to capture and control us. Undoubtedly, the seduction of our imaginations (and our brains) has been achieved, making stories a weapon far more effective than lethal heat-ray guns or clouds of mesmerizing gas.

Story Transportation: Big Business

Given the integral role story played in the evolution of Homo sapiens, it's not surprising something as frivolous as story-based entertainment is so central to our lives. It's unclear how our hours of reading and watching stories have any bearing on the survival of our species. Yet, we while away our time escaping into fictional worlds of all kinds, going into dark movie theaters on sunny days to cry, tremble, exult someone else's triumphs, or feel sorrow at their downfall. There must be more here than meets the eye.

The numbers are staggering. The film industry alone took in nearly $43 billion in 2019.[13] Monthly traffic to streaming video services accounts for over thirty thousand petabytes of data, and that's before the COVID-19 pandemic.[14] How much is a petabyte? It's enough storage for about 341 million three-minute MP3s. You do the math. YouTube expects viewership will continue to rise a staggering 100 percent every year for the foreseeable future.[15] It's hard to imagine all of the servers in the cloud needed to accommodate all of that story data. We fly right past the realm of petabytes into territories known as exabytes, zettabytes, and yottabytes.

Book publishing, including digital and print editions, is also on the rise. Readers bought almost seven hundred million books in 2017, a 10 percent increase over 2013.[16] Reading is by no means dead.

Then there is the never-ending stream of multiplayer video games like *World of Warcraft* growing at an annual 18 percent clip.[17] Interestingly, some of that revenue is attributable to players using real dollars to purchase imaginary script to buy computer-generated products like real estate only existing in the world of the game. Who could have imagined a story could be so entertaining it would convince someone to pay precious money for a fictional address in an imaginary world? It lends new meaning to the old phrase "If you believe that, then I have a bridge in Arizona to sell you."

By 2021, the entertainment and media markets globally will be worth $2.1 trillion.[18] Storytelling is big business. It behooves us to understand how and why we so readily rely on it to transport us out of our current circumstances.

The Roots of Story Entertainment

As we have pointed out, stories can create simulated experiences comparable to and perhaps more enticing than interacting with the world around us. Let's face it. For most of us, our daily routines are relatively sedate and banal. Spending two hours escaping into a "once upon a time" world is understandably a welcome diversion from a life filled with tedious, dull, and never-ending responsibilities. Perhaps this has always been the case.

Historically, hunting-and-gathering societies spent their spare time going to their version of the movies by gathering around a central fire to tell stories. As far as we can tell, they, too, loved a good yarn. When the sun and the moon began to rise, the fire did more than just warm and protect them from the dangers of the night. It catalyzed reflections on the experiences of the day and musings about past times when those among them did something heroic and exceptional. In addition to telling stories for teaching or planning purposes, perhaps they, too, turned this capacity to the task at hand—avoiding boredom. It was especially true when the winter days were short, and the nights were long. In the absence of today's electronic wizardry, our ancestors used the most potent story simulator ever invented—the human mind. They discovered they had an internal screen in their heads, only needing the words of a gifted raconteur to set its pictures into motion. Once storytelling switched on that internal TV set, they never turned it off.

The earliest storytellers, no doubt, shared awe-filled tales as the characters of their stories confronted life's mysteries. Most probably, they were peppered with humor and reflected listeners' innocent foibles and foolishness. They were also bursting with all the action of comic superheroes as hunters courageously subdued dangerous beasts ten times their size. Perhaps most importantly, they were laced with wisdom about what it means to live in harmony with the physical world while respecting the invisible realms inhabited by powerful gods. Is it any wonder ancient people found delight in these stories? Was this not a form of adult play? Are we, contemporary humans, any different?

Being playful may predict how well we're suited to survive. Studying Alaskan grizzly bears, researchers Robert and Johanna Fagen found, "Young bears that played more tended to survive best to independence. Our data support play as a survival factor ... over and above obvious factors such as food, litter size, condition, and differences among mothers."[19] Who would have thought play is so crucial to a bear's, and perhaps our, well-being? Could the vibrancy of our health be predicated on being transported away from the mundane world's responsibilities into an imaginary universe?

The Imperative of Story as Play

Unlike the flow of our days filled with so many trivial details, a story can become a form of shorthand for life experience. It compresses time, eliminates everyday detritus, and burnishes reality. Perhaps most importantly, stories can romanticize our existence, elevate the meaning of events, and accentuate the good and bad qualities of people. Stories both resemble our world but have an otherworldly quality. Who would not want to take an excursion into this fabricated reality where you can leave your troubles behind for an hour, an evening, or longer through ballads and tales spanning many days in the telling?

Unlike contemporary times, most of our ancestors likely never traveled far from their homes. Only hunters and scouts got to see the lands just over the horizon. Through listening to their stories, though, their clansmen could embark on heroic journeys, slay dragons, overcome all kinds of danger, experience the wealth of kings and queens, inhabit a palace, or trek across expanses of desert and tundra. Through story, they could virtually cavort with the gods and traverse across the galaxies. It was the next best thing to being there in person.

This form of play is like taking our brains to a feast and filling our plates with a smorgasbord of sensory delight. Not only does it nourish us bodily, emotionally, and spiritually, this virtual repast became as important as the food itself.

The research on play is serious stuff. Stuart Brown, the founder of the National Institute for Play, defines it as purposeless, free from time constraints, and often improvisational.[20] Research on the effects of play suggests it also affects brain functioning in significant ways, especially in early development, making us better adjusted socially and our brains more adaptable later in life.[21] Finally, the English psychiatrist Donald Winnicott suggests that play and being creative are the best avenues to self-discovery, allowing us to tap into essential parts of our personality.[22] It just may be the case that play is the key to the development of our brains, a phenomenon that doesn't necessarily stop in adolescence, but may continue well into adulthood as we share stories.

The Tall Tale:
The Incomparable Adult Entertainment

While the tall tale did not originate in the Americas, there's plenty of evidence suggesting early colonialists and settlers perfected it. These stories blended just enough truth with bald-faced lies, leading listeners to take the bait hook, line, and sinker to the endless enjoyment of all those in the know. It's not surprising strangers to this new frontier were primed to believe fantastical tales. For dozens of years, visitors to this continent plied Europeans with descriptions of enormous bounty in the frontier territories. They portrayed races of strange people the earliest visitors mistook to be from the Indian mainland. The abundance of wild game led to exaggerated claims you could simply walk into the woods and grab a large buck by the horns for dinner.

In the European continent, the elite ruling class owned the land. But in America, commoners could own enough property to put the estates of royalty to shame. Europeans had logged most of their forests over the previous centuries. But in America, old-growth forests covered the hillsides, boasting trees stretching as far as the eye could see. Physical monuments like Niagara Falls simply had no parallel in the homeland. Visitors ran out of superlatives to describe them. While the oppression of serfdom subjugated the masses of Europe, in America, it was possible to experience real freedom without an overseer telling you what to do. At least that was the story, even if the reality of indentured servitude was still alive and well, not to speak of the morally abhorrent practice of slavery.

Here was born the myth of the backwoodsman who could comfortably live off the land through his wits and brawn. In truth, the likes of the Dutch and English East India Companies employed many of these men to bring furs to the market. They may have looked like mountain men, but were company men through and through, not much different from the blue-suited IBM employee of the twentieth century. This story became part and parcel of the great American myth. A man, if he had the will and the desire, could pull himself up by his bootstraps and succeed with just the shirt on his back. The reality, as we now know, was an entirely different story.

Tales written by the likes of Benjamin Franklin and Mark Twain made their way across this continent and as far east as Russia. They extolled bigger-than-life heroes who were distinctly American. But the tall tale wasn't just the province of literary giants. It became a badge of honor for any ordinary Joe or Jane to pull the leg of a visitor from the Old Country. One's ability to tell a convincing tall tale could build their stature among family and friends. Lying for fun became both an art form and a way of life as people gathered around pot-bellied stoves and on front porches. Who could top the whopper of a friend who faced down a grizzly bear and lulled it to sleep with a sweet melody taught to him by his grandma? Who could fill their tale of a fish getting away with more and more suspicious details describing its size and ferocity? How could one man or woman perform impossible feats with one hand tied behind their back, like lassoing a bucking bronco blindfolded? Nothing was off limits. The bigger the tale, the bigger the laugh, especially after gullible souls nodded in belief and wandered off contemplating what they took to be the gospel truth.

Benjamin Franklin plied his trade as a raconteur, exaggerating this land's magnificent natural wonders. In one story, he claimed the sheep here have so much wool on their tails they had to attach small carts with wheels on them to support their weight. Another account reprinted in the European press is a perfect example of a tale rampantly out of control:

Ignorant people may object that the Upper Lakes are fresh and that Cod and Whale are salt-water fish; but let them know sir that Cod like other fish when attacked by their enemies, fly into the water where they think they can be safest; that Whales when they have a mind to eat Cod, pursue them wherever they fly; and that the Grand Leap of the Whale in that Chase up the Fall of Niagara is esteemed by all who have seen it, as one of the finest spectacles of Nature!—Really, Sir, the World is grown too incredulous.[23]

People living in the Americas were portrayed in these tales to be meaner and more brutal than their cousins in Europe. Europeans perpetuated this myth by assuming that only evil criminals and reprobates could survive in such an inhospitable place. Isaac Weld, visiting the Americas around the time of the Revolution, reinforced these suspicions by claiming he encountered "four or five invalids whose testicles—so he was told—had been torn off in combat with barbarous neighbors." Weld goes on to report to his fellow Englishmen, "I have been credibly assured that in the Carolinas and Georgia the people are still more depraved . . . and that in some particular parts of these states, every third or fourth man appears with one eye."[24] You can only imagine his American hosts doing everything they could to suppress their laughter in the face of such ridiculous yarns. We are residents of North Carolina and Georgia, respectively, and can assure you Weld's account is untrue. Only one out of every ten men we know has lost an eye in a knife fight or had their testicles ripped off in a spat with their neighbors.

Yes, life was challenging in those early years. Many settlers succumbed to virulent diseases and the hardships of severe winters and failed crops. Surviving these perils became a point of pride, and they didn't hesitate to accentuate their difficulties, partly in jest, and partly as a form of comic relief. With every telling, last winter's snowdrifts piled higher and higher, soon topping the tallest pine. Going without basic staples for prolonged periods led to feats of resourcefulness, like boiling everything in sight for sustenance, including the wooden furniture. Suffering became elevated into the highest form of art. These farfetched tales produced a wry smile on the teller as unsuspecting, naïve visitors attempted to imagine how they survived in sixty-foot-high snowdrifts. They also reinforced their self-concept as hardened survivors because each tale contained a kernel of truth.

In the 1860s, Mark Twain built on this tradition with his famous tale *The Celebrated Jumping Frog of Calaveras County*. It was about a man named Jim Smiley who had a severe gambling problem. He'd willingly place a bet on almost anything, including odds on whether a good friend's wife recovering from a grave illness would die by week's end. He had no shame or, apparently, any conscience. The biggest bet of his life came when he captured a frog one day and taught him how to jump higher and farther than any frog in the county. A stranger visiting the town was impressed and challenged Jim Smiley's frog to a contest. The only problem was the stranger didn't have a frog to compete. Smiley was more than happy to oblige the man by leaving his in the man's possession while he went out to the pond to catch a frog for him. Unbeknownst to Jim, this man spoonfed Smiley's frog quail shot until he became heavier than a doorstop. Naturally, Smiley's frog could hardly move when the contest commenced, and the stranger walked away with Smiley's cash. Smiley, suspecting something awry, soon discovered the stranger had severely handicapped his frog, besting him at his craft.

Of course, in the style of the tall tale, this story was told with the straightest of faces, in a somber tone, with all the dignity one could expect if they were telling you an accurate account of a tragic accident. Twain mastered this approach and took great satisfaction in the fact no one was ever really sure if he was lying. "I never told the truth that I was not accused of lying, and every time

I lie, someone believes it. So, I have adopted the plan, when I want people to believe what I say, of putting it in the form of a lie. That is the difference between my fiction and other people's. Everybody knows mine is true."[25]

All it took for the unsuspecting to believe Americans' tales was a dose of sincerity married to a credible source. Newspapers writing up these fictions in the 1700s and 1800s were eagerly read and accepted as real. They echoed the fantastic tales detailed in publications like today's *National Enquirer*. Did you hear they spotted Elvis with aliens driving in a convertible down Broadway in New York City last week?

This tradition of tall tales is still very much alive. Perhaps you've stopped at a gas station while driving out west and perused the postcards for sale. There, right beside iconic images of the Grand Canyon, Arches National Park, and Old Faithful, are pictures of a unique animal supposedly found only in the Southwest—the jackalope. This rare species resembles a rabbit with deer's antlers and has engendered all kinds of serious musing, leaving many a new visitor to these parts keenly on the lookout for the jackalope's rare appearance. If you have a sliver of skepticism about its existence, the Douglas, Wyoming, Chamber of Commerce will quickly silence your doubts. They issue hunting licenses for jackalopes, good only one day of the year from midnight until 2:00 a.m. Some vendors even sell jackalope milk. You can only wonder what it takes to catch a jackalope, much less milk one.

Why do we have such a penchant for tall tales and go to such extremes to produce entire lines of merchandise about a mythological animal probably hatched by cowboys one night around a campfire? What can we learn about living vibrantly by exercising our wits to make up bald-faced lies? We contend this is an evolved way for adults to play together. It's both a sign of mental health and resilience. This kind of storytelling serves an essential function of allowing our imaginations to take off on flights of fancy. Tall tales reveal possibilities where none appeared previously as we somberly assess how to get out of some self-inflicted pickle. Recounting these preposterous tales with a straight face also gives us the capacity to build connections with strangers who, once they recognize the joke, can let down their guard as we have a big belly laugh together. There is so much to be serious about in this world. The tall tale is the perfect antidote to downturned faces, impending catastrophes, and the bad news permeating today's media. As we have learned about our profound need to play, the tall tale can reacquaint all of us with our playful nature, transporting us beyond the mundane details of everyday life to fantastic worlds filled with joy and mystery.

The Implications of the Power of Stories to Transport Us

As we explore the power of story to transport us, we must turn our attention to its profound implications stretching beyond play and entertainment. *Homo narrare's* brain is an immensely powerful simulation machine. If we wish to enhance the EQ of our family members, students, colleagues, and leaders, we must magnify our exposure to narratives filled with rich and complex characters having life experiences conspicuously different from our own. In this way, amplifying our Story Intelligence activates our EQ, better preparing us to discern the emotional realities of others.

In the last years, much has been made of virtual reality devices giving the wearer a visceral sense they are someplace else entirely, allowing them to interact with lifelike characters in this make-believe domain. As we have seen, story's transport qualities do an equally credible job of taking us to new places, allowing us to experience life through another's eyes. Plus, it's low-fidelity and low-tech. We must wonder how we can use this unique transportation property of stories to intentionally address a host of challenges we face in our global economy. Now more than ever, we must learn to get along with others whose cultures are quite different from our own. Could sincerely listening to each other's stories transport us into their world, teaching us we are not as dissimilar as we are the same, while also helping us develop empathy for our differences? For our entire lifetime, leaders have extolled the virtues of world peace, but there hasn't been a plausible pathway to bridging our cultural divides. Developing the Story Intelligence of peoples worldwide could prove to be the remedial cure for conflict, providing a path for reconciling what on the surface looks like irreconcilable differences.

Lastly, this invaluable transportation characteristic of stories suits it flawlessly to achieve what Jules Verne predicted—time travel. While we concede predicting the future is a complicated affair, those with highly attuned Story Intelligence will be better equipped to anticipate alternate futures and better prepared to manage the challenges each poses. While experience is no guarantee of future success, it does give us an edge if the difficulty in front of us is similar to one we have faced before, in real time or in story time.

Journey Deeper

How to Create a Compelling Story

There are many things to consider when taking a raw experience and turning it into a story you can tell and share. First of all, you must establish the time of the story to facilitate transporting your audience to a different world with different values. For example, "When I was a boy, my father and I set out on a trip across the country in our old jalopy . . ." Or, "When I worked in the Sarasota office, there was another technician named Jeb Smith. I never met anyone more committed to getting the job done right. Once, he . . ." Starting the story with "when" immediately provides context for audiences—something their brain is craving as they listen.

It's also imperative to establish the place of the story and the personalities involved. And what's the story's mood, e.g. distant, intimate, humorous, melancholy, fanciful, suspenseful, etc.? Also, to turn good anecdotes into stories often requires that you convey events through conversations and actions rather than straight narration. Here are a few suggestions:

1 **Start with a dramatic opening** or a heroic deed. Few listeners can resist a story with a good beginning.
2 **Verify your facts**, especially if you're going to use the story in a business or organizational context.
3 **Identify the problem the story solves** to expand an anecdote into a bona fide account.
4 **Keep it brief**, something you could tell in two or three minutes.
5 Have your story **illustrate one theme or idea.**
6 **Unfold your story according to events**, not explanations, descriptions, or summations.
7 **Keep plot details simple and easy to remember.**

8   Remember to **reveal characters through their actions**. Also, use real names if possible. If you need to protect privacy, change the names and identifying characteristics.
9   Remember that the important thing is the story—**let events speak for themselves**.
10 Provide your audience with **a satisfying ending**.
11 Give it a **good title**.
12 **Project the image like a film in your imagination.**
13 **Share the story with a friend or colleague** and evaluate what worked and why. What didn't work? Why?
14 **Refine the story** based on this feedback.

More on Creating a Good Story

The following are some of the best tips we have ever heard about developing and writing a story from Richard's former business partner and writing coach, Philip Golabuk. He now runs PhilosophyCenter (www.philosophycenter.net). Follow these wise steps and your stories are sure to improve.

Story Development as Dictation. When we write or develop a story for telling, it should feel like taking dictation. Some may refer to this as being seized by the inspiration of your muse. In this sense, we don't have to make ourselves write as much as *let ourselves write*. Think of yourself as a scribe. What does the story you're developing want to say to its audience? Listen. Transcribe. There will be plenty of time later to go back and edit and polish.

The Quality of a Story Is Dependent on Its Predicament. A story has a precipitating event, a conflict, a resolution of conflict, and a point. But what precipitating event? Which conflict, and how to resolve it? And what is the point? Whatever form the story takes, imbue it with the life you or the story's contributors know. What has moved you or them to this point? If you miss this, your account most assuredly will not impact the listener or the reader.

Remember, you don't need to fabricate drama. Every life has drama. The gift you can bring to the story is to discern this drama and expand, accentuate, and articulate it in an informative, authentic way for your reader or listener.

Conflict: An Essential Ingredient. A story needs a through-line that's anchored in a central conflict or predicament. This conflict should build, as opposed to being random or episodic. Having an anvil falling out of the sky on Wile E. Coyote is not conflict. Two people who desire to possess an anvil made of gold and are willing to risk their lives to obtain it, that's the beginning of a good story. The bigger the problem, the better the story. How the character resolves the issue is the crux of the matter. Without conflict or a challenge to organize and structure the story, it will wander aimlessly, like a lifeless zombie. Without conflict, the story's emotional impact is as flat as a tire punctured by a nail. Ultimately, stories are about the troubles and efforts of characters to resolve them.

At the Heart of Things: The Universal in the Particular. The art of developing or writing a story depends on our capacity to recognize the universal in the particular. Imagine being almost run over by an ambulance that came tearing down the country road. The ambulance could represent, in a sense, the double-edged sword of technology. How ironic it is that the very things that we depend on to save us may end up killing us. Can you see how this "point" goes even beyond the context of technology, to a farther-reaching point? This is an excellent example of the universal in the particular. Because the universal resides in the particular (holographically), your predicament is your material. If you can make your vision coherent enough, like the laser light used to create a hologram, you will discern the universal theme or themes in your particular experience, or that of someone whose story you are creating.

Stories Have a Discernible Rhythm. A good story beats with its own life and rhythm. You find this rhythm by looking honestly and willingly at the here and now and reporting what you see with as little judgment or censorship as possible. Stick with what occurred and dispense with lofty pronouncements or platitudes. Stylistically, it's more like journalism, even if it's fiction or a screenplay. Imagine you have a stethoscope and listen for this heartbeat while writing. What is the story's drumbeat? Whatever truth you're aiming for, let it reside in the words and actions of your characters. Not in deductions about their psychological state.

The Story Is Contained in the Details. Forget about grand ideas. Focus on the small details that embody these ideas. By concentrating on the particulars of experience, see if you can arrange them to capture something universal. This is at the heart of what it means to write artfully. On the other hand, be sure you don't become so microscopic in your attention to detail that you create an irrelevant trail of crumbs that does nothing to help your reader find their bearings.

The Story's Structure. Every story has a premise. Usually, it starts something like this: "What would happen if . . ." You can fill in the details. What would happen if every person in America was guaranteed a living wage? What would happen if the polar ice caps melted? What would happen if we weren't able to find a workable vaccine for a virulent virus? Each question propels you down an exciting path with a beginning, a middle, and an end.

The Beginning, or the Precipitating Event: Something happens to launch the series of events that unfold in the forward motion of the story (plot). Identify this event early in the piece. In a short story, usually, the first few paragraphs establish the precipitating event or situation, sometimes the first few lines. It can be subtle, a precipitating psychological shift, or something more obvious like the landfall of a major storm, which triggers some external change.

The Middle, or Character Arc: The precipitating event sets into motion a chain of causes and effects that carry the protagonist seamlessly through some significant change or changes. Remember, readers are interested in characters who "arc," going through some critical change. No arc, no story, no audience! That arc can show up in multiple ways. Someone rich loses everything and becomes poor, like in *Trading Places* starring Dan Aykroyd and Eddie Murphy. Or someone can be a coward but they witness a busload of children roll over into a ditch and catch fire. Now, that person must summon up something from their depths to face death and save the children. Or, someone can be a moral character but they choose to align themselves with an evil person, like in *Wall Street*, when Charlie Sheen decides to divulge insider information obtained from his father to Michael Douglas because he wants to make it big. Likewise, someone can spend most of their life in selfish pursuits but has a change of heart before they die and dedicates their life's fortunes to improve the world of those who were born with minimal opportunity.

The End, or Resolution: Resolution does not mean that everything gets wrapped up neatly. Some endings are the beginnings of another story. The resolution will rarely be conclusive, but it must be dramatically *just* or *right* in the audience's mind. What we mean by that is the ending seems fitting for what happened leading up to it. It has integrity with the heart and rhythm of the story.

What Is Plot? The plot is not a series of unrelated episodes or scenes. It's not fragments that create a mood or stir the senses but lack focus and direction. Anything gratuitous like humor, weirdness, intellectuality, character quirkiness, or drama doesn't make for a good plot. Arbitrary conflicts—with or without resolutions—that don't serve a broader context of conflict and resolution aren't plot.

The plot is a through-line, decisive forward motion, the thread that strings together the dramatic beads of the story, a meaning-arc that gives the reader a sense of closure and completion, and is the soul of the story (words are the body).

Capturing the Audience's Attention. If it's a written story, it's essential to bring the reader into the story right away, to create a world with an emotional atmosphere and gravity that puts the reader's feet on the metaphorical "planet" where the story occurs. You must primarily transport your readers to this new world. Universally, the most iconic way to transport them and engage their "willful suspension of disbelief" is in the opening words of your story. Traditional tellers from cultures worldwide employ a short motif or moniker to signal to their listeners that they're about to enter a storied time and place. Most of us English speakers are familiar with "once upon a time." But this motif isn't unique to just European cultures. The Japanese also start many of their classic fairytales this way.

In business settings, you might find it a handicap to use words like, "Let me tell you a story." People in serious, no-nonsense environments may associate negative connotations with "story." So, you might want to use words like, "Imagine with me for a moment if our customers could . . ." and then describe for your company executives an idea for a new service that could impact customer satisfaction. Or, "Looking back over the past twelve months of sales, let's explore some of the core narratives that have impacted our success." Or if your child has been offered two different jobs in two other cities, you could engage them with a thought experiment: "Imagine it's three years from now, and you're living and working in Burlington. Describe for me the quality of things going on in your life. Now, tell me the story of what it would have been like taking the job in Atlanta."

Some Final Pointers. Good writing uses words economically. As Churchill said, "Use the shortest word that will do the job." There's another quote relevant to this that is often attributed to

Mark Twain, but probably initially uttered by Blaise Pascal: "If I had more time, I would have written a shorter letter." Dispense with purple prose. Simplify. Experiment with underwriting. As the saying goes, "Less is more."

Before you start to write, can you identify a single sentence that embodies the theme or point to your story? If you can't, you have more preparation to do.

Think of language as colors on a canvas. Does it colorfully demonstrate what is happening to your characters? Does it vividly paint the picture in the audience's mind?

Use Sticky Notes to Storyboard

Over the years, we have found it useful to visually map out our stories, whether it's a short story, a screenplay, or even a presentation. You may be aware of storyboarding used by filmmakers. They employ artists to draw in detail every scene to assist the director in preparing the shot. The following list is some useful technical tools now available that can help you with this level of detail, even if you don't have an ounce of drawing skills.

What we have found more straightforward and useful is to use sticky notes to organize my ideas. Here is a step-by-step method that you'll hopefully find helpful.

Step 1: Find a vertical or horizontal surface you can work on with a fair amount of space.

Step 2: Identify all of the critical components of the story. We suggest you use the elements of the story as your headers. Write on each sticky note the essential story element, e.g. Setting, Characters, State of Affairs, etc.

Step 3: Using sticky notes, write as much information as you can under each heading. Don't worry about the order or organization at this stage.

Step 4: After doing this for each heading, then arrange and consolidate.

Step 5: Now, you're ready to either practice honing the oral story or developing the written version.

Storyboarding Resources:
- www.storyboardthat.com
- www.milanote.com/product/storyboarding
- www.post-it.com/3M/en_US/post-it/ideas/articles/how-to-make-a-storyboard-with-post-it-products

Create a Cèilidh in Your Home

In Ireland and Scotland, there is a venerable tradition still alive today. People from all walks of life gather in someone's home or a community hall to tell stories, recite poetry, sing ballads, and dance. They call these gatherings *cèilidhs*, an ancient Gaelic word pronounced "kay-lee." Years ago, we held cèilidhs in our home, and they proved to be a big hit. We'd select a theme for the evening, like "travel to exotic places," or "biggest mistake," or "most unusual experience you've ever had." The response was always positive, but several people would say they'd come and listen, preferring not to speak. Invariably, though, they would be reminded of a story and share it, and they were off to the races telling a spellbinding account of something exotic and quite extraordinary. We had no stage. Everyone just sat around listening and enjoying each other's company. The tough thing was getting people to leave as we approached the midnight hour. We wanted to go to bed. Sharing in this way nurtures people's souls in ways they don't even know they miss.

In addition to inviting people to come and share a story, have them bring a favorite song or ballad, an instrument to play, a poem to read, or teach everyone a traditional dance. Expect to build a depth of community that's hard to replicate through most any other activity we know. In this time of social distancing, you can easily replicate *cèilidhs* online as well.

Tall Tale Contest

Help your friends tap into a true American tradition, perhaps combining it with the most American holiday, Independence Day. Ask them to come prepared to tell the biggest, most plausible whopper they can. Mark Twain and Ben Franklin would be proud.

The Moth

In 1997, George Dawes Green came up with the idea of The Moth StorySLAM, inviting friends to his home to share their tales. At the first public venue in New York, which continues today, ordinary people off the street have told over six thousand stories. Today, The Moth events are popping up all over the US and overseas. You, too, can get in on the action either as a listener or a teller. To learn more, call 1-877-799-MOTH or check out their website at www.themoth.org.

StoryCorps

In the early 2000s, David Isay, a radio producer, became interested in efforts in the 1930s to collect and record oral histories. The work of Studs Terkel also inspired him. Terkel spent his life collecting the stories of ordinary working people all across America. Isay decided to set up a recording booth in Grand Central Terminal in New York City and invite anyone who had a story to be recorded. The idea took off. Today, tens of thousands of people have sat down with a relative or friend to be interviewed and tell their stories, and they're being preserved at the National Archive in Washington, DC. There's probably a StoryCorps recording booth in your hometown. Also, there's now an app, making it easy for you to upload your story to www.storycorps.org. Check it out. The stories are moving, authentic, and engaging.

More Fun

For extra fun and imaginative resources for jumpstarting your story-making, go to www.storyintelligence.com.

Books We Recommend

Creative ideas are the fuel for every personal and professional endeavor. *The Book of Doing: Everyday Activities to Unlock Your Creativity and Joy* by **Allison Arden** will light the fire of your imagination and transport you to new possibilities.

We all need to be reminded daily of the importance of dreaming and fantasizing. If you're needing a good reminder, give your hand to **Dr. Seuss** and read *Oh, the Places You'll Go!* Be prepared to become a child at heart all over again.

Lateral Thinking: Creativity Step by Step by **Edward de Bono** is the bible for all those who want to break out of the ruts of every-day thinking and see issues and problems in a whole new light.

Gianni Rodari transformed the way children were being edu-cated in a small Italian village, opening their minds with fun games that ignited their genius. Ever since, educators from all the great learning institutions have travelled there to discover the secret to his magic. *The Grammar of Fantasy: An Introduction to the Art of Inventing Stories* is one of the best manuals we've read on how to make education interesting and exciting. It's filled with fun, imaginative tools for all ages.

In *A Whole New Mind: Moving from the Information Age to the Conceptual Age*, **Daniel H. Pink** makes the case for the idea that creatives will rule the world of the future. In this concise and fun read, he opens the door to a host of different approaches you can pursue to enhance your creativity. No surprise, storytelling is one of the keys!

2

The Power of Story to Communicate

The ability to powerfully present a message to build a bridge to your audience and catalyze change.

The mystery of storytelling is the miracle of a single living seed which can populate whole acres of human minds.

—Ben Okri

A wise storyteller once told us if you want to convince anyone to adopt a new idea, much less change their behavior, the first step is to tell an entertaining story. As we explored the ways stories transport us in the previous chapter, hopefully, you'll agree. Nothing entertains better than a tale giving your audience permission to suspend their disbelief and journey with you to a different place and time, whether it's traveling to the past or an imagined future. In this chapter, we'll explore the power of story to enhance and supercharge every facet of your communication by transporting your audiences to places filled with new ideas and possibilities. There is no better approach to connecting with others than through a well-told, engaging story. Nothing does a better job of disarming the listener or the reader, sometimes lightly and at other times abruptly shaking them from their current way of seeing, thereby opening their minds to an alternative perspective.

Contrast this with the prevalent cultural model of informing people with numbers and data, expecting it's sufficient to get them to change their minds. If knowing something was adequate to modify our behavior, those of us who struggle to lose a few pounds would quickly consume fewer calories or restrict our intake of carbs. People would not text while driving. Countries would hurriedly adopt steps to stop global warming. Patients would comply with every directive from their health provider. But none of these things have been significantly impacted through the sharing of information. Most efforts at educating people with facts with the expectation they'll alter their behavior have been relative failures. Our country has gotten fatter. People still text while driving even though they intellectually recognize the danger. Our planet grows warmer by the day as businesses and governments wrangle with small, incremental changes. Patients continue to disregard medical advice in alarming numbers, getting sicker.

As we delve deeper into the power of story to communicate, we'll see how informational strategies fundamentally fail to engage our brains. This is especially true when contrasted to how telling and listening to stories produce significant neural repatterning. We'll also investigate the many ways stories are ideal for the vast and varied arena of human communication in all of its variations.

One thing is certain about *Homo narrare*—we spend most of our waking hours communicating in some form or fashion. When it comes to day-to-day conversations, researchers have devoted their time to counting, believe it or not, the number of words we speak on average. James Pennebaker figured out a way to inconspicuously sample people's speech to determine if there's any truth to the common belief that women are chattier than men. Not surprisingly, men tend to talk more about concrete things, whereas women tend to talk more about other people. But all in all, there was no gender difference. Men and women speak, on average, about sixteen thousand words a day.[1] When you consider the typical novel might have about a hundred thousand words, that means every week, without fail, we each spew enough words to fill a romantic paperback or, at the least, a guy's guide to how to fix things around the house.

If we're spending so much time talking, we must be spending nearly as much time listening to others. Or, are we tuning out? Paula Underwood, a Native American mentor of ours, used to say we're responsible for 100 percent of everything we say, but only for 25 percent of what people hear. You see, most of us are weak or inefficient listeners. We can blame this shortcoming partly on the strict physical limits on how much we can digest at any given moment. According to Mihaly Csikszentmihalyi and Robert Lucky, our conscious brains can only process about 120 bits per second.[2] Our processing speed limit sets up an interesting quandary. How do we decide what we should pay attention to? If we're the ones speaking, how can we best capture the limited listening real estate?

Just listening decently to one person requires processing sixty bits of information a second. Listening to two people puts us right up against our processing limit. Forget about listening to three people talking at the same time or trying to follow four friends' conversation in a noisy restaurant. Talking to someone coherently while also attempting to text is virtually impossible. Simultaneously driving, speaking, and texting is comparable in attention degradation to knocking back a couple double martinis before getting behind the wheel. Given these considerations, concerted listening to and comprehending the world of another requires tangible concentration.

How do we cope with these physical limitations? We become very selective. Csikszentmihalyi calls this phenomenon an "attentional filter" and sees it as a boon to our functioning in the world, at least most of the time. These filters work in the background of our consciousness, weeding out all the trivial debris in our perceptual grid. As Csikszentmihalyi explains, this is why we can drive for hours on the interstate and be unable to provide any relevant description of the landscape that's whizzing by at seventy-five miles per hour. If you became too distracted by the fall foliage, you'd not see that tractor-trailer in front of you suddenly braking. This level of filtering keeps us alive.

There are some decided disadvantages, though, to filtering mechanisms. Once a filter's in place, it impairs our receptivity to new information. We can miss important clues and evidence pertinent to our interests and survival. Filtering mechanisms can also create chasms of misunderstanding between us and others who have different filters, leading them to construct an entirely different story from the same raw data.

While we're relatively limited as speakers on what we can do to impact the listening of others, we do have power over one thing—our words. If we want people to listen to us, it's incumbent upon us as speakers to do as good a job as possible on our side of the equation. In this chapter, we'll show you how to expand your Story Intelligence to better engage others, achieve your goals, persuade someone of your point of view, and explain technical information to nontechnical audiences. Improving your SQ can also enhance how you share knowledge, involve people with a cause, sell someone a valuable service, build meaningful connections, inspire collective action, and lead.

Neurons That Fire
Together Wire Together

Not surprisingly, attentional filters have a corresponding physiological underpinning. The Canadian neuropsychologist Donald Hebb coined the adage, "Neurons that fire together wire together."[3] Essentially, every experience triggers the firing of thousands, perhaps millions, of neurons. If we repeat something over and over again, the brain quickly learns the pattern, automatically firing the same neurons. This is how our brains seek ways to become more efficient. Hebb's findings demonstrate that as neurons fire, they release neurotransmitters that communicate essential information that's absorbed by adjacent cells. This synaptic transmission can strengthen over time as similar messages travel down the same neural pathways. Soon, they become automatic. Disrupting an automatic response like this proves to be complicated. That's why if we want to replace an old habit with another new one, it can take weeks of daily practice before the new skill becomes engrained. We must wire together new neural connections.

In the psychological realm, this evolutionary phenomenon can have a profound downside. Once we learn a dysfunctional response and repeat it frequently, we have a strong tendency to continue to rely on it even though new circumstances are radically different. We stop responding to the immediate environment. Instead, we react based on our idea of what the situation means, living primarily in the past. For example, if your parents physically abused you as a child, it's likely that the fight-or-flight response became hardwired and associated with all physical contact. Even in circumstances that are potentially nurturing and safe, any hint of physical contact will elicit the fight-or-flight neural patterns in your brain.

In a milder example, perhaps you grew up in a hypercritical, judgmental household. In college, even when a teacher praises you for an excellent job, you'll likely be stuck in the old story of not being good enough. Despite this positive input, you'll discount it and think your assignment is lacking, concluding that the teacher is just taking pity on you. Ignoring the praise, you'll find ways to prove that you're not adequate to the task at hand. God forbid that a professor gives you some critical feedback, or perhaps you fail an exam. The negative stories you tell yourself can spin out of control, leading to rumination and perseveration. The more you imagine how inadequate you are, the worse you feel. The worse you feel, the more you believe you're worthless and incapable of succeeding at anything. Depression, anxiety, panic, and obsessive behaviors set in, further impairing your performance. The negative hole is so deep that you have no internal resources to short circuit this hellish loop. You need professional help from someone not entangled in this story.

This neurobiological phenomenon impacts our decision-making and even our political views. It's why people are often so resistant to reasonable arguments and irrefutable data. The good news is the right kind of story can disrupt faulty neural wiring.

The Intimate Dance of the Listener and Teller

Adopting a new story can change our brain's wiring. When we tell stories, we alter the brain functioning of listeners as well. Uri Hasson studied this phenomenon using fMRI scanners to track brain activity while people were telling and listening to others' real-life stories. As an actor told a story, "the neural responses in all of the subjects begin to lock together and go up and down in a similar way."[4] As far as we know, listening to a lecture chock-filled with data and charts accomplishes none of this. Nor does this coupling occur when we're listening to the head of our company rattle off bullet after bullet to explain the coming year's strategic priorities.

The idea is not new that our genetics predispose us to engage with others. For years researchers have been studying "limbic resonance,"[5] in which the limbic system of a parent and infant synchronize through nonverbal cues. As a mother holds her baby with their faces approximately eighteen inches apart, something remarkable occurs. Both of their limbic systems achieve resonance. This system is responsible for a host of internal functions, including how we feel and relate to others, and for our self-regulation. Both eye contact and loving touch contribute to this phenomenon, and we now know this intimate interaction, or the lack of it, plays a significant role in children's brain development.

Just as children deprived of contact develop a host of dysfunctional issues, a parallel phenomenon may occur if our environment deprives us of story. Angeles Arrien, an anthropologist, explored for years the role of shaman healers in indigenous communities. Suppose you were feeling out of sorts and unwell. A shaman healer would most probably ask you four questions: When did you stop singing? When did you stop dancing? When did you stop taking time to be silent, whether through meditation or sitting quietly in nature? And, when did you stop taking time to be enchanted by listening to and telling stories?[6]

As we grow older and begin listening to adults tell stories, research suggests the intimacy of the relationship between the teller and the listener also produces a form of limbic resonance. This finding has enormous implications for how we communicate, how we build connectivity between people who hold different viewpoints, how we educate our youth, and how we can heal ourselves and our divisive culture. The more we create spaces where people can hear each other's stories, the more likely they'll experience neural synchronization and limbic resonance. Hopefully, their capacity to connect and understand each other will grow along with their well-being.

The Fictional Roots of Empathy

Let's explore how a phenomenon called "mirror neurons" in our motor cortex may be at the evolutionary root of how empathy is possible. The early work of Giacomo Rizzolatti[7] attempted to localize the actual neurons firing when macaque monkeys grasp a piece of food and bring it to their mouths. Ingeniously, they were able to place probes into the brains of the monkeys in the areas controlling motor actions and link these up to a speaker. Every time the monkeys reached for some food and ate, the neurons in that area fired, and the electronic interface generated a crackling noise over speakers in the room.

One day a researcher ate a snack in front of the monkeys. To his surprise, the speakers crackled. They concluded the monkey's neurons were "mirroring" the activity of the researcher as he ate. Dubbing these "mirror neurons," they hypothesized this process is the neurobiological roots of how empathy evolved within our species. It could also be the basis for how we can learn from each other through the action of listening to or reading stories that recreate an experience for us without our ever having to go through something firsthand.

To this end, Raymond Mar examined what happens in our brains when we're reading a fictional text.[8] As Mar's subjects read, the areas of their brains responsible for hearing, smell, touch, taste, and even their sense of motion all fired in a fashion similar to people having "real" experiences. Mar concluded, "A ready capacity to project oneself into a story may assist in projecting oneself into another's mind in order to infer their mental states."[9] This would appear to explain our ability to feel another's pain and to walk a mile in their proverbial shoes.

Contrary to the stereotype of the bookworm who is so absorbed in literature they lack social skills, Mar found, "Frequent readers do not report smaller social networks or more loneliness and stress. Reading narrative fiction was associated with more social support, and reading expository nonfiction was related to less social support and more stress."[10] Given this, it doesn't bode well for young people, as our education system deemphasizes the humanities in favor of more "practical" subjects such as engineering and computer science. We may unwittingly be contributing to their social ineptitude.

In another study, Mar found narratives powerfully impact emotion and personality when the authors fill them with sympathetic characters and events brimming with conflict and challenges. He calls this "cueing of emotionally valanced memories." Once evoked by the story, these emotions can, in turn, influence a person's experience of the narrative, having lasting consequences even after the person has concluded reading. Moreover, "The distinction isn't really between fiction and nonfiction, but between stories and exposition. Making something narrative in nature—a story—regardless if you label it a true story or a fictional story, the more absorbing it is, the more people will be absorbed and immersed and possibly the more persuasive it will be."[11,12] Imagine a story describing a character kissing his or her amour for the first time. The neurons in our brain fire as though we're kissing our first love, exploding with a corresponding flurry of activity.

In another study, researchers found that the verbs in stories actuate the motor areas of the brain.[13] Just as mirror neurons are intimately involved in our ability to empathize with another human being, they are also the mechanism whereby we identify with characters in a story. That's why fictional characters can become as real and intimate to us as our family. Extraordinarily, we become the characters with which we identify. This hazy distinction between fictional and factual stories is even more significant as we explore the many ways stories can profoundly influence our world view.

Does Story's Power to Transport Us Hinge on the Truth?

In addition to taking us on flights of fancy, we have seen how stories can take us to places we'd likely never visit and introduce us to people whose paths would never cross ours. But do accounts like this have to be true to allow us to experience genuine empathy for the human condition? Melanie Green and Timothy Brock[14] examined this question along with whether stories can change beliefs. To measure this, they created a piece of literature describing a gruesome tale—a murder of an innocent child in a shopping center perpetrated by a psychiatric patient. Would this story affect people's beliefs about the safety of malls, the supervision of people with mental health conditions, and whether the world is moral given a blameless child was the victim?

They told one group this was a true story, and the other group it was fictional. Then, they assessed the degree to which this story transported readers to get to how we tend to identify with the characters in a story, regardless of how different they are from us. They asked questions like, "Could you easily picture the events taking place?" and "How aware were you of other activities going on in the room while reading the story?"[15]

They found that as people immerse themselves in a story, they are "less aware of real-world facts contradicting assertions made in the narrative. [Moreover], transported readers may experience strong emotions and motivations, even when they know the events in the story are not real."[16] Interestingly, the tale's veracity simply had no differential effect on its effectiveness. Factual and fictional stories transport readers to an equal measure. More importantly, "Highly transported participants showed beliefs more consonant with story conclusions as well as more positive evaluations of the story protagonists. Becoming involved in a fictional world seemed to have measurable consequences. A likely possibility is individuals altered their real-world beliefs in response to experiences in a story world."[17]

Is it possible that a simple story is powerful enough to change our beliefs? Their findings suggest that when a story transports us into the world of a character, we identify with them and hesitate to disbelieve a claim congruent with the character's beliefs. There may be other mechanisms at play here as well. "First, transported readers may be less likely to disbelieve or counterargue story claims, and thus their beliefs may be influenced. Next, transportation may make a narrative experience seem more like a real experience. Direct experience can be a powerful means of forming attitudes, and to the extent narratives enable mimicry of experience, they may have a greater impact than non-narrative modes. Finally, transportation is likely to create strong feelings toward story characters; the experiences or beliefs of those characters may then have an enhanced influence on readers' beliefs."[18,19]

We don't have to look far for an example of this experiment operating in real life. Every time President Trump told the story of an innocent person murdered by an illegal alien, he transported his audiences into an account where they identified with the crime's victim, thereby elevating their fear of anyone Latino or with darker skin. News pundits countered this claim citing the many ways illegal aliens contribute positively to their communities and commit a far lower percentage of crime than the general population.

These arguments fall on deaf ears. Compared with rhetorical techniques, narrative persuasion has rhetoric beat hands down for one decisive reason—emotion. When a story arouses people's feelings, they allow themselves to identify with the characters willingly. Rhetoric, on the other hand, relies on logic. It presumes humans are rational, sensible creatures. If we can just give people all the data, they will see the light and come to a reasonable conclusion. Unfortunately, this supposition is false. We're irrational beings as much as we'd like to think otherwise—most decisions we make from the gut, not the head.

Add Suspense to Heighten Emotional Engagement

Suspense can make our communication exceptionally powerful. Shakespeare long ago recognized its hypnotizing impact in this short monologue by Hamlet.

I could a tale unfold whose lightest word
Would harrow up thy soul, freeze thy young blood,
Make thy two eyes, like stars, start from their spheres,
Thy knotted and combined locks to part
And each particular hair to stand on end,
Like quills upon the fretful porpentine.
—William Shakespeare, *Hamlet* (1.5.15–20)[20]

In contemporary times, Alfred Hitchcock is the unmatched master of suspense. If you have ever seen his classic movies, you know what it means to sit on the edge of your seat with sweaty palms anticipating something terrible is about to occur. As Janet Leigh in *Psycho* steps into the shower, the hairs on our head do "stand on end" as we anticipate impending doom. When Jimmy Stewart in *Rear Window* suspects his neighbor of murdering his wife, he begins taking pictures of him across the apartment's courtyard. We can only imagine what will occur if his neighbor suspects Stewart is spying on him. Once his neighbor does see him, we along with Stewart feel our blood "freeze," and our eyes "start from their spheres." Why was Hitchcock so successful at scaring us to death?

Matt Bezdek put Alfred Hitchcock to the test by having subjects lie in an MRI machine and watch his classic films.[21] Surrounding the film image was a checkerboard pattern. They hypothesized as suspense increased, viewers would become much more focused on the imagery

 in the movie and less aware of the peripheral visual array. For example, during Hitchcock's famous *North by Northwest* scene, the brain narrowed its visual focus as the airplane bore down on Cary Grant. As uncertainty intensified, viewers were transported, creating a corresponding neural signature. When he hid in the cornfield and suspense decreased, the neural activity reversed course, and attention broadened to include the checkerboard pattern.

There are a variety of devices available to build suspense into a story. Just a mere title can snag a reader's attention. For example, if you were attempting to focus someone's attention on issues

related to climate change, compare these two titles: "Climate Change and What You Can Do about It" versus "The Environmental Clock Is at 11:59 p.m. Can Humans Avert a Climate Disaster?" I don't know about you, but the second title would do a better job of getting me to pick up the magazine or tune in to the TV. By injecting the element of a ticking clock, we turned up the tension and the suspense. The second hand counting down is a timeworn device used by authors and filmmakers alike, suggesting something tragic is about to occur.

Another method is inserting a secret into your plot. A character knows something the rest of the characters, including us, are trying to discover.

One tantalizing suspense builder is flashing on the screen "To Be Continued" just as a central character is facing extreme danger. We all want to know if our heroine got out of the building before it exploded and will wait with anticipation until the next week's show airs.

Not only does suspense drive deeper engagement, but a growing body of evidence also suggests injecting suspense into a story leads to better memory of story-related information. Researchers like Anneke de Graaf and Lettica Hustinx found participants reported higher instances of story-consistent beliefs when a narrative contained a suspenseful structure.[22] If you want your listeners to focus intently on an issue and open themselves to a new way of understanding and believing, building suspense into your story is the perfect recipe for getting the job done.

Story: The Best Vehicle for Conveying Emotion

Whereas many in the political arena revert to explicit arguments to win people over to their point of view, the most influential politicians have long recognized there's nothing more effective than a good story to influence voters. If messaging doesn't carry with it an emotional component, it's dead on arrival. Story may be the best thing we've come up with over hundreds of thousands of years of evolution to move us to change.

Taking this a step further, Paul Zak has explored the impact of how stories stimulate our brains' natural production of the biochemical oxytocin and the effect that has on our impulse to help others.[23] He contends this is the chemical substrate for what we call the Golden Rule. To test this, his team created two short animated videos. They based one on a true story about a young boy, Ben, playing joyfully outdoors. He's happy and feeling good because, for the first time in months, his treatments for brain cancer have concluded. His father watches him play but is decidedly sad because he knows something Ben doesn't—Ben is dying. The doctors have given him at most six months to live. Trying his best to play with Ben and show good humor, we see his dad weighed down by the thought of his son's mortality. It's more than he can bear.

The second film portrays Ben and his dad having a fun time at the zoo. Nothing much happens as they go from display to display viewing the wild animals. There's no mention of Ben dying or his father's conflicted feelings.

Before they watched the videos, Zak measured the participants' levels of cortisol, a chemical associated with stress, and oxytocin, which produces the feeling you'd like to help others.[24] The story of the dad and his son facing cancer produced an increase in both of these biochemicals. In contrast, the group who watched the narrative lacking any real plot had no change. As the viewing concluded, an experimenter asked the subjects if they could help him out with a few bucks. Those who watched the movie with Ben's dad watching him play knowing he was dying were more than generous with their help. The other group's subjects were not so willing to lend a hand. Why?

As you recall, we're wired to seek information structured in the form of a story. The first film satisfied our minds' craving, featuring a "dramatic arc," whereas the second was more anecdotal.

It didn't go anywhere, and it lacked conflict, climax, emotional response of a character to a dilemma, and a denouement or outcome. It didn't reach the threshold of being a complete story.

Could exposure to a complete story be the key to producing oxytocin, and in turn, cause people to behave more pro-socially? To test this, Zak showed subjects public service announcements (PSAs) to highlight pressing social needs. Before viewing the PSAs, they injected one experimental group with forty IUs of oxytocin; the other received a simple saline solution. They also paid the subjects five dollars to participate. At the conclusion, a screen on the computer came up asking them if they'd like to contribute their five dollars to the social cause discussed in the PSA. Those who received the oxytocin gave 56 percent more money to the charity than the group given the saline solution.[25] This finding represents a straightforward causal role linking story, oxytocin, and empathy for those suffering and in need. Zak suggests stories are so effective in eliciting an oxytocin response from the brain, their effect lingers. Could it be the more we hear stories of others' trials, the more they bathe our brains in oxytocin, forever making us more empathic creatures, more social, and might we say, better people for it?

Story: The Perfect Antidote to How We Think and Make Decisions

In 2015, the World Bank commissioned a report entitled "Mind, Society, and Behavior"[26] to examine recent research on the ways psychological and social factors impact behavior. They found three factors impacting our decisions. First, we think automatically. Daniel Kahneman explores this concept in his seminal book *Thinking, Fast and Slow.*[27] Automatic thinking falls within Kahneman's rubric of more emotionally-based fast thinking. We already explored this concept through another lens when we looked at how neurons firing together wire together. Fast thinking relies on neural patterns informed by heaps of experience with a topic. Automatically we default to a wired-in, habitual response. We have also seen how emotions play a central role in the choices we make, trumping logic nearly every time.

Second, we think socially. Our shared networks, societal identities, and social norms all impact our thinking, influencing us more than we'd like to admit. We only need to survey the world of social media to see how quickly the crowd can shape our viewpoint on a topic.

Finally, we use mental models to think. Our narrative about the world becomes a frame that colors every belief and opinion.

What does this all have to do with how to persuade someone to change their attitude or behavior? First, as we have discussed, presenting "the facts" to convince people is naïve at best. The field of behavioral economics demonstrates people don't make decisions by weighing evidence in a detached, rational manner. Our actions are often opposed to any semblance of logical thought.

Within decision-making, story provides the perfect intervention to address fast, automatic thinking, social context, and altering mental models. For example, Dave Gold details all the ways Democrats have faltered because they mistakenly attempted to persuade the electorate through facts and data, thereby suffering historic losses for four consecutive election cycles.[28] Note that he wrote his analysis before the 2018 congressional elections, which reversed this trend.

How can we win over others with what we perceive to be a better way of seeing the world? According to Troy Campbell, who studies how social movements produce change, story is the answer. But not all narratives are created equally when it comes to their capacity to change minds. We must start with the understanding that our beliefs deeply inform the way we interpret the world. When new information contradicts these beliefs, it's likely to be dismissed out of hand. How do we sidestep this impediment? The best stories, he says, are the ones that "bypass the brain's insistence on keeping the facts separate from our opinions."[29] To accomplish this, he recommends stories must be familiar in structure for the targeted audience and have traditional character arcs. This engenders receptivity. Familiarity promulgates engagement, especially if it highlights the beliefs we already possess. These kinds of stories are particularly successful when they "show how these beliefs are still compatible with new ways of seeing a problem."[30]

Campbell offers a couple of persuasive examples. We have long forgotten there was a time in this country when women were not permitted to vote. Men, the ones in power, generally believed women were weak, unintelligent, and incapable of the rigors of self-governance. This made for a strong headwind for women to change prevailing norms and laws.

By organizing themselves in massive marches, they demon-strated their ability to exert political muscle in ways exceeding the best efforts of their male counterparts. What emerged was a coun-tervailing narrative that profoundly contradicted the view they weren't particularly competent at much else than household chores and cooking.

They also adopted the famous description of Joan of Arc—a heroine in the Hundred Years' War in which she supported Charles VII to oust the English from French soil. In the Siege of Orléans, she led the men into battle and succeeded in freeing the city, which in turn emboldened the followers of Charles to tri-umph. Joan embodied beauty, strength, and the capabilities of the fiercest fighters. This symbolic narrative allowed men to see their wives, mothers, and daughters in a new light, yet didn't contradict their view of them as soft and virtuous. It merely added to the narrative. They could be all that and more.

More recently, we look to the example of Ireland, which was the first country in the world to approve gay marriage through a popular vote rather than by legislation or judicial decision. It was a stunning reversal given that Pope Paul VI in 1946 described Ireland as "the most Catholic country in the world."[31] How did

Ireland's Gay and Lesbian Equality Network accomplish this feat? They got people from all persuasions and walks of life to tell stories on social media sharing why they supported the legislation, tying voting for the new law to traditional Irish values promoting fairness and citizenship. Campbell sums it up, saying, "A vote for marriage equality ultimately became synonymous with a vote for the rights of Irish people."[32]

To move beyond the frames that condition our thinking, we need a story catalyst to break the mind's constraints. In the context of pressing issues like climate change and social and economic inequality, our very survival may be at stake if we can't enhance our SQ and find ways to use stories to change perceptions.

Numbed by Numbers

Researchers for the past three decades have been waking up to the notion that numbers alone do a poor job of persuading people. They're most often counterproductive. It's surprising how misguided number-crunching business managers are when it comes to motivating people. If you have ever attended a critical gathering announcing a new initiative requiring everyone's support, it's most likely they swamped you with loads of information laced with numbers. Why do they continue to fail miserably?

Martin and Powers[33] wanted to get to the bottom of this phenomenon. When they initiated their study in 1983 at the height of a recession, a select number of Fortune 500 companies were attempting to convince their staff and prospects they were genuinely committed to their well-being, even in hard times. Contrary to conventional business practices, they were maintaining staffing levels amid belt-tightening in other areas. It was a wise strategy. When economies rebound from downturns, companies that don't cut staff are better positioned to ramp up and steal market share.

The only problem with this strategy was most of their employees didn't believe their claims. Too many people had been laid off too many times at other companies to think the same was not inevitable. Martin and Powers wanted to see what the best strategy was to overcome this wave of skepticism. They compared four approaches. With one group, they used just a story. In the second, they provided the statistical data to substantiate the claim. The third group got the statistical data and the story. The fourth got a policy statement earnestly delivered by a senior company executive. Have you guessed which method worked best? Most people we share this study with are inclined to choose option three—the story accompanied by the data. But they would be wrong. The story alone was the most convincing. While it's counterintuitive to our rational minds, as we'll see in the following examples, numbers interfere with our adopting a new behavior or belief. In every case, it's the power of a story flying solo that accomplishes what data alone or data and a story combined cannot achieve.

The Universal in the Particular

There is another side to how numbers and facts interfere with our decision-making, a challenge that simple stories are ideally suited to overcome. Nonprofit organizations of all stripes have been attempting for years to get your attention and win your allegiance. The causes are as varied and as numerous as the stars in the sky. All these organizations are dependent upon us to open our checkbooks to support their efforts. For those who succeed, there is one common denominator. They rely less on data and numbers to portray the enormity of the problems they're solving, trusting almost exclusively the power of story to persuade you to become a regular donor.

Paul Slovic, a social scientist, has been studying this phenomenon for years, concluding that the extent of the world's suffering does not motivate us to help. It paralyzes us and constricts our willingness to provide aid. Consider the civil war in Syria where the estimates of civilians killed are somewhere in the four-hundred-thousand range, many of them children. In 2016, the UN identified nearly thirteen million Syrians requiring humanitarian assistance. Roughly half are internally displaced within Syria. Millions more wallow away in refugee camps in other countries.[34] Some nations have attempted to address this humanitarian catastrophe. But many politicians in the US and Europe have turned their backs on the problem. Why have we been so complacent? Slovic says, "People don't ignore mass killings because they lack compassion. Rather, it's the horrific statistics of genocide and mass murder that may paralyze us into inaction. Those hoping that grim numbers alone will spur us to action in places like Darfur [and Syria] have no hope at all."[35]

It doesn't work to tell people in TV commercials or print advertising the numbers of unjustly murdered civilians. Knowing stats about how many hungry children or abandoned pets there are in our communities is ineffective as well. Telling me about how global temperatures are rising by our pumping tons of CO_2 into the atmosphere doesn't motivate me to reduce my carbon footprint. The more generalized numbers we hear, the less inclined we are to donate regardless of our financial resources.

While numbers indeed tell a certain kind of story, it's not the right kind of story to engage us. The problem with numbers is they appeal to the head and bypass the heart. For most of us, our hearts are compassionate organs. As we have seen previously, a story elicits an empathic response when we hear about individual suffering. When we listen to reports of a million people suffering, we feel overwhelmed and helpless to effect change. We stop feeling and start thinking, and this short-circuits the impulse to help. Here's how Slovic sums it up:

"If I look at the mass I will never act. If I look at the one, I will."
This statement uttered by Mother Teresa captures a powerful

and deeply unsettling insight into human nature: Most people are caring and will exert great effort to rescue "the one" whose plight comes to their attention. But these same people often become numbly indifferent to the plight of "the one" who is "one of many" in a much greater problem.

There is a concept particularly relevant to this dilemma. It's "the universal is contained in the particular." What we mean by this is the story of one particular person contains within it the DNA of the bigger problem. By focusing on the one, we're able to tap into our human inclination to help. For most of us, that's the only way we can grasp the intimate social impact of an issue and make a difference. Stories taking us into the world of the individual allow us to enter into the problem with our hearts wide open. It works something like this:

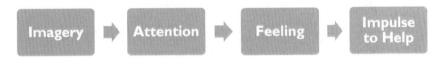

Slovic also found something counterintuitive. If you were the publicity head for a nonprofit attempting to eradicate childhood poverty, for example, you might think, *If one picture can tell a thousand words, wouldn't multiple images of impoverished children do even more to pull on our heartstrings?* Let's try an experiment, and you be the judge. Consider the following pictures. Imagine them beneath a headline in a print ad. Scan the images and note how you feel.

Won't You Help End Childhood Poverty?

Which picture grabbed your attention? Did you find yourself torn between more than one image? How did you feel as you scanned the photos?

What Slovic discovered was multiple images tend to divide our attention. When our focus is divided, we become split internally and torn by the enormity of the problem. Paralysis sets in.

Now, compare your experience with the following.

Won't You Help End Childhood Poverty?

Can you feel the difference? Slovic's research unequivocally demonstrated that ads featuring just one subject not only were more impactful emotionally, they also resulted, hands down, in higher donations. Ads with two photos instead of one photo fell dramatically in response. Slovic calls this the "identifiable victim" syndrome. We can relate to one victim. Add another, and our capacity to feel empathy decreases.

What about the idea of showing a single picture and then accompanying the ad with data about the numbers of people impacted or afflicted? Wouldn't that be more effective than just the one picture accompanied by a compelling story? As we saw in the previous studies comparing storytelling with storytelling plus data, the story alone is the most effective.

Our tendency to frame problems as massive, intractable crises incapacitates us and keeps us from decisively acting. Take climate change, for example. If you're like us, the enormity of the problem quickly sinks you into a feeling of helplessness.

An antidote to this powerless feeling may lie in exemplars of how individuals are forging solutions that can turn the tide. We recently attended the UN Environment Programme's annual recognition dinner and heard story after story of how young entrepreneurs innovate solutions to thwart the effects of climate change. For example, one startup is developing coral that can thrive in warmer waters. They're experimenting with planting it in reefs bleached by rising sea temperatures. We left the event uplifted, for the first time more optimistic than pessimistic, feeling that perhaps we each can make a difference to create a more sustainable world.

When it comes to using numbers in the tales we tell, there may be exceptions worth noting. A growing cadre of entrepreneurial philanthropists is interested in making a broad impact on global issues. Bill and Melinda Gates may be the best known, but they are not alone. These donors are less swayed by the unique case and more interested in substantially moving the needle. When communicating the need with them and making a case for support, it may still be wise to use an identifiable victim to exemplify the depth and reach of the problem. This story becomes a means of summarizing key issues and concepts simply and quickly. It can also connect the potential donor to their core values and their emotional relationship to the topic. When you then segue to the more significant numbers and explain how their support can have a substantial impact on millions just like the one represented in the story, you have created a clear pathway helping them justify their investment in your cause.

Sometimes transposing numbers into metaphors can be useful in the tale-telling. The Advocacy Institute at the Berkeley Media Studies Group[36] has been experimenting with translating big problems into bite-size stories and pictures. For example, it's difficult to mobilize people to take political action who live near a chemical plant emitting tons of pollutants. For the average person, taking on a giant corporation seems overwhelming. Lawrence Wallack offers this alternative metaphor to help people grasp the enormity of their circumstances. Instead of harping on the tons of pollutants emitted every day, break it down into smaller units, such as describing it as twenty-five balloons full of toxic pollution for each school child in the town.[37] This visual metaphor is understandable, plus it reminds the listener this problem affects what is most precious to them—their children.

Whether you're in charge of development for a nonprofit, marketing a discrete product or service, or merely attempting to convince your leadership of a new, more productive direction, your success will hinge on the degree to which you make use of the "universal in the particular" principle. But it's not always as easy as it sounds, especially if you're a nonprofit with a diverse portfolio of offerings, for example. We have been fortunate to work with organizations such as the Red Cross and the YMCA. If you know anything about either, you understand their dilemma. For example, the Red Cross provides international disaster relief to support the victims of tsunamis and hurricanes, fires, and earthquakes. You probably don't know that when someone's house catches fire in your hometown, Red Cross volunteers and staff are often the first on the scene. They provide food, clothing, and shelter for a family who may have lost everything. The Red Cross also offers life-saving CPR and first aid classes through businesses and other organizations. Plus, they teach people how to swim, certify lifeguards, and train CNAs for home healthcare. How do you tackle all that in a singular story about one person? The answer is, you don't.

The Power of
Knowing Your Audience

Pertinent to the issue of what story to tell when your work or services cross multiple domains, in our workshops, we teach people a lesson connected to a Native American practice. If you were a Native storyteller, you likely would carry a medicine pouch on your belt. In it, you'd find several precious or sacred objects such as a unique stone, an animal claw, a rare herb, or a bird's feather. Each would have a story associated with it. Your job as the informal chief storytelling officer of your organization is to have a metaphorical pouch filled with stories about individuals your organization has helped, or about people in your organization who have devoted their lives to helping others.

If you're trying to raise money for a cause you feel passionate about, how would you know which story to pull out of the pouch when sitting with a donor? That requires that you know their story. Imagine you were involved with your local Red Cross and discovered the potential donor loves water sports. Perhaps she even had a near-catastrophic drowning accident as a youth. Based on this knowledge, you might tell her the story of how someone who had recently attended a CPR class heard yells from her neighbor's backyard one afternoon. She rushed out to discover her neighbor's grandchild had fallen into the canal running behind their houses, where he found her floating facedown. Her grandfather jumped in to retrieve her and pulled her up on the lawn, but she wasn't breathing. Luckily the neighbor had recently completed the Red Cross' CPR class and knew exactly what to do while the grandfather ran to call 911. By the time the EMS crew arrived, she had restored the child's breathing. The little girl survived. She probably wouldn't have made it if not for the quick intervention of a knowledgeable neighbor. If the Red Cross development officer asked that donor to support the Red Cross to ensure they could train more people like this neighbor, this story would likely hit the mark, and she'd readily pull out her credit card.

As a communicator, your job is to know as best you can who your audience is. The more you know, the better equipped you'll be to select the right story. It will increase the odds of unlocking your listener's heart.

But what if you're speaking to a diverse crowd? How do you know which story to tell then? The best way to explain this is through a short story.

Once a king was riding through his realm seeking expert archers to join his legions. One day he rode into a small village. There on the side of a barn were three bull's-eyes with arrows in the dead center of each. He commanded the villagers to bring him the man who shot these arrows. A few minutes later, they brought him a young boy.

The king was dumbfounded. "Young man, you shot these arrows?"

The child nodded yes.

"How did you become such an expert archer at such a young age?"

The boy shrugged. "It was easy. You see, first, I shot the arrows into the side of the barn, and then I painted the bull's-eyes around them."

Sometimes we are flying blind and have to make our best guess about the right story for a broad audience. While the story may not hit the center of the bull's-eye for everyone, likely, it will at least hit the side of the barn and evoke something important within most of the people attending. Prepare to be surprised about what it arouses. Whereas your objective may have been X, you will find invariably the story's richness prompted Y in many people. While it might not have been central to your purpose, it got them closer to you and your work, and they will be surprisingly thankful for it.

How Stories Can
Change Public Policy

Stories of individuals who have been adversely or positively affected by a given public policy or law can often turn the tide for legislative action. We once had a colleague who worked with the head of the Tennessee Valley Authority (TVA). She had to go to Congress and ask for a renewal of hundreds of millions of dollars in funding. There had been a growing chorus of naysayers advocating defunding the TVA and privatizing it. Instead of marshaling a laundry list of reasons for the renewal supported by data and charts, she simply told a story of how dependable electricity uplifted one rural family's life. Moreover, the TVA's management of rivers and lakes had averted major flooding this past year, saving this family from devastation.

The chairman of the committee had been briefed by his aides to play hardball with this administrator. But in light of the story, that tactic seemed at best insensitive and misguided. He didn't want to appear to constituents that he was heartless and didn't care about their plight. Without a chart filled with data, the committee renewed funding for the TVA.

For those of you who grew up watching Mr. Rogers on public television, if it hadn't been for his storytelling abilities, we might not have public television today with the rich array of programming that so many appreciate. Back in the late 1960s, there was a move afoot in the Senate to defund PBS. At the time, the Vietnam War was raging. To pay for it, President Nixon proposed slashing PBS's budget in half—a move eliminating much of its valued programming, including *Mister Rogers' Neighborhood*. Senator John Pastore was the chairman of the budget subcommittee on finance. He agreed with Nixon and was pushing defunding legislation. Pastore called witness after witness to defend PBS but summarily dismissed them after a few minutes of making their case. It was clear he was just going through the motions of feigning interest in their testimony so he could get on with what appeared to be a foregone conclusion.

Fred Rogers was PBS's last hope. He didn't bring in any charts or data. Even though Rogers had prepared a lengthy statement, he chose not to read it, saying he trusted Senator Pastore would do so later. What he wanted to tell him was why his show was so important for children and their development. In his disarming style, he explained how children who tuned in wanted a shoulder to lean on. Most of all, they needed to learn how to deal with their difficulties.

> This is what I give. I give an expression of care every day to each child, to help him realize that he is unique. I end the program by saying, "You've made this day a special day, by just your being you. There's no person in the whole world like you, and I like you, just the way you are." And I feel that if we in public television can only make it clear that feelings are mentionable and manageable, we will have done a great service for mental health. I think that it's much more dramatic that two men could be working out their feelings of anger—much more dramatic than showing something of gunfire.

After this preamble, he asked the senator if he could tell him the words of a song he composed, inspired by a young boy who didn't know how to deal with his angry feelings. Pastore was disarmed and nodded for him to continue as he leaned in to listen.

> What do you do with the mad that you feel?
> When you feel so mad, you could bite.
> When the whole wide world seems oh so wrong,
> and nothing you do seems very right.

What do you do? Do you punch a bag?
Do you pound some clay or some dough?
Do you round up friends for a game of tag
or see how fast you go?

It's great to be able to stop
when you've planned the thing that's wrong.
And be able to do something else instead.
And think this song:

"I can stop when I want to. Can stop when I wish.
Can stop, stop, stop anytime . . ."
And what a good feeling to feel like this!
And know that the feeling is really mine.

Know that there's something deep inside
that helps us become what we can.
For a girl can be someday a lady,
and a boy can be someday a man.

Pastore had never had anyone come to testify before his committee telling a story like this. Or singing a song. His dismissive demeanor evaporated. "I'm supposed to be a pretty tough guy, and this is the first time I've had goosebumps for the last two days," he said. "Looks like you just earned the $20 million."[38] PBS was saved by a story genuinely told that opened a skeptic's heart.

How Stories Can Inspire Collective Action

Stories can also inspire collective action and motivate large numbers of people to get behind a cause. Frederick Mayer in *Narrative Politics: Stories and Collective Action*[39] details a wide array of instances where a story was the decisive factor in getting people to come together to make a difference. We have already seen how well stories transport us into the world of others. They do this so effectively we identify with the actors in the story. In this case, they're suffering due to some injustice or benign neglect of governmental leaders. We, in turn, become the protagonists in the story. What harms the lead actors in the tale is, in effect, done to us. A moral injury becomes personal. Suddenly, an injustice that had been out of sight and out of mind becomes real and tangible. Our indignation grows to the boiling point, and we put down the story or walk out of the theater motivated to join others to make change happen. If there are enough people who have shared the same experience, you have the makings of a movement. It's how patriotism is born, and ideologies take hold of the consciousness of whole communities. A compelling story can shape an entire group's world view, values, and orientation toward others. When this occurs, a community's biography can take hold of and inhabit our autobiography.

In recent times there are many examples of this phenomenon. When 250,000 people descended on Washington, DC, in August 1963, marching for jobs and peace, the narrative of racial inequality coalesced not only blacks but people of all ethnicities to join them. It was a narrative shared in some shape or form by many others, including Italians, the Irish, and the Jews. They, too, had found many doors closed to them since arriving here in large numbers at the turn of the twentieth century. Countless other groups had experienced the same prejudices. Admission quotas at the country's finest educational institutions were no secret. Private clubs and organizations had clear rules precluding membership. Many neighborhoods and communities prevented them from purchasing homes there.

What Martin Luther King Jr.'s iconic "I Have a Dream" speech accomplished was to acknowledge the painful narrative of the past, then forge a fresh storyline embodying renewal and hope, healing, community, and inclusion. King's words became the on-ramp for the possibility of a story that had been foreign to this land until that day. "When we allow freedom to ring, when we let it ring from every village and every hamlet, from every state and every city, we will be able to speed up that day when all of God's children . . . will be able to join hands and sing in the words of the old Negro spiritual: Free at last. Free at last. Thank God Almighty, we are free at last."

A different kind of story can lead to collective action in unexpected ways. When Donald Trump in the *Access Hollywood* tape brazenly declared all of the ways he had taken advantage of women during his career, he unwittingly unleashed a pent-up narrative brewing for decades. Since the passage of the Nineteenth Amendment, women have been fighting for equal pay and freedom from oppressive male behavior for over a hundred years. When major news outlets rebroadcast Trump's words, the #MeToo movement was born. Following his inauguration, we had the most significant peaceful protest in the history of this country, with somewhere between two and four million people marching in multiple cities denouncing his behavior and, more generally, discriminatory practices.

This growing narrative wasn't just a flash of protest. In 2018 women claimed 102 of the House's 435 seats, including a Native American, women of Muslim faith, and women who identify with the LGBTQ community. Twelve women won Senate seats, plus women won nine governorships. This doesn't even take into account the number of women elected for the first time to state legislatures and leadership positions in local and municipal governments across the country. Is this the dawning of a new era of women's participation in politics? A new age of equal rights? If the events of the last few years are any indication, it would appear a caustic story casually relayed on a bus by a man who eventually became our president has evoked a bigger story. It has changed the landscape of women's place in American society for generations to come.

When the video went viral of a white policeman kneeling on

George Floyd's neck, slowly suffocating him, white people around the world finally woke up to the many ways white-dominated societies have institutionalized racism. Overnight, Black Lives Matter went from a fringe group, disparaged by many whites, to being accepted and almost universally affirmed. What has made this moment catalytic when so many previous heinous events disappeared into the relentless news cycle? It's difficult to say, as it's difficult to ascertain how communities and politicians will seize the day and turn the page on this country's long history of hate and inequality. What is certain is the story has shifted. Within this new story, there is an opening for profound transformation.

Caution: Stories Can Have Dangerous, Unintended Consequences

While we extoll the power and value of stories to change minds and hearts, there are some caveats. Using narratives in public policy arenas can have adverse, unintentional consequences. Francesca Polletta[40] chronicled instances where decision-makers created laws or policies based on a compelling story that turned out to misrepresent the nature of the larger reality.

Recall the story of the woman who pulled into a McDonald's drive-thru window to get a cup of coffee. As she drove away, it spilled, burning her leg. She then sued McDonald's and won $3 million in damages. This narrative was fodder for activists in the late 1990s who pushed tort reform to restrict the number and size of lawsuits consumers could bring against corporations. They claimed this event was just the tip of the iceberg. The case of the spilled coffee became the poster child for everything wrong with the American jurisprudence system. The contention was that unreasonable claims to obtain settlements in the millions were driving up the cost of insurance for all of us. Whatever happened to people taking responsibility for their negligence, decried the reformers.

Her story was just one of many. There was the case where a woman went into a hospital for several tests, then sued, claiming the tests were responsible for her loss of psychic powers. Perhaps if she was so telepathic, she could have foretold these dire consequences! Then, there was the burglar who attempted to break into a man's home through the ceiling skylights. The skylight gave way. The man fell, injuring himself, then sued the homeowner for his suffering and hospital bills. Another ridiculous claim came from a man who strained his back while pushing his lawnmower. He held the manufacturer responsible for all of his physical therapy and orthopedic visits. As lawmakers heard these tales, the more outraged they were by the ways consumers were harming the system.

As it turned out, the reality in many of these situations was far more complicated and nuanced. The woman who spilled the coffee wasn't only complaining because of a painful scalding of her leg. She had third-degree burns leaving permanent scarring over 16 percent of her body. This injury prevented her from working for the next two years. Moreover, for over ten years, McDonald's had received hundreds of complaints about scalding-hot coffee but had done nothing about it. The real capper was, in the end, the punitive damages were reduced to closer to $600,000 from the original verdict.[41]

Of more significant consequence was how lobbyists erroneously explained skyrocketing malpractice insurance rates. Frivolous lawsuits weren't causing them. Instabilities in the investment marketplace were producing escalating prices. Insurance companies were trying to hedge their bets by passing on the cost of their errors to doctors. Nevertheless, the tort reformers used these narratives to obfuscate the facts and sway legislators, thereby succeeding in getting tort reform passed in almost every state. Chalk one up for big corporations abusing the power of story.

Sometimes the universal isn't contained in the particulars—the particulars simply turn out to be a rare example of one person's experience that doesn't speak to those in the broader class of people who share their problem.

Arthur Frank points out that when advocates tell individuals' stories for a particular effect, they are often open to alternate interpretations, and can lead to unanticipated consequences. A great example of this is the story of the Dreamers—people brought to this country as children or infants who only know the US as their home. Most of them have gone on to be productive contributors to our society, yet many in this country want to expel them and send them back to their country of origin. The tragedy is that the narrative that characterized them as innocent and deserving of protections and citizenship has been turned against their parents. "These stories were used as justification for arresting and deporting their parents, who by definition were then not 'innocent.'"[42]

If you wish to transform society by influencing policymaking, storytelling can be your ally and a useful tool for change. But we all must learn to become more insightful about the stories we tell and their consequences. Fredrick Mayer warns us:

> The same tool that King used so masterfully to move a nation to overcome the evils of segregation was used by Hitler to enlist the German people in the evil collective action of Nazism. And we can be called by false prophets as well as true. Like all powerful tools, narrative is dangerous. And for that reason, in our time, it is all the more important to understand the power of narrative and to use it with care and humility as we seek collective responses to the challenges that confront us.[43]

Perhaps the broader lesson is it's incumbent on us as listeners to consciously develop our SQ and become better attuned to the pitfalls individual stories contain. We can learn to carefully extract value from them while at the same time cautiously generalizing from one person's experience to inform our beliefs, policymaking, and legislation affecting the lives of millions.

Why Economists Need English Majors

When was the last time you read the newspaper and attempted to make sense of an economist forecasting the future? The keenest minds can be muddled by complex sets of facts and numbers neatly organized into tables to show some historical trend. In all of my years of reading, only a handful of economists have articulated why things are going awry with the economy or have explained the factors portending the next recession.

Robert Shiller, in his new book, *Narrative Economics*,[44] makes a compelling case for the value of story in understanding and explaining economic forces and events. He also suggests, at times, it's quite simply the narratives people have adopted that cause a recession. "We have to consider the possibility that sometimes the dominant reason why a recession is severe is related to the prevalence and vividness of certain stories, not the purely economic feedback or multipliers that economists love to model."[45] Shiller goes on to liken narratives to contagions acting just like a virus, spontaneously mutating and taking on a life of their own, spreading rapidly like COVID-19. The truthfulness of these stories is incidental, and often they can be founded on whimsical thinking with no grounding in economic realities whatsoever.

As an example, Shiller offers this explanation for why the Great Depression built up steam into an unstoppable force starting in 1920. During World War I, manufacturers inflated prices for all kinds of consumer goods due to the scarcity of raw materials. When the war concluded, companies continued wartime pricing. Newspaper stories began circulating, claiming selfish profiteers were taking advantage of the public. The public responded with moral outrage. People started postponing many of their purchases, believing this would force manufacturers and merchants to lower prices. When prices began to fall, the public saw this as a good sign but continued to defer buying, believing the bottom was still way off. Prices did tank eventually, and the deflationary effects spread like wildfire throughout the system, leading to the crash of the stock market.

Shiller suggests the turning point came with the injection of a new narrative in the form of a fireside chat by President Roosevelt. He used his moral standing to convince people they were not patriotic by withdrawing all their funds from their banks, thereby leading to banks' precipitous closure nationwide. His words were inspiring and had all the bearing of a general marshaling his troops on the battlefield. "You people must have faith. You must not be stampeded by rumors or guesses. Let us unite in banishing fear."[46] It worked. The run on the banks ended, money began to flow again, and the complete collapse of the economy was averted.

Interestingly, following the events of 9/11, then-President Bush deployed a similar narrative strategy, downplaying the effects of this tragedy and encouraging people to go to the mall and buy something. Such an appeal felt surrealistic, but it did get people off of the sidelines. Instead of waiting for the next terror attack, they went back to work, and most importantly, back to spending money.

As we are writing this chapter, a growing financial crisis is once again enveloping the country, caused by the coronavirus pandemic. President Trump's early attempts to assuage people's and investors' concerns sounded emptier and emptier as the infection rates in Europe and here in the US multiplied at an astounding rate. Pictures of ICUs in New York City filled with sick patients overtook the calm narrative he was attempting to project, unveiling it as wishful thinking utterly uninformed by the advice of epidemiological experts. As of now, the administration's failure to manage the pandemic has hobbled our economy, and the end appears nowhere in sight. It's a shifting story impervious to proclamations by a leader whose primary strategy seems to be grounded in denial. Until scientists discover a cure or an effective vaccine, no story told by the administration to get people back to work and children back in the classroom will be persuasive in the face of a hidden, deadly virus that pays no heed to the tenor of a narrative.

Stories All Leaders Should Be Equipped to Tell

We want to conclude this chapter by highlighting a few critical stories you need to develop and have at your disposal in the metaphorical story pouch you carry with you wherever you go. Your communication success depends on it.

Revealing Your Authenticity. It is incumbent on every leader to answer this question: Who am I? Now, you may be the kind of leader who believes you don't want to be too transparent with your team. People getting to know you personally may make it doubly tricky down the road if you have to make the tough decision to let someone go. If leaders are to earn the trust of those who are following them, our bias is they must be authentic. Authenticity comes from knowing yourself and your story. While it's not necessary to wear your biography on your sleeve, by sharing facets of your life at the right times, you will be perceived as more accessible and caring by your staff, all of which lead to greater trust.

There are a host of ways you can go about this. One hospital CEO we knew of would weekly put out a note to the entire staff sharing what had occurred in the previous days with his family. If his daughter had fallen and broken her arm and ended up in the hospital's ER, he'd share what the experience was like for him as a concerned dad. If his son kicked the winning goal in the previous weekend's soccer match, he'd proudly recount his excitement. If his wife had brought in a record crop of tomatoes from her garden, he included a photo of a ripe tomato sliced up in their evening salad. Invariably, as he walked the halls of the hospital, people he didn't even know by name would stop to congratulate him or express concern for something difficult that had just occurred. That opened the door for him to ask about how things were going for this employee. It also allowed him to forge a new relationship on a first-name basis. You can bet when the hospital faced difficult times, and he had to ask people to make an extra sacrifice for the good of the institution, they rallied around him because they felt he was like them.

Roots Matter. Your organization's history can be a source of inspiration and identity for every member of the team. Included in that is what we call your "Foundation Story." It details how you got your start and the many challenges you had to overcome. These kinds of stories remind everyone what you stand for and give new employees a sense that they were there in the beginning.

There is one challenge with these kinds of historical tales, though. Companies change over time. Frequently the stories about the past no longer reflect the culture and values of the company today. Our friends who were part of the Disney organization in its early years in Orlando lament the changes they have seen since Walt passed out of the picture. It's a different company today, and the lore of yesterday now seems quaint. At worst, it's entirely out of step with the twenty-first-century conglomerate Disney has become. Every organization must reckon with its evolution, preserving what is best about the past and jettisoning things not reflective of contemporary reality.

Making Values Real. Your organization's values are abstractions at best. Reproducing them in posters on your walls or printing them on a card to be carried in a wallet will do little to reinforce them or help people when there's a tough decision at hand. We once worked with over a hundred managers of a large healthcare organization. When we asked them what the organization's values were, people began calling them out. Then, someone would yell, "That was last year's value." Not until someone fished a card out of their purse and read the current values could we be sure what they were. The bottom line is such devices do little to emblazon the organization's values on the hearts of the people working there. In contrast, finding stories embodying those values and frequently telling them will make them real and tangible.

David Armstrong,[47] who heads up Armstrong International, decided years ago to eliminate his policy and procedures manual. He replaced it with a book of stories capturing the company's values. As an example, Armstrong exalts the creativity of its people. Because they manufacture several complex steel products, safety is also valued. One day a shop steward accidentally spilled alcohol on the concrete floor. He could have easily wiped it up with rags, but then what was he to do with the highly flammable cloth? He had the bright idea to burn it off, which he did successfully. And, they summarily fired him. Yes, it was a somewhat creative solution to his dilemma, but he endangered the lives of hundreds of people because of his actions. Imagine if you heard this story during your orientation. You'd have little doubt what you'd need to do if ever faced with a challenge crossing the line between two competing values. Safety would always come first.

Where Are We Going? When you ask a team of people or an entire organization to follow you, that requires a considerable degree of trust. Before I head off into the wilderness with hiking buddies, it's natural I'd want to know what our destination is. And how do they propose we're going to traverse that raging river in the distance or climb up rugged terrain without any belaying equipment? Your team members need a picture of where you're expecting them to go and the challenges you anticipate they're going to have to overcome. There's no better way to accomplish that than a clearly articulated story. We'll shed more light on this topic in the last chapter of this book, focusing on using storytelling to envision the future.

Customer Success Stories. Your customers are your lifeblood. Teaching your staff to treat them as precious resources is crucial to your success. There is no better way to get this point across than through the sharing of customer success and service recovery stories. A good story can accomplish way more to attune your team to the complex needs of the customer than a written script.

In the early days of Universal Studios Orlando, someone got the bright idea tourists would love to have breakfast with Woody Woodpecker. Tour operators would make the reservation weeks in advance. The morning of the event, buses filled with tourists eager to meet Woody would pull up to the entrance gate around seven a.m. before the park opened.

One morning due to someone's blunder, a bus pulled up, but there was nothing in the books saying they were coming. The cooks hadn't clocked in, nor had the person who regularly donned the Woody Woodpecker costume. Only a couple of custodial staff cleaning up were there. When the guard called back to announce a busload of hungry guests was at the gate, no one would have blamed them if they responded there would be no breakfast. But they didn't do that. They told the guard to let them in. One of them went into the kitchen, put on an apron, and prepped scrambled eggs and toast for forty people. The other slipped into the costume and was there to welcome the guests to the backlot, keeping them entertained long enough to give his partner time to get the breakfast ready. The tourists left happy and excited to have gotten in on something exclusive and unique. The two custodians recognized that everyone, regardless of their role, is in the business of making the guest happy. To not collect and share these kinds of stories is to fly into a competitive storm at your peril.

How We Do Things. Finally, there's an informal sharing of stories occurring in every company, letting people know how to get the work done. A staff member's account can capture insights into complicated processes and how she solved a thorny problem.

You no doubt have heard the iconic story of how Xerox copy maintenance specialists used to gather at a local coffee shop each day to share shortcuts to fixing these complicated machines. Their tales led to greater efficiency and effectiveness. If there were a hall of fame for "how we do things" stories, this would certainly win an Emmy. When an efficiency-minded VP heard his guys were taking time off for coffee instead of servicing customers, he called a halt to the practice. Not surprisingly, their effectiveness declined. When Xerox's leadership recognized the error of their ways, they instituted these kinds of knowledge-sharing skull sessions, not just permitting them. They encouraged them. How are you promoting the sharing of "how we do things" stories in your company?

Finally, if you were sitting with a new manager, what would be the best way to convey to him or her how to be a good boss? A few years ago, we had the privilege of interviewing managers at a large aeronautics company. A wave of the senior folks was about to retire, and they feared they'd be losing the lessons of how to manage teams effectively. They had recognized one manager we interviewed as one of the best in the business. Because she was a woman in a predominantly male culture, her success was even more notable. When we asked her what the key was to her success, she told us about her first manager. Everything he did was ass-backward. He was an exemplar of how to demotivate a team and get the least from them. Today, when faced with a challenging management issue, she thinks of that first manager and contemplates what he would do. Then, she does the opposite.

The key here is it's essential to encourage the informal sharing of stories. These tales carry your organization's spirit. The more robust the sharing, the healthier and more resilient your organization will be.

Journey Deeper

13 Rules for Supercharging Your Presentations

Rule #1: Know Your Audience

Here are some things to consider, especially when making technical presentations.

- What is the level of expertise of your audience?
- What do they currently know about your topic?
- Are they complete neophytes, or do they already have a basic knowledge of the topic?
- How sophisticated are they?
- What's their education level?
- Do you need to frame the presentation as though you're speaking to a room of PhDs? Or, sixth-graders still stuck in the Newtonian view of the physical world?
- What's the expectation about how much time you have? A reasonably good presentation will crash and burn if you don't respect people's time and run past your allotted period.
- What's the predisposition of your audience? What story are they living in regarding your topic? If you're preaching to the choir, that conditions the type of presentation you'd make in contrast to making a presentation to a room filled with naysayers.
- Finally, what do they want from you, and what do you want from them? Getting clear on this will make a big difference in how you structure what you say and how you position your "ask."

Rule #2: Start with the End in Mind

Before creating your first PowerPoint slide, and even before you decide your key messages, take a step back and ask yourself: What's the purpose of my presentation? What's the question I want my audience to contemplate? Do I simply want to inform people, do I want to teach them something they can use, or do I want to persuade them to do something, like fund a proposal or an initiative? If you're seeking to get them to do something, what would success look like? And if they take the steps you're advocating, how will the world be a better place as a result?

Rule #3: Harness the Whole Brain's Mentalware

Our brain is hardwired for story. Recognize that your audience will be more inclined to stick with you and engage with your presentation if you frame it as a story. Remember, story is our native language. Everyone speaks it. Everyone understands it. When you tell a story, it ensures that you and your audience's brains entrain. It gets you both on the same proverbial page.

Rule #4: Organize Your Presentation Like a Story

You must understand what constitutes a good story. As we have seen, a story minimally has characters, a setting, a plot, a conflict, and a resolution. When structuring a presentation, we've found it useful to use the narrative schema structure as a loose guide for developing it. This plot structure makes for an excellent presentation structure. The narrative schema are:

- Introduction of setting and characters
- Explanation of state of affairs
- Initial event
- Emotional response/statement of goal by the protagonist
- Complicating action
- Outcome
- Reactions to the outcome

Rule #5: Build Your Presentation as a Series of Stories

Be sure that each story has an exact point that contributes forcefully to the overall conclusion you'd like your audience to make due to hearing your presentation.

Rule #6: Pictures Outperform Words Every Time

If, for example, you wanted to present the history of DDT use in the United States, what you wouldn't want to do on a PowerPoint slide is cover it with tons of copy. Instead, show your audience pictures, like an eagle and her eaglet, and tell them how the widespread use of DDT endangered them. Place all that copy in your *notes* instead.

Rule #7: If You Must Present Words and Data, Use an Infographic

They're the most compelling way to present vital information.

Rule #8: Capitalize on the Power of the Universal in the Particular

Remember, most decisions are grounded in emotion! If you're seeking a positive response to your presentation or argument, recognize the universal is always contained in the particular. It's the best vehicle for engaging audiences at an emotional level. Remember, data creates resistance; stories build engagement and consensus. If you want to present data, do it in the form of a simple infographic.

Rule #9: Use Video Sparingly

Video is a powerful means of demonstrating complicated ideas, but if you let it dominate your presentation, you miss out on the opportunity to make a personal connection with your audience. Use it sparingly, and don't rely on it to tell everything. There are tons of video resources on the web to enhance your presentations. Use them. As powerful as a video is, you want your audience connecting personally to you through your storytelling. If you relegate the storytelling only to a video, there will be less engagement and probably less buy-in. You can't overestimate the power of the personal touch and the entrainment building between you and your audience when telling an oral tale.

Rule #10: Create a Logline to Inform Your Title

If you're unfamiliar with the term, it evolved in the movie industry to create a shorthand of sorts to give a broad-brush sense of the story for someone listening to your pitch. It should be memorable and, hopefully, stick with them long after they have forgotten the details of what you shared. Here are some examples from iconic films of the past.[48]

- *The Godfather*: The aging patriarch of an organized crime dynasty transfers control of his clandestine empire to his reluctant son.
- *Forrest Gump*: Forrest Gump, while not intelligent, has accidentally been present at many historic moments, but his true love, Jenny Curran, eludes him.
- *The Shawshank Redemption*: Two imprisoned men bond over several years, finding solace and eventual redemption through acts of common decency.

Now, compare the title of the following scientific article with the logline we suggested to replace it when presenting to nontechnical audiences: *Controlled-release of Bacillus thuringiensis formulations encapsulated in light-resistant colloidosomal microcapsules improves our ability to manage lepidopteran pests of Brassica crops.* Here's the logline: *The story of how a little-known bacterium can make agriculture safer and more productive.* Which one would grab your attention?

We have already seen how suspense can build engagement. If you're going to be giving a talk within your organization or to a broader audience, take a bland title and inject it with suspense to build interest and curiosity. Look for an edge to pique prospective attendees' attention. Or, reframe the title using a provocative question. Here are a few examples:

Economic Lessons for Today
vs.
Thirteen Ways Economics Can Make You Wealthy

Bioethical Considerations in Healthcare
vs.
*How You Address These Bioethical Issues
Will Impact Patients' Perception of Care*

Climate Change and Its Impact on the Economy
vs.
*Will the American Economy Collapse by 2050
Because of the Effects of Climate Change?*

Today's Political Landscape
vs.
Will Political Polarization Destroy American Democracy?

Rising Tuition and Its Impact on Higher Education
vs.
*Can Higher Education Survive if Graduates
Are Unable to Repay Their College Loans?*

*Rule #11: There Are a Hundred Ways to Leave
a Lover and a Hundred Ways to Tell the Same Story*

With apologies to Paul Simon, explore telling your story, whatever the topic, in various ways. Before you settle into a particular framing of your narrative, come up with at least six possible distinct approaches. Then, thinking of your audience, which one do you think will have the most impact with this crowd?

*Rule #12: Don't Be Afraid to Entertain
Your Audience — They'll Appreciate You for It*

As we have seen, we're all hungry to be entertained. Even if your audience is a serious lot, bring some levity to your presentation. The exception is if the topic is solemn, such as sexual abuse or increasing levels of crime in the community. In these cases, being lighthearted would be deservedly interpreted as insensitive or crass.

Rule #13: A PowerPoint Show Is Not a Handout

Time and again, we have seen presenters construct their show as though it's going to be the handout or leave-behind. If you follow the rules 1 through 12, your slides will have minimal copy and be predominantly pictorial. They won't be useful as a handout. Instead, take all that information you used to cram into your slides and put it in the notes section. It's your reference for the presentation, but you should never read them verbatim. If you think it's important to leave something behind, take the time to design the handout with your audience in mind. Hit the high points you want them to remember. Use white space liberally, so the reader isn't overwhelmed when they first pick up the document. Infographics are always helpful. And yes, use pictures to tell the story where appropriate.

Build Your Narrative Assets

Anyone interested in influencing others can benefit from a concerted effort to collect, catalog, and share their stories with internal and external audiences. The problem we hear most from nonprofit board members is they need stories to share when approaching potential donors. More often than not, those tales are stuck in the heads of the people in the organization. There are a lot of ways to address this issue. At the least, appoint someone in the organization to be the chief storytelling officer. Their job is to collect the stories. That can be accomplished easily by recording interviews with key players. Just as you carefully manage your financial and human assets, these are your narrative assets, and they deserve just as much attention. The recordings can be simply transcribed using any number of transcription services on the web, or you can try out some of the free artificial intelligence transcription sites. Then, decide on terminology for classifying the stories and make them accessible to staff and board members. We like a straightforward system by topic. Be sure to give each story a descriptive title. You can also identify some critical words to help a prospective searcher know a little more about the story and its relevance to them. Place those under the title. If you have the resources, put them on the web and make them password protected.

How to Find and Use Stories

In your many years of experience with your organization, you have undoubtedly had a wide array of experiences that potentially could become compelling stories, useful for influencing and impacting various stakeholders. Here's a series of questions that may prompt you to remember events and anecdotes that you can turn into good stories:

- What has been your organization's most significant setback, and how did you overcome or solve the problem?
- Who are the people in your organization whom you admire the most? Why?
- Which staff members have impressed you the most? Why? What have they done to win your admiration and respect?
- What stories have you heard within the organization that made the biggest impression?
- What is the most extraordinary story you have ever heard that expresses your mission and values?

Your coworkers can also be a source of stories that you can add to your organization's repertoire. First, to find these stories requires that your staff knows you're in the market for a good tale that illustrates a principal organizational value and involves some degree of heroism. Second, ask each of your staff members, from the secretary on up, if they have a good story for you. Third, regularly seek new stories. It's an excellent way to stay in contact with all your staff.

If someone brings you a good story, write up the story, then distribute it around the office. It's a great way to recognize the hero of the story and reinforce your organization's values, vision, and concerns.

Tips on Interviewing and Getting the Story

1   Get clear on the goal of the interview. What do you hope to elicit from the person(s) you're interviewing? Be sure to let the interviewee(s) know why you're interviewing them and what you're going to do with this story.

2   Decide whether you want to allow the interviewee to review the story before you use it. If so, make that point up front and find out to what extent they want to have editorial input.

3   If the person is comfortable with recording the interview, do so; otherwise, take precise notes. There are some terrific AI options available today for transcribing digital audio recordings for free.

4   Keep it conversational while also focused and on track. Be sure before you wrap up the interview you have learned everything you can from this person. Are there others you need to interview to round out the story?

5   What questions do you have? Write them out. To end up with the guts of a compelling story, find out everything you can through the design of your questions. The following are some examples:

    a   The setting: What's the backdrop to your story?

    b   State of affairs: What is going on that led to this happening?

    c   Who are the principal characters? Who are the supporting characters? What's their backstory? Who are the antagonists, if there are any?

    d   What was the precipitating event that set this story into motion?

    e   How did your characters react? What did they want to happen? Why do they care about this?

    f   What were the obstacles they faced? How did they go about addressing them?

    g   What kinds of complications did they have to face and overcome?

    h   What was the resolution?

    i   How did your characters respond when there was a resolution to the problem or conflict?

    j   What and who has changed as a result?

    k   If this is an ongoing story, what is on the horizon?

6   Give the interviewee space to think and reflect. Silence is often an indication that they are mulling over what to say next. Give them enough space to do that before barging in with another question.

7   Leave the door open to come back and ask for clarifications and additional information. You may learn things from others that shed light on this story and prompt you to ask further questions.

Understanding Your Audience

Who are the key audiences that you must be aware of when you deliver your message? What story are they living in? Can you broadly describe each of these audiences?

As an exercise, identify an individual or stakeholder group from one of those audiences who could potentially be a strong supporter of your work or be the audience for whom you're creating your story. What are their key concerns, and why does your work make a difference to them? What is it about a specific story that you might tell that would resonate with their story and background? Write two to three paragraphs. Be sure to describe this individual as a means of understanding why they'd want to help.

Now, consider each of your audiences. Which of your stories would best meet their profile, needs, and background? Which account is most likely to motivate them to support your work?

Books We Recommend

When we first began introducing business leaders in the early 1990s to how they could use story in the workplace, we were paddling out in the ocean waiting for a big wave. Well, it came in the form of a number of fine books on story and organizational life, and our colleague Stephen Denning had a hand in a number of these great reads, all of which we recommend:

Storytelling in Organizations: Why Storytelling Is Transforming 21st Century Organizations and Management by **John Seely Brown, Stephen Denning, Katalina Groh, and Laurence Prusak**

The Leader's Guide to Storytelling by **Stephen Denning**

The Secret Language of Leadership: How Leaders Inspire Action through Narrative by **Stephen Denning**

A key to understanding the many ways story intelligence infuses every facet of our thinking is recognizing the different modes of thought. **Daniel Kahneman in** *Thinking, Fast and Slow* has blazed new trails that you'll find both fascinating as well as practically relevant to how you can become more effective in every facet of your communication with others.

If you're interested in understanding how others can see the world so differently than you, or how you can better communicate with those with an opposing political view, *Don't Think of an Elephant!: Know Your Values and Frame the Debate* **by George Lakoff** will be a mind-opener and a must-read.

If storytelling is the language of the imagination, then metaphor is one of its foundational elements. In *Metaphors We Live By* **by George Lakoff and Mark Johnson**, you'll enter into the rich feast of metaphorical language and learn how you can use it to transform your communication effectiveness.

While we have pulled back the veil on the intricate way stories engage us, **Brian McDonald in** *Invisible Ink: A Practical Guide to Building Stories That Resonate* will take you into the subtle and powerful DNA of any story.

There are a few great speakers whom we know who are truly master of their art, and **Nido Qubein** is definitely one of them. In *How to Be a Great Communicator: In Person, on Paper, and on the Podium,* he reveals how he has made communicating both an art and science and used it to support his phenomenal success.

3

The Power of Story to Enable Learning

The ability to thoughtfully enrich others' capacity to learn by integrating story into every subject matter.

Education is the kindling of a flame, not the filling of a vessel.

— Socrates

To native peoples, using stories to enable learning is a foregone conclusion. The Oneida tradition stressed it's impossible to teach anyone anything. The closest word to "teach" they had could best be translated as "enabler of learning." They understood the best we can do is establish the conditions for learning, then trust this will enable the student to discover new worlds, deepen their understanding, and grow. One of the keys to facilitating learning rests in story's power to evoke new perspectives and insight. Mastering this art is at the heart of Story Intelligence and is essential to parenting, classroom instruction, and training in business settings. To succeed at this power, though, we must be willing to swim upstream against deeply entrenched cultural norms when it comes to education.

In most instructional settings, we have grown away from narrative and embraced more prescriptive approaches to learning. Perhaps it's because of our successes in the realms of mechanization and industrialization. Classrooms have become places to "train" minds and exact conformity of understanding. The goal is to demonstrate a predetermined proficiency level in regurgitating information and performing tasks to ensure graduates go on to the next level. Historically, this path prepared people to excel in their factory jobs. As a result, we have erroneously come to think of learning as a process of inputs and outputs, viewing humans and their brains as mechanical devices. If we can just get the inputs right, know which dials to turn and how much, then humans will learn the proper lessons and apply them in every context of their lives and work. Unfortunately, humans and their brains aren't so simple. If this approach were correct, we'd be seeing many more successful schools and more competent, confident, and accomplished students graduating. As we're discovering, this old paradigm for learning and teaching is less and less relevant in today's ever-changing world. Today, one's ability to continually learn may be much more important than what you know, because the pace of knowledge obsolescence is fast approaching the rate of species extinction on the planet.

The challenge here lies in what Jerome Bruner[1] frames as two divergent approaches to cognition: propositional thinking versus narrative thinking. Propositional reasoning focuses on the abstract and theoretical. It's all about the construction of logical arguments devoid of context or feeling. For example, propositional thinking is invaluable when it comes to calculating the speed of light or figuring out which stock or bond will boost my return on investment. Scientists, engineers, and business analysts excel using this form of cognition.

But our everyday lives are concerned with things decidedly more human and practical. Narrative thinking helps us succeed in a variety of tasks. For starters, it provides us a wealth of understanding about ourselves, others, and the world. Simply put, the human enterprise and interpersonal relationships lend themselves elegantly to the power of story. In this milieu, context is everything, as are intentions, personal goals, character, morality, feelings, time, and place. Nothing is tidy and linear in this world. Knowledge derived from narrative thinking is fuzzy around the edges, imprecise, and complex. It deals with complicated relationships and focuses on internal motivation and actions. This kind of knowing tends to render a more holistic perspective about the way things are and why. As we have seen, we tend to define our lives narratively, and this kind of thinking is hardwired.

If this is the case, why aren't we tapping into the power of narrative thinking in our educational institutions and our places of work to enhance our capacity to achieve, learn, and share knowledge? And, how can we all benefit from this power of story-based thinking to solve our most vexing problems and address the enormous challenges facing our societies?

The Role of Language and Story in Human Development

From the beginning of our lives, our parents babbled at us. Most of us were read to as well and told stories about simple things. Titles like *Where the Wild Things Are, The Giving Tree, Goodnight Moon,* and *Green Eggs and Ham* are staples in most middle-class homes. Perhaps one of these was a childhood favorite of yours or is now a favorite with your kids. Bedtime is also a great occasion to make up stories with children. In a program we taught years ago at an Elderhostel event (now called Road Scholars), a participant told us a story he had been telling his children and grandchildren for years. It had colorful characters named Joe Pfufnik, Joe Fabitz, and his girlfriend, Molly Begonia. Perhaps your parents, too, made up farfetched tales populated by exotic characters like these.

In the simplicity of telling and reading stories, something profound happens in the child's brain. Their mind makes connections where there were none. Neural circuitry starts to wire itself, helping the child see they are like the story's protagonists. With time, they learn their actions have consequences, just as the story's actors benefit from wise decisions and suffer because of poor ones. They also begin to understand that if a character postpones gratification, there are more substantial rewards waiting around the metaphorical corner in contrast to choices they make without the future in mind. In this way, storytelling becomes an important vehicle to help children develop impulse control.

This is not the case for many, though, who grow up without books, without parents reading to them, and without a rich lexicon of spoken language permeating their daily interactions. Those who grow up without exposure to stories can teach us much about the importance of narrative in human and brain development.

The phenomenon of generational poverty cuts across racial divides and contemporary societies around the globe. We're talking here about families who have been living below the poverty line for multiple generations. More often than not, in today's American culture, these are single-parent homes where the mother may be working more than one job, barely making ends meet. It's a rarity in these homes to find the warm interactions we so often associate with a mother cradling and nurturing her young child. Instead, a not-so-benign babysitter has replaced nurturing relationships—the television.

When assessing the tenor of their interactions with their parents and other adults, it's generally not constructive. More than middle-class households, parents communicate with rebukes or punishments for transgressing some invisible line. In most cases, these parents simply lack interpersonal or parenting skills to positively manage their relationships. Words like "stop that," "no," and "shut up" become representative markers for the interactions between parent and child, pointing to an even bigger problem—

these parents simply talk far less to their children than parents in middle-class homes.

The differences are stark and revealing, affecting the future of children in profound ways. Dr. Dana Suskind, who started the Thirty Million Words initiative, began recording interactions between children and adults across the socioeconomic continuum. Children from wealthier, college-educated families typically heard, on average, over 2,100 words an hour. The number of words children heard from underprivileged cohorts was astonishingly paltry—an average of 616 words an hour. Add that differential number up over the first three years of a child's life, and it reaches into the thirty-million range.[2] This data point alone seems to be the most significant determinant of differences in IQ test scores at ages three and nine.

The scarcity of language exposure is like a prison sentence for children from low-income families, ensuring the cycle of poverty is replicated generation after generation. Suskind began wondering if they could reverse this trend. Her team came up with a device called LENA, which stands for Language Environment Analysis. It works much like a pedometer, tracking the number of words parents speak every day, and gives them immediate feedback.

The results in the early tests have been encouraging. Once parents become aware of not communicating often enough, they increase their communication levels by over 30 percent. Only time will tell if these higher levels of communication will be adequate to stimulate brain growth and help their children break the bonds of poverty. The challenge, though, is that increasing the quantity of communication may represent only part of the equation to uplift children's development.

Martin Joos,[3] a Dutch linguist, began digging deeper into the differences in language between children who come from impoverished households and those who come from families with more considerable socioeconomic resources. Joos identified what he calls five "registers" in people's language,[4] regardless of the culture:

Register	Characteristics	Examples
Frozen	The words are always the same.	The Lord's Prayer, The Pledge of Allegiance
Formal	The word choice and sentence structure used by the business and education community. Uses a 1,200-to-1,600-word spoken vocabulary.	"This assignment is not acceptable in its present format."
Consultative	A mix of formal and casual register. Used in conversation.	"I can't accept the assignment the way it is."
Casual	Language used between friends, which comes out of the oral tradition. Contains few abstract words and uses nonverbal assists—a 400-to-800-word vocabulary.	"This work is a no-go. Can't take it."
Intimate	Private language shared between two individuals, such as lovers or twins.	"Sweetie, would you give nuggins a little . . ."

It turns out children from households experiencing poverty for at least two generations rarely use the formal register in their speech. No wonder these children struggle to make the grade—formal register is often the register of choice in the classroom.

Language register also plays a vital role in the realm of how these impoverished students see their world. Formal register carries with it a traditional story structure with a beginning, middle, and end. People develop an internalized schema with an expectation the story will have a character, a setting, an initial event, action by the character in response to the event, complicating action as the character attempts to resolve the conflict, a conclusion, and a reaction to that conclusion.

In contrast, children growing up in households characterized by generational poverty rely almost solely on the casual register. As you can see in the previous chart, the vocabulary within this register is relatively limited and tends to be laden with emotionally charged words. Thinking and speaking within this framework upends the traditional story structure. The child simply jumps to the conclusion or point of resolution, whichever has the chief emotional charge.

Relying solely on the casual register when tracked out across a child's life can be devastating. According to Ruby Payne, a lack of story structure in children's lives can impact their ability to plan, take responsibility for the consequences of their behavior, and can often lead a person down a path of criminality. "If an individual depends upon a random episodic story structure for memory pattern, lives in an unpredictable environment, then . . . the individual cannot plan. If an individual cannot plan, he cannot predict. If an individual cannot predict, then he cannot identify cause and effect. If an individual cannot identify cause and effect, he cannot identify consequences. If an individual cannot identify consequences, she cannot control impulsivity. If an individual cannot control impulsivity, she has an inclination to criminal behavior."[5] While growing up poor does not predestine a person to a life of crime and imprisonment, an alarmingly high percentage of people incarcerated today are illiterate. In the US, 85 percent of juveniles who interact with the court system are functionally illiterate, and 60 percent of the inmates can't read.[6] We know this outcome is a slow-moving train wreck beginning early in life with predictable outcomes that have huge consequences for individuals and society. According to Christopher Zoukis, "Children who struggle to read in first grade are 88 percent more likely to struggle in grade four. And those who struggle in fourth grade are four times more likely to drop out of school. The great irony is that prisons base some of their future planning on third and fourth-grade literacy rates."[7]

The absence of a future story is another factor differentiating these children from those in middle-class households. Children growing up with few resources are continually stressed and in survival, living in neighborhoods that aren't safe and often overrun by gang violence. They live from moment to moment, uncertain if there's going to be a tomorrow. Who has time to plan for the future in these circumstances? Yet, being able to conceive the future is crucial when it comes to planning and preparing assignments in school. Questions like, "What do you want to do when you grow up?" are foreign to these students. Ruby Payne, an educator, spoke with an eighteen-year-old student and asked him what he anticipated life would be like when he turned twenty-five. His answer was startling. "He said he would be dead. I asked him how he knew that, and he said everyone like him is dead by that age."[8] When we live without a future story, why would we care about what happens in Mrs. Jones' third-period English class? Or care about the importance of a college education? Or consider what it would take to create a better life?

How Stories Help
Children Develop Impulse Control

Stories can play an instrumental role in helping children learn how to develop impulse control through a relatively simple mechanism—behavioral modeling. Through a story, children witness characters who often don't manage their emotions effectively, thereby suffering adverse consequences. They also get to see exemplars of productive behaviors and how these actions can benefit the story's protagonist. Through these stories, children can quickly learn what it means to manage their emotions.

Perhaps the best example of how a story can benefit impulse

control comes from the Inuit tribes in northern Canada. In the 1960s, Jean Briggs, an anthropologist, traveled to the Arctic Circle and convinced an Inuit community to allow her to take up residence. Very quickly, she became aware of a profound difference between how these people approached parenting and the prevalent culture in North America. Inuit adults never expressed public displeasure through angry words or gestures. It's not to say they didn't feel irritation or anger. They simply didn't show it in any demonstrative manner. Events that might have made us curse up a storm and send our blood pressure soaring just didn't have the same impact on Inuit adults. For example, "One time someone knocked a boiling pot of tea across the igloo, damaging the ice floor. No one changed their expression. 'Too bad,' the offender said calmly and went to refill the teapot. In another instance, a fishing line—which had taken days to braid—immediately broke on the first use. No one flinched in anger. 'Sew it together,' someone said quietly."[9] It's difficult to imagine American parents responding in such a positive manner. As a young boy, I regularly knocked over a glass of iced tea at dinner, causing my mother to blow a gasket. This kind of adult behavior would be a rare exception in the Inuit communities. How did the Inuit develop such a level of control over their feelings?

When their children got angry, Briggs discovered that the Inuit used storytelling to discipline and teach them. Instead of reprimanding them when they misbehave, Inuit parents playfully tell the child a story designed to mold behavior in real time. If a child plays too close to a dangerous ocean wall, they don't yell at the kid to get away from the water. Instead, they pull the child aside and tell her a story about a sea monster living just under the water's surface. He waits for children to fall in and places them in a slimy pouch. Just that thought is enough for most kids to heed warnings about the sea's hazards.

They also use storytelling to teach children about self-care in the harsh arctic winters. When the Northern Lights fill the sky with their mysterious glow, parents tell children if they don't wear a warm hat at night, the lights will reach down and use their head as a soccer ball. While they tell such stories good-naturedly, most children don't take them too literally. But they convey the message, and it's no doubt remembered.

Even when a child throws a tantrum, lashing out angrily at someone, parents patiently wait for the emotional storm to subside. Then they enact a story drama with the child:

> Typically, the performance starts with a question, tempting the child to misbehave. For example, if the child is hitting others, the mother may start a drama by asking: "Why don't you hit me?" Then the child has to think: "What should I do?" If the child takes the bait and hits the mom, she doesn't scold or yell but instead acts out the consequences. "Ow, that hurts!" she might exclaim. The mom continues to emphasize the effects by asking a follow-up question. For example: "Don't you like me?"[10]

By lightheartedly inviting the child into the event's reenactment, without an emotional charge or severe judgment, the child gets to see that hitting hurts, and they don't want to be someone who injures others. They also begin to develop an ability to disassociate their feelings from behavior. After repeating the drama until the child quiets down and gets the lesson, the parent is modeling for the child what it means not to let your feelings take over and lead you to do something socially unacceptable or harmful. They also learn nothing in life is so important or grave as to warrant lashing out at another, especially if it leads to losing a valued relationship.

How Story Can Shape Moral Development

Contrast the previous approach with the way contemporary educators have relied on propositional thinking, verbal discussions, and punishment to shape and teach morality and ethics. Only now are social scientists "rediscovering" what ancient prophets and teachers always knew—the way to reach people's minds and hearts is through parables.

You're no doubt familiar with the fact that Jesus, a Jew, used parables to convey essential principles to the masses. He came by story honestly, given the Old Testament is filled with one story after another about the Jewish people, their journey to freedom, and their struggles to develop a deeper, more ethical relationship with God and their fellow human beings.

Research is now shedding light on how stories accomplish this, and what kinds of stories have the most impact. For example, one group of researchers showed how hearing classic moral tales like "Pinocchio" and "The Boy Who Cried Wolf" doesn't impact the degree to which children ages three to seven lie about their transgressions. In contrast, the story about how George Washington cut down the cherry tree does decrease lying. The authors suggest, "The reason for the difference in honesty-promoting effectiveness between the 'George Washington' story and the other stories was the latter emphasizes the positive consequences of honesty, whereas the former focus on the negative consequences of dishonesty. When they altered the 'George Washington' story to focus on dishonesty's negative consequences, it too failed to promote honesty in children."[11]

Other research suggests children's age plays a crucial role in their willingness to fess up when they've done something wrong. Smith and Rizzo presented four-to-nine-year-old children stories of kids engaged in various inappropriate behaviors. They included stealing candy from a friend to pushing another child to the ground to access a swing. They then concluded each story with branching storylines. In one, the transgressor lied about their actions; in the second, they confessed. In the latter storyline, they asked the child about how their mother would feel about the confession. On the whole, older children tended to attribute the emotion of remorse to the protagonists in these tales and associated positive feelings with fessing up. In contrast, younger kids were much more predisposed to have a positive attitude toward the children in the stories who didn't tell the truth to their mom.[12]

Interestingly, in the vein of how the Inuit respond to their children, the authors of this study concluded that a low-key parental response to misbehaving might be the healthiest approach to teaching children ethical and moral behavior. When children grow to expect their parents will not overreact to a misdeed, and may even react positively, they are more likely to confess to things they did wrong. By behaving in this manner, parents can extol the virtues of honesty.

So, if you're a parent, what is the best strategy for downloading your moral values and preparing your children to become more responsible citizens? And, what should you do if your child lies about egregious behavior? First, share stories with them extolling honesty and the benefits of telling the truth versus creating a climate of fear and punishment regarding dishonesty. If you can't find suitable stories from your religious tradition or folk literature, get creative and make them up. Ask them what they might learn from the story. When you affirm the child's insight into the characters' behavior, you make it safe to positively explore her thinking about a challenging dilemma without fearing remonstration for getting it wrong.

Second, realize if a child does something unkind like hitting someone or stealing, this doesn't mean your child is on the road to becoming a sociopath. It's a natural part of their moral development. The less you overreact, the more likely they'll recognize it's safe to come clean when they do something inappropriate. The data is reasonably emphatic—focusing on negative consequences for lying or crossing an ethical line rarely has a lasting positive impact on children's behavior.

Third, like the Inuit, be willing to get playful with teaching your child how certain behaviors are hurtful and inappropriate.

Ultimately, their bond with you is more important than the pay-offs for misbehaving. Trust that they'll quickly learn the value of postponing gratification for the things they want. Moreover, when they do screw up, they'll develop that same playful compassion for themselves, endeavoring to do better the next time. In the end, none of us benefit from a double dose of guilt—the first imposed on us by many of our parents, the subsequent guilt self-inflicted as adults without any prodding.

What We Can Learn from an Ancient Story Tradition

One of Paula Underwood's learning stories, *Who Speaks for Wolf*,[13] couples the power of story with a reflective process to engender deep learning. The Oneida believed this is the only way to learn anything of importance. They placed such a high value on learning that they kept a continuous record of it through their oral tradition and had thirty-four different words to describe it. These people gave serious consideration to what it means to develop a deep understanding of themselves and their world.

Paula's great-great-grandmother was a healer among the Oneida tribe living in Western Pennsylvania nearly two hundred years ago. When she was a child, an old man was the "Keeper of the Old Things"—the oral history of the Oneida, their lifeways, and most important for our discussion, the ancient learning stories. The Oneida's customs were quickly changing because of the pressures exerted by white settlers. Younger people were losing interest in the old ways and becoming much more attracted to these new peoples' customs from another continent. Who would carry on the traditions? Would there be anyone interested in preserving the ancient stories? Did anyone have the patience to listen arduously to and learn these tales? In Paula's ancestor, he found just such a person, and he proceeded to patiently download all he knew to her, hoping to preserve this knowledge for future generations. Older generations eventually passed these tales down to Paula's father, and he, in turn, patiently taught them to her. She then chose to write them down. In the recommended books at this chapter's conclusion, we have listed many of these stories and other writings by her.

A few years ago, with Paula's death, her daughter picked up the mantle and is sharing the stories and lifeways Paula conveyed. Her children are embracing and telling the stories as well. Hopefully, these tales will be preserved for generations to come for all those who have, as Paula would put it, "listening ears."

The Oneida framed the story of *Who Speaks for Wolf* to pass on essential learning necessary for the tribe's survival. As the story goes, Paula's ancestors had outgrown the place where they lived and recognized they needed to find a better home. The tribe's leaders sent out scouts to identify a new land with the most resources. One of these scouts was named Wolf's Brother. The tribe revered him for his intimate knowledge of wolves, like the meaning of their howls, why they behaved much like humans, and especially the way pups played like our children. At night it wasn't uncommon for wolves to come to the edge of the fire's light, apparently as curious about us as we were curious about them.

When the scouts returned, they were each certain they had identified the best place for growing crops, hunting, and situating their longhouses. The people listened attentively. Then the experts among them who knew the most about agriculture, hunting, fishing, and longhouse construction commented. Soon a consensus emerged. The chief expressed what they were thinking. No one objected, except one person who pointed out they had not heard from Wolf's Brother. It was unclear why he hadn't yet returned. The chief pointed out perhaps he had died in his journey, or a late winter storm had delayed his return. He dismissed the objection, insisting they had to decide given they had to send an advance party to prepare the land.

A few days later, Wolf's Brother did return. When he heard of the place the tribe had chosen, he counseled against this decision. You see, he knew a large community of wolves lived in that region. The chief minimized Wolf's Brother's concerns, saying they had accommodated Wolf all these years; certainly, Wolf could make room for them this one time. He further justified his stance by pointing out the preparation party had already departed, and the people had commenced making preparations to move. Wolf's Brother objected, saying he feared it would take a lot more energy to change a wrong decision later than to do so now. But the chief closed his mind and would not listen.

Wolf's Brother's prediction came true. Soon after they arrived in their new home, wolves began sneaking into the village and taking food when none were looking. When this occurred, the people resolved that giving them a little food was a small price to pay for the land, and they started leaving leftovers at the village's edge. Wolf became bolder and was soon wandering among the longhouses. The women were alarmed to have wild wolves in such proximity to their children. So, they reversed course and stationed men at the village's perimeter to drive Wolf off. It worked, but it, too, had unforeseen consequences. In the fall, the woman in charge of winter's stores came to the chiefs to inform them that there would be insufficient food to get them through a long, hard winter.

The people gathered to consider their options. They readily saw feeding Wolf had contributed to the problem—it was precious food they could have stored away. They also saw having sentries posted around the village was keeping these same men from hunting. Someone suggested they could kill off all the wolves, but others spoke up to say they didn't want to be the kind of people who needlessly killed rather than move.

This could just be a story about a people who, after a hard winter, decided to relocate and, perhaps, from then on, consider Wolf when making significant decisions. But they saw there had been something deeply flawed in their approach. They failed to take into account the energetic impact of every decision. Also, they recognized there were many things they could not foresee when making a decision. From then on, after they explored every possibility when confronting a problem, someone in the tribe would rise to speak for all they did not know that they did not know, and ask, "Tell me now, my brothers, tell me now, my sisters, who speaks for Wolf?"

After sharing this tale, the teller would ask a simple question of the listeners: "What might we learn from this story?" No one would offer up a prepackaged lesson, as is our custom with fables. Or judge the response of the listener. They understood a child of three or four would glean lessons filtered through their limited knowledge and insight. As the child grew and heard the story again, say at age twelve, their understanding would expand. As they grew into adulthood, they would garner new lessons tempered by their years of experience. Every insight was welcomed, affirmed, and appreciated.

What the Oneida understood is we each have a learning edge upon which we can build our knowledge and from which we can grow and expand our understanding. Attempts to short-circuit this process or jump ahead to tell the learner what they should learn are ineffectual at best. Such insights fall on fallow ground. Once you suggest to the listener what they should know, the process ceases to be one of personal exploration and devolves into one in which the student is now trying to figure out what answer you're expecting.

In contrast to our Western tradition of fables, the Oneida learning stories don't provide answers. Instead, they're designed to engender questions and contemplation. This process stimulates what Paula refers to as "interlobal" communication within the brain. From what we now know about neural connectivity, the process undoubtedly begins laying down new neural pathways. In this way, story becomes a vehicle for self-initiated learning independent of a teacher. We're tapping into the brain's natural mode for self-exploration and discovery.

The insights of the Oneida into the process of learning are many. For starters, they saw how marrying language with imagery is essential to constructing a compelling story. These two facets of the story are integral to each other. For whole learning to occur, both are needed. The Oneida also understood the value of repetition. When Paula introduced *Who Speaks for Wolf*, it was embraced by the US Department of Education as a program of excellence. Teachers were encouraged to read the story to their students a minimum of three times during the school year. Paula described it as once for each ear, and once for the heart. Sometimes it takes a long while before a story penetrates our filters and preconceived notions. I've had stories work in me for years and keep gleaning insights each time I revisit and reflect on them.

Reflecting on the Power of Reflection

There's a lot to unpack when reflecting on reflection. First, it's a form of thinking in its own right, distinct from conceptual, creative, or critical modes. Usually, we direct it at some facet of our experience. Often, it's focused on understanding better an opaque, complicated, and perhaps incomprehensible problem. Most importantly, reflection helps us to create a feedback loop to evaluate our actions and thoughts. Without it, we'll replicate our mistakes ad infinitum. In that sense, it's a unique platform we have developed for course correction.

Likewise, reflecting on stories can be as beneficial for our growth as reflecting on our life experiences. From the given facts and circumstances of a story, reflection enables us to deduce a new perspective that we'd never have seen. Confucius said over two thousand years ago, "By three methods we may learn wisdom: first, by reflection, which is noblest; second, by imitation, which is easiest; and third by experience, which is the bitterest."[14] Story's true gift to us is it allows us to learn without the bitter suffering.

Aristotle suggests a life of reflection leads to wisdom, insight, and hopefully, better action and superior outcomes.[15] Story and reflection become, then, the pathway to better living.

In contemporary times, John Dewey, the twentieth-century philosopher, extolled how reflective thinking creates an uneasy edge within us. Perhaps this is why many people resist leading a contemplative life. "Reflective thinking is always more or less troublesome because it involves overcoming the inertia that inclines one to accept suggestions at their face value; it involves willingness to endure a condition of mental unrest and disturbance. Reflective thinking, in short, means judgment suspended during further inquiry; and suspense is likely to be somewhat painful."[16] In light of Hebb's insight that "neurons that fire together wire together," reflection represents a form of swimming upstream against familiar neural pathways. Breaking away from these points of view can indeed create a challenging mental/biological dissonance. As you'll see later, stories can ease or even bypass this painful process of looking at ourselves.

At a more personal level, Peter Pappas, an educator, writer, and instructional designer exploring the frontiers of teaching, has developed a useful taxonomy.[17] You'll see it starts with a story and moves from the past to the future. From this perspective, reflection and meaning-making cannot thrive without storytelling.

Taxonomy of Reflection	
Creating	What should I do next?
Evaluating	How well did I do?
Analyzing	Do I see any patterns in what I did?
Applying	Where could I use this again?
Understanding	What was important about it?
Remembering	What did I do?

McDrury and Alterio[18] stress storytelling, coupled with reflection, has considerable advantages for adults engaged in learning a professional practice. It offers them a way to explore their new experiences, generalize them to other situations, decide how to translate their learning into future actions, and then evaluate the result of their actions. They investigated this by exposing learners to a talented practitioner's stories about the complex and diverse situations they encounter in everyday practice. Furthermore, storytelling offers many of the merits of experiential learning. First, it creates tacit knowledge for the learner as though they had been there in person. Second, it creates for the learner episodic memories similar to actual experiences stored in long-term memory, which can then be more easily retrieved. To this end, they offer a five-stage model for reflective learning through storytelling:

1   Find emotionally evocative stories, especially those based upon the learner's prior knowledge.
2   By listening, create the opportunity to make sense of the story's context and the human experience within the story.
3   Expand on the story to make more connections to prior knowledge. Active reflection allows new knowledge into their cognitive structures. In this step, dialogue between the teller and listener increases. Together they begin to construct meaning from their experience of the story.
4   Encourage story processing and questioning in which the teller and listener can explore multiple perspectives and dig underneath the narrative to get at the concepts represented in the story. In this stage, learning deepens and expands.
5   The listener and teller reconstruct the story in light of their own experiences. Not only are they reflecting on the story, but they also reflect on their own beliefs, thinking, and behaviors. As a result, they may experience a kind of personal transformation that permanently changes them and their practices, leading to real personal growth.

Failing Is the Secret to Wisdom

There's a humorous old story in which a seeker of truth climbs to the mountaintop to meet with a wise guru.

"O wise one, how might I develop wisdom?"

The guru contemplates this question for a moment and answers, "To achieve wisdom, my son, you must develop good judgment." The seeker departs on a quest to develop good judgment, but after two weeks, returns perplexed.

"How can I develop good judgment?" he asks.

"Ah," says the guru. "To develop good judgment, you must acquire experience."

The seeker departs only to return a few weeks later. "I have attempted to acquire experience, but feel no closer to developing good judgment, much less wisdom. How can I gain experience?"

The guru chuckles. "My son, it is simple. To gain experience requires bad judgment."

Are experiences and all of the inevitable bad choices we make sufficient to learn and develop wisdom? To get to the bottom of this question, Giada Stefano[19] compared individuals who focused on merely acquiring more experience versus spending time to reflect on the skills they had accumulated. They wondered whether the additional experiences are more beneficial to performance. Is there a point where we have amassed an adequate amount? Are we better off spending time codifying and articulating what we know through the process of reflection? We've all grown up hearing that there's nothing more valuable than on-the-job training. Could on-the-job reflection be just as useful? For example, if you were training to be a brain surgeon, just reading about this topic would inadequately prepare you. Is there a tipping point, though, where spending more of your precious time performing surgeries is less beneficial than reflecting on what you have learned from the surgeries you have already completed? Stefano frames this as the opportunity cost of one's time:

> Articulating and codifying prior experience does entail the high opportunity cost of one's time, yet . . . thinking after completing tasks is no idle pursuit: It can powerfully enhance the learning process, and it does so more than the accumulation of additional experience on the same task. [In fact, there is an] increase in the ability to successfully complete a task when individuals are given the chance to couple initial experience with a deliberate effort to articulate and codify the key lessons learned from such experience. In explaining the performance outcomes associated with reflection, deliberate learning efforts affect how one approaches the same task afterward, both cognitively and emotionally.

Reflecting on our experience has distinct and powerful advantages not just for individuals, but for organizations as well. Just taking fifteen minutes at the end of each day can propel your learning. It not only will build your confidence in what you have learned, but it will also improve your ability to apply knowledge and drive increases in your performance by as much as 22 percent. While these numbers are compelling, many industries have not embraced this practice, including healthcare, one of our fastest-growing sectors. Let's now examine if a story coupled with reflective learning can be the antidote to patient harm.

How Ancient Wisdom
Can Help Us Today

Industries have long embraced the lessons of quality improvement and learning from the past. In examining defects in the manufacturing process, teams can build a better story in the future.

Likewise, after even routine practice missions, military squads assemble to debrief what went well and what could be improved next time. The hallmark of a capable team is its ability to step back and, at times, literally stop the line. Only then can they discern through reflection and study why errors continue to persist in the end product.

In contrast, hospital teams rarely pause to reflect on what happened and how they can do a better job for future patients. Healthcare is just beginning this journey, but for the most part, it's struggling. This resistance to organizational learning has its roots in deeply held beliefs unconsciously codified in the industry's culture.

A colleague of ours once told us that the near misses are the real gold in reducing patient harm. If mined, these data points can be powerful predictors of where the next sentinel event could kill someone. Near misses can be the proverbial canary in the coal mine to avert a human tragedy. Surprisingly, though, hospital teams rarely take the time to stop and see what they can learn when things come within a hair's breadth of harming a patient, or actual harm occurs.

To create a product called StoryCare, we and our colleagues at IDEAS, a former Disney division, teamed up with Synensys, a healthcare consulting firm dedicated to reducing patient harm and error. The product's premise was simple. Healthcare is a team sport filled with experts—doctors, nurses, technicians, and administrators. They each spend years honing their craft. Unfortunately, little in their education and training prepares them to practice effectively as an expert team. The data bears this out— breakdowns in leadership, teamwork, and communication are the root cause of most patient harm. The numbers are scary, and most patients and families have no clue how dangerous a hospital stay can be. We're talking about an estimated four hundred thousand people dying annually from preventable harm while in the hospital, making it the third-largest killer in America after heart disease and cancer. Nearly triple that number is hurt but go on to recover.[20] It's a big problem and is the equivalent of a jumbo jet crashing every day. We thought if we could get teams taking time out to reflect on their practice of medicine as a team, they could improve and hopefully save lives.

Considering *Who Speaks for Wolf* as a template, we went to work writing and recording over one hundred stories about regularly occurring near misses and fatal mistakes. The idea was to create an inexpensive way to provide these stories to teams in situ. Healthcare professionals are busy people, and the dynamics of a hospital make it difficult for entire teams to remove themselves from patients' care to watch a video in a nearby meeting room. With the stories implemented as audio only, we could deliver them to the team at a nurse's station, playing them from a cell phone while preparing to take over from the previous shift.

To enhance their effectiveness, we had our audio engineer "sweeten" the tracks with sound effects. Suppose a story's setting was a bustling ER. You'd hear in the backdrop calls for doctors over the intercom, beeps and bells emitted by equipment, and the general noise of people yelling to colleagues halfway down the hall as they attempt to triage multiple patients at the same time.

The idea was simple. The team would listen to the story then debrief it using a few reflective questions. When compared to high-fidelity medical simulations in which a team practices on sophisticated mannikins replicating a host of physical problems, this is also a simulation, but is about as low fidelity as you can go.

You're already familiar with the first question the facilitator of the simulation would ask: What might we learn from this story? This simple question's impact is as profound for modern medical teams as it was for ancient peoples like the Oneida. As you would expect, as team members debrief the events occurring in the story, they gain more profound insight into the universal problems represented in the story. Without prompting, the team members begin to draw parallels between the story and their patients. If they don't make the leap, though, the facilitator can follow up with additional questions, such as, "What's one thing we as a team could change in our practice based on what you've learned?" or, "What one thing could you personally do differently to improve outcomes based on what you've learned?"

One of the stories we developed detailed how a car hit a bicyclist, and he coded during surgery. They induced a coma to give his lungs a chance to recover from the trauma of the accident. Over a couple of weeks, they slowly weaned him off a pivotal medication to bring him back to consciousness. In the middle of a nursing handoff one evening, a code was called for another patient. An hour later, they had stabilized that patient, and the day nurse slipped out without reviewing the doctor's orders for the bicyclist. The night nurse sat down and was examining the chart. Something caught her attention and didn't make sense. The doctor had ordered that she increase the critical medication, not decrease it as they had been doing over the last days. She called the day nurse and asked her what she knew about this. It perplexed her as well, so they phoned the doctor at home, a daunting task because he had a nasty reputation. The rap was he'd make your life miserable for phoning him for issues he considered inconsequential. At first, he was irritated by the call. But they forged ahead and asked if the medication increase was correct. He immediately knew it wasn't and searched his memory for what could have happened that afternoon to distract him and cause such a significant mistake. The story concludes with his thanking them for the call and for setting the record straight. If you'd like to listen to this improvement story and watch a team debrief it, visit StoryCare's website.

This particular story is about cross-monitoring. All team members need to be willing to be questioned about decisions, because, quite simply, we're all human and prone to making mistakes. If you're ever hospitalized, you'll want this kind of cross-monitoring. Unfortunately, the culture of healthcare is such there is resistance to learning these principles. Practices like this intended to fill the gap created by human error are the exception, not the rule.

These stories can accomplish what is so difficult for healthcare teams to do on their own—spur reflection. Whereas teams may find it painful to take a cold, hard look at their deficiencies, it's much easier to identify a hypothetical team's screw-ups in a story. Hatton and Smith[21] identified essential issues that this "distanced" approach achieves. First, reflection allows healthcare teams to bring clarity to complex or ambiguous problems and test alternative interpretations. In so doing, they can adjust and modify their course of action in real-life situations. Second, it allows them to gain a perspective about themselves that's difficult to deduce when they're doing something. Syd Lieberman, one of the country's best storytellers, once described this to us as looking at one's life from across the street. With that kind of distance, we have the room to learn in a lighthearted manner. In fact, not taking ourselves so seriously may be a necessary predicate to insight. Third, discussing an event with a group facilitates understanding.

With that said, the story of StoryCare is still evolving. It came into focus when we worked with obstetrical teams from hospitals in North Carolina and Virginia. These two states had some of the worst outcomes for baby and mom when an emergency C-section was required. Using StoryCare and higher-fidelity simulations, we taught these teams how to debrief an emergency C-section and carry this practice back to their respective institutions. Before the training, they effectively had a zero-rate of debriefing. After the training, they increased their debriefing to nearly 75 percent of the time. As we expected, harm to moms and babies fell precipitously.

Nursing schools have demonstrated interest in StoryCare as well. There may be no better way of teaching new practitioners about the nuances of teamwork and communication than through compelling stories coupled with reflection. These kinds of stories allow learners to ask themselves, "How might I have acted in this situation?" They won't find this in a discursive textbook. The question helps them embark on a journey of self-discovery and explore their relationship to complex, challenging professional dilemmas they are sure to face within the first days of joining a healthcare team. As they care for sick people suffering from multiple complications, there are rarely black-and-white answers. How they navigate their relationships with their fellow caregivers may be as significant a determinant of their patients' outcomes as anything they memorize from a textbook.

Imagine how a learning tool, such as StoryCare, could help teams in all kinds of high-risk environments to improve their performance. Suppose we could regularly allow teams to take time out and reflect on their practice spurred by fictional, yet realistic, stories. As a result, diverse, high-risk industries could begin lessening the impact of human factors that often lead to less than optimal outcomes.

Journey Deeper

Ideas for the Learning Organization

Who Speaks for Sustainability? With the growing recognition humans are harmfully impacting our environment, sustainability is becoming an essential cornerstone for business today. But it's often an afterthought. Tell your teams the *Who Speaks for Wolf* story, then ask them, "Who speaks for sustainability?" In this way, you can build awareness of this crucial issue in your planning and decision-making.

Create Learning Stories for Your Organization. StoryCare brought to life pivotal universal problems about patient safety through focused stories, giving teams a catalyst for reflection and learning. You, too, can identify the Achilles' heel of your work and create narratives engendering reflection and learning for your employees.

If you don't have the resources to have them recorded, simply write them down and ask a team member to read the story at a staff meeting. Follow that with two to three incisive questions to stimulate deeper thinking about the challenges they face. Don't forget to include the pivotal question "What might we learn from this story?"

Take Time Out to Reflect. Organizations giving individuals and teams short, focused windows to reflect will find their performance on future tasks significantly improved. Just fifteen minutes a day of reflection can make all the difference.

The Rule of Six. To arrive at a more holistic perspective of reality's complex nature, the Oneida devised a method for reflecting on problems. They were, perhaps, the first to develop a "systems" approach to thinking. They also understood there are two distinct ways we can ponder any problem. The first, which we often associate with right-brain thinking, is to open up the possibilities creatively. The second, which we associate with left-brain thinking, is to assign more definitive probabilities to those possibilities to help us discern a course of action.

Here's how it works. For any phenomenon, see if you can think of at least six *plausible* explanations. Each in their own right could reasonably explain why things are the way they are. For example, why would people leave their homes in Guatemala and travel over a thousand miles by foot to seek asylum in the United States? Here are six plausible reasons for their making this harrowing, life-threatening journey:

1   They come from neighborhoods controlled by criminal groups that continuously threaten them. Women especially fear rape, assault, and extortion.
2   There is a drought, and there is not enough food.
3   The US government has magnified the problem by supporting unsustainable agricultural practices unsuitable for Guatemala's climate.

4   The country's government is so corrupt, aid and attempts
to remedy these problems don't work. Officials are getting
rich at the expense of the poor.
5   People continually hear stories that there is an opportunity
to earn a decent living in the US and keep their children
out of violent gangs.
6   Parents are hoping their children can receive a quality education not available in Guatemala and hopefully have a
better life than they have there.

You will find after you get to about six explanations for why
things are the way they are, the pickings for new reasons become
slim.

Now that you have your six explanations, assign each a probability weighting—none can be 0 percent, and none can be 100
percent. For example, to explanation #1 (people are coming
because of threats to their life), we might assign an 85 percent
probability that this is a substantial contributing factor. To explanation #2 (drought is causing migration), we might give a 65 percent probability. For explanation #3 (the US has magnified the
problem by pushing nonsustainable farming practices), we might
assign a 20 percent probability factor, because it would appear the
drought is impacting agricultural practices far more than the
ideas the USDA is promoting. Regarding #4 (the government's
corruption), we might assign a probability factor of 50 percent.
There's plenty of evidence to support this claim. To explanation
#5 (people hearing stories about life being better in the US), we
might assign a 30 percent probability factor, in large part because
people aren't coming here mainly for economic advantages but
rather to flee violence. Finally, when it comes to educating their
children, Guatemala's problem isn't that schools are so awful; it's
that their children can't attend school without falling prey to
gangs. We'd assign a 20 percent probability factor here.

With this picture in hand, if our government wanted to stem

the tide of immigrants showing up at our border, we might focus our attention and dollars on solutions back in Guatemala rather than waiting for people to make the trek north. To start, we might take a multipronged approach putting our attention mainly on those factors we scored having higher than a 50 percent probability. Like all things, it's complicated.

Tap into the Genius of African Dilemma Tales

This ancient African tradition uses stories to engage groups with what often appears to be thorny and intractable problems. These stories' beauty is that they don't have an ending—that's the audience's task. Dilemma tales take the listener into the heart of a problem and catalyze them to see it from multiple perspectives. By encouraging the audience to wrestle with contradictions and competing values, they're collectively given a chance to craft the conclusion. Here's where the magic of dilemma tales occurs. The ensuing discussion leads participants deeply into the difficulty of seeking robust solutions that can resolve disparate interests.

Such tales can help groups explore issues that divide them. These stories can also help people think more robustly about steps they'd like to take in the future. Instead of asking, "What might you learn from this story?" which is the hallmark of Oneida learning tales, these stories ask, "What would you do, and how would you do it to arrive at the best solution for all concerned?" To learn more, see the recommended books section of this chapter for a great resource.

Ideas for Personal Exploration

Rethinking Old Family Narratives. We often repeat some of our family stories so often they lose valence and potency to help us see anything anew. After someone shares a family anecdote, breathe new life into the story by asking, "I wonder what we might learn from [insert the subject of the tale]."

Reconsidering Failure and Success. Whether things go as planned or crash and burn, see each event in the light of what you might learn from it. Debriefing your successes in this manner will reveal areas where you could have done even better. There is always room for improvement. Seeing your failures in the light of learning can redeem a difficult and perhaps painful experience, allowing you to see all was not entirely lost if you can learn from it.

I Come from a People Who . . . And from Them, I Learned . . . Ask people in pairs to complete these two phrases. It's a powerful way to bring people together who don't know each other. There are many ways you can reflect on who your people are. You can go very wide and speak of large groups with whom you may identify, such as, "My people are of Irish descent." Or you can think of your country of origin or religious upbringing as defining characteristics. You can also complete the phrase in a narrower manner by describing your immediate family, such as, "I come from a family with a great sense of humor, even in the face of the most trying experiences." Most of us have never reflected on our people of origin. When we do, we inevitably uncover something important we learned from our people—a trait, a skill, or a world view we never before considered. The exercise will not only give you a greater appreciation for who you are; it will connect you powerfully to others through their learning.

Young Eyes, Old Eyes. Paula Underwood wrote extensively about how her people cherished learning and wisdom, elevating it to the highest value. One could have no greater purpose than to learn. The Oneida also understood that wisdom is not always associated with the number of years of experience we have. Young people can see things we older folks don't see because of our acquired filters, mindsets, and the wiring together of our neurons that keep us stuck in seeing the world from just one perspective. To open up your reflective learning processes, ask yourself, "How would I understand this problem if I were looking at it through my child or grandchild's eyes?" Take climate change, for example. For those of us in the last quarter of our lives, we may see it as a worrisome development, but it probably will not impact our lives significantly before we check out. For a young person, though, they see their lives being powerfully affected. For them, it's an existential crisis. Who speaks for them when our leaders consider the steps we need to take today to avert a global disaster?

Walk the Four-Step Path. How do we gain better insight into our circumstances each day? How do we discern wisdom amid conflicting stories or tumultuous change? Paula Underwood describes how the Oneida developed a concrete approach for building clarity. They call it the Four-Step Path. If you have ever walked a labyrinth while 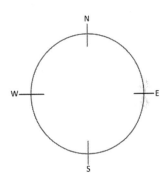 contemplating a question, the Four-Step Path is similar. You can physicalize it by creating a medicine wheel on the ground, with each of the four directions demarcated. As you walk around the circle, consider the following questions as you arrive at each of the four directions:

- *In the East,* consider the element of courage. What do you need to muster within yourself to take a courageous step? What do you need to become, or learn, to fulfill your authentic destiny?
- *In the South,* consider what ways you need to open up your heart, especially to those whom you have closed out, or those who are difficult people in your life. What feelings are holding you back from growing?
- *In the West,* look within and consider what you need to reflect on to resolve this situation. What qualities do you need to cultivate within yourself?

- *In the North,* consider what is most true for you. What actions can you take that will most nurture your spirit?
- *In the Center,* consider what you need to maintain your humility. Confront the fact that there are many things you may not know. It is a place of uncertainty where you live deeply within questions that may not have ready answers.

Pay Attention to the Lit Fuses. As we listen to or read a story, it's natural to free-associate and be reminded of things we have long ago forgotten. These can often act like lit fuses in our imagination. From this point of view, storytelling is the perfect knowledge-management catalyst, igniting associations with the things we know about a particular topic, which we may not even know we know. In this way, listening to stories can help us build a lattice-work of knowledge, connecting what we know with what we're currently learning. The effect is multiplicative. So, pay attention to what emerges in your imagination as you listen and learn. These seemingly disparate bits of information are the building blocks for deepening future understanding.

Hone Your Reflective Power

Ask these six questions distilled by Peter Pappas to sharpen your capacity for reflection and improve your performance:

1 *What did I do?* This is about *remembering.* What story are you weaving about this event or situation? Is there another way to weave together the same facts and tell the story from a different perspective?

2 *What was important about it?* This is about *understanding.* How does this action or event connect to other facets of your experience? Can you see this event through a different set of eyes and arrive at a different conclusion?

3 *Where could I use this again?* This is about *applying.* Scan your life and wonder how this lesson has applicability in other dimensions of your world.

4 *Do I see any patterns in what I did?* This is about *analyzing*. Remember, story is all about patterns and frames. Is this experience a repetition of previous themes in your life? How?

5 *How well did I do?* This is about *evaluating*. In what areas could you improve your performance?

6 *What should I do next?* This is all about *creating*. How can you use this learning as a platform to grow?

Books We Recommend

Practically every culture around the world uses story in a unique way to shift our thinking. In *African Dilemma Tales* by **William Bascom**, be prepared to enter into an intriguing approach to engaging large groups with ethical and moral dilemmas that will open people to whole new approaches to self-exploration.

Every once in a while, a book comes along that can get us thinking in entirely new ways. In *Unlocking Leadership Mindtraps: How to Thrive in Complexity* by **Jennifer Garvey Berger**, you'll discover invaluable approaches to improving your ability to lead, especially in these times when we need fresh thinking more than ever.

Paula Underwood was an important teacher for us, and her stories and commentary on them still inform and illuminate our understanding of what it means to be an effective learner. In *Three Native American Learning Stories: Who Speaks for Wolf, Winter White and Summer Gold, Many Circles*, she shares three tales that were pivotal to her people's survival and learning. *Three Strands in the Braid: A Guide for Enablers of Learning* is an invaluable resource for exploring and using these tales. *The Walking People: A Native American Oral History* will take you back ten thousand years and trace the learning of her people and demonstrate how crucial their stories were to enduring the vagaries of living in an unpredictable world. Finally, in *The Great Hoop of Life, Volume 1: A Traditional Medicine Wheel for Enabling Learning and for Gathering Wisdom*, Paula shares a unique approach to embodying wisdom.

4

The Power of Story to Create Meaning

The ability to use story to make sense of our life experiences and live more purposefully.

The business of stories is not enchantment. The business of stories is not escape. The business of stories is waking up.

— Martin Shaw

Imagine the first time a curious human peered into a small pond on a moonlit night some 250,000 years ago. Seeing her reflection next to the image of that white orb awakened something. A question, like those shadowy statements emerging in a Magic 8-Ball, formed in her head: *What does it all mean?* From that first moment of self-reflection, humans have been preoccupied with their significance in a mysterious universe. From where we stand on earth, the sun and the moon and unimaginably distant stars and planets, roiled by powerful forces, seem to have little regard or need for our frail existence. In this context, how do we find meaning?

In more recent times, philosophers and religion have co-opted what was once the purview of tribal shamans. Countless sages have all taken their bite at the apple of meaning. Aristotle claimed it all comes down to *eudaimonia*, loosely translated as happiness, and looking for the "good" in all we do. In 350 BC, Socrates proclaimed the "unexamined life is not worth living."[1] For Eastern thinkers like Confucius, meaning is derived principally from harmonious relationships in society. Buddhists see life's ultimate purpose is to master the art of rising above personal suffering. For Hindus, awakening to one's divine nature is the ultimate goal. Judaism enshrines meaning in the lofty aim of bettering the soul through the embodiment of the Torah, which Jews see as the word of the living God. Christianity focuses on loving oneself, others, and God, while Islam has spun a variant of this message, emphasizing Allah's glorification.

In the twentieth century, Albert Camus framed personal meaning as a question of whether it makes sense to choose life. The Japanese have given this issue a distinctive name—*ikigai*, translated loosely as "that which most makes one's life seem worth living."[2] It turns out those who self-describe as having *ikigai* have a demonstrably decreased risk of mortality from ischemic heart and cerebrovascular diseases. Recognizing one's life is worth living isn't just a beautiful thing to have. It's a necessity for health and vitality.

Each of these philosophers, theologies, or cultures uniquely approaches the definition of meaning. They have in common a sustaining metanarrative to help us make sense of our world, ourselves, and where we fit in the cosmic order of things. Unfortunately, in Western, industrialized cultures, many of us have lost connection with these grand metanarratives. This is the result of a phenomenon we call *destorification*. As we have objectified the natural world and reduced it to a "thing" to serve us, we have posited the world as something separate from ourselves, an object to be manipulated to meet our needs. We have also found powerful ways to depreciate storytelling in our lives—the very thing making human civilization possible.

It's akin to clearcutting a forest to harvest its "resources," doing untold damage to the ecosystem. Even if we replant trees, the abundant, interconnected life rarely returns. Neat rows of pines can't reproduce the complex environment supported by towering oaks and maples and a rich and varied undergrowth, along with the animals and microbes that depend on this diversity. Likewise, when we stop sharing stories with our community around a central fire, on our front porches with our neighbors, and in our living rooms with our children, something dies. This ritual practice has nourished us for millennia. From time immemorial, stories have been the carrier of the metanarratives. Without it, our soul becomes as barren as a denuded old-growth forest.

Jerry Mander[3] in the early 1990s chronicled how technology has destroyed traditional cultures and the process of oral storytelling, all in the name of a mythical thing called "progress." We have replaced ancient rituals of story sharing with a different fire—the television screen. In the 1980s, the Canadian government pushed Inuit tribes living on the tundra in the far western reaches of the country to get wired for cable TV. They painted an ideal picture of modernization—connection to the rest of the country, being informed about events in the wider world, and economic improvement. It all sounded logical and desirable. Mander had started the first nonprofit advertising agency to assist native peoples in North America to tell their story when controversial political issues threatened their way of life. One community's elders invited him in to consult on the prospect of bringing TV to every home. He counseled against getting connected, fearing TV would have unseen and harmful consequences for the Inuit. The voices favoring progress drowned him out, and the people voted to have cable TV installed.

In these communities, it was not uncommon for three generations to live under the same roof. While the parents were out hunting and fishing, the grandparents provided a steady hand in raising the next generation. But when they installed TVs, grandparents began spending ten to twelve hours a day watching, especially daytime soap operas, neglecting their grandchildren's oversight. In these stories, they saw dysfunctional lives filled with despair, not realizing that they were fictional. The characters on *As the World Turns* soon made it onto their prayer lists, for surely these people needed divine assistance.

The destorification of their culture became readily apparent on many other fronts as well. Children were also watching TV all day and into the night, comparing their lives with fictional characters who had enormous financial wealth on shows like *Dallas*. We can only imagine what that did to their self-concepts. Behavior problems never before seen in their schools began emerging. Mental health issues started rearing their ugly heads. Traditional crafts that they had practiced for centuries came to a screeching halt, literally dying overnight. Most importantly, people stopped telling ancient tales. With one click of the remote, the culture became virtually extinct.

In our modern world, the effects of technology have insidiously accomplished what occurred to the Inuit. It has been achieved through a slow drip beginning in the nineteenth century, building up steam in the late twentieth, and blossoming most recently with the advent of social media and the internet. Traditional cultural rituals and containers for human connection and sharing have been mutilated or destroyed. Unseen in this destructive fire has been the extinction of metanarratives that once brought meaning and relevance to our individual lives.

When Friedrich Nietzsche proclaimed in 1882, "God is dead," he referred to how metanarratives reigning full tilt since before the Christian era had lost their hold over contemporary life. The theology of the Greeks implied a pantheon of gods was predictably ordering the world. An omnipotent Judeo-Christian God replaced these gods. Fast-forward to the end of the nineteenth century, when many in the West began to question God's reliability. When humankind lost all semblance of sanity and perpetrated the heinous crimes of the Holocaust in World War II, we hammered the last nails into the coffin. The casket was lowered into the grave after further atrocities over the last years in places like Srebrenica, where the Bosnian Serb Army slaughtered eight thousand Muslim boys and men, and the Rwandan genocide, where marauding Hutus murdered upward of a million Tutsis in thirty days. If an omnipotent, kindly God can no longer be relied upon to prevent injustices of this magnitude, where can we securely stand? In what story can we put our faith?

In many respects, metanarratives operated at the unconscious level to unify our world view and provide us with solace to face the challenge of living in a changing, scary universe. Parry and Doan, leaders in the narrative therapy movement, suggest, "In the demise of all grand narratives, we now live in a world in which personal narratives essentially stand alone as the means by which we pull together the text of our own lives, as well as the 'intertextual' overlappings of those lives that enter ours. Although this may be frightening without the legitimating guidance of the grand narratives, it is also a liberating possibility. It frees us from the totalizing tyranny of the grand narratives."[4] Within this freedom, though, are some disheartening statistics, which we shared earlier. Too many Americans have not discovered a satisfying life purpose or have a strong sense of what makes their lives meaningful.

Surprisingly, we haven't seen any societal efforts aimed at assisting people in discovering a meaningful purpose. While the Declaration of Independence promises us life, liberty, and the pursuit of happiness, the country's founders provided few clues on how to find it. The responsibility is ours to discover a road map for creating new venues for the sharing of stories. Hopefully, this chapter will help you map out the possibilities, assisting you to develop your Story Intelligence to illuminate your *ikigai* and build a more durable source of meaning and personal fulfillment.

The Story-Meaning Connection

Let's start our journey by delving into what we mean by meaning. As it turns out, this question has a lot of nuance with important implications for how we each can use the power of story to carve out a life of significance and value.

The word comes from the Old High German *meinen*, to have in mind.[5] The implication is that meaning doesn't reside independent of human endeavor, nor is it somehow divorced from our mental activity, living a life in some lofty locale. To ask the question, "What is the meaning of life?" is grasping at the wrong end of the stick. To understand meaning, we must understand our role in its creation and examine how we mentally connect the dots and represent and interpret our world.

So, what constitutes a meaningful life? The theorists we gravitate to suggest there are three fundamental components: coherence, purpose, and significance. We'll explore this territory to discover how developing our Story Intelligence can assist us broadly in this endeavor.

Coherence has everything to do with the cognitive maps and stories we create to make sense of our day-to-day experiences. We're wired to search out patterns, always fitting new information about ourselves, others, and our environment into a preexisting schema to understand our world. To make our experiences relevant and manageable, we'll create stories about even the most abstract,

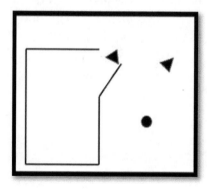

disconnected processes, imputing human motives, and drama into things objectively divorced of any personal relevance. A classic study by Fritz Heider and Marianne Simmel[6] beautifully exemplifies this. They invited people to describe what's going on in a short film of a square, two triangles, and a circle moving haphazardly on the screen. Without prompting, participants projected a human drama onto these inanimate objects inferring all kinds of motivations and emotions wholly absent to the objective eye. As far as we know, geometric shapes don't think, feel, plan, or have any kind of subjective experiences at all. But try to tell that to the people observing the film.

The way we make sense of our world isn't so different from this psychological exercise. People present us with all kinds of behaviors, often ambiguous in intent, yet we're quick to infer their emotions and motivations. In the blink of an eye, we make up a story and add meaning to what they did, then act on these assumptions. The stories we create with minimal data often turn out to be as fictional as the accounts the participants attributed to inanimate objects. A guy swerving in and out of traffic is a jerk. At our favorite shop, the clerk provides minimal attention to our needs. We conclude she's undeserving of respect. During a meeting with your boss, a colleague heaps praise on your work. You suppose he's a prince among men.

But how often do these initial stories prove to be entirely off base? What if you knew the guy who's swerving in and out of traffic is trying to reach the hospital, where an ambulance just took his daughter after a disastrous accident? Or, the clerk is struggling with financial woes threatening to bankrupt her? Or, your colleague is buttering you up because he has an ulterior motive and wants a favor? What story would you tell now?

Without our ability to create stories out of the disparate experiences flooding our awareness moment by moment, life would be fragmented and filled with a sense of randomness. There would be no through-line relating one occurrence to the next. We would have little way to comprehend or order the relevance of significant life events. Connecting the past to the present to the future would be impossible. Learning would be absent as well. At most, we would be subject to the vagaries of operant conditioning, responding impulsively to painful or pleasurable stimuli.

With a story, though, we're able to superimpose a structure onto the haphazardness of life, rendering it, to a degree, knowable and predictable. This structure, in turn, brings us comfort and an abiding sense of safety. It also may be a key to our health. Over forty years ago, Aaron Antonovsky began examining what produces health in people versus disease. His research pointed to this very issue of coherence. He even coined a name for it: "*salutogenesis*—of the origins *(genesis)* of health *(saluto)*."[7] Making sense of our world can make us whole.

Does It Matter Whether a Story Is True?

Whether our stories are, in fact, true may be less relevant than the sense of control a good story provides. James Hillman addresses this conundrum in the tale of identical twins adopted by two different families at birth.[8] As young adults, they were each fastidious, always ensuring every little thing was in its place. When asked how they developed such habits, though, each sibling told a unique, contradictory story to explain how they came to be who they are. One twin spoke that she learned these habits from her parents, who were particularly fussy when it came to keeping things ordered and clean. The other twin, though, told a story about how her mother was a complete slob, and the house was always disheveled. According to her narrative about herself, her need for order resulted from her reaction to her mother's unkempt practices. Hillman's contention, though, is these twins came into this world precoded with this predisposition for cleanliness and order. Their distinct stories were a retrospective attempt to explain their environment and upbringing as the root cause for these traits. Through this lens, we all come into life with a great deal of who we are already programmed. Then, we engage in making up stories that are works of fiction to make sense of who we are. It's an interesting hypothesis, isn't it?

The Role of Story in Self-Knowledge

To further this discussion, let's look at the etymology of "story." The word has its roots in the Latin *narrare*, meaning to tell, relate, or recount, which in turn has its PIE (Proto-Indo-European language root) in "*gno," meaning to know. To story our experiences is fundamentally one of the most powerful ways of knowing our world and ourselves.

As children, we first understand our world through others' eyes and the stories they tell. It's a frothy soup of tales about us and our birth, about our parents and other family members, and about the way the world is and how it works. This hearty stew becomes the inherited filter through which we interpret so many facets of our experiences. We forge our personality and world view out of them, yet they are not of our own making. Even though we claim them as distinctively our own, our parents' and society's fingerprints are all over these tales.

Marshall Duke and Robyn Fivush have been studying this phenomenon for the past thirty years. They discovered some critical ways that the stories children hear and know impact personality. It's no surprise that we acquire much of our narrative ability through conversation with adults, most notably our parents. Family members sharing stories about the past provide young minds a context for their place in the world and a scaffold upon which to construct their own stories. Fivush calls these "intergenerational narratives," leading to what she refers to as "autobiographical reasoning," in which children begin drawing parallels between their parents' stories and their own life experiences.[9] This ability to connect accounts of the past to our definition of ourselves is a crucial development phase, giving us self-awareness.

Duke and Fivush's research into this topic led to a surprising finding. The best predictor for children developing a high sense of self-esteem and strong resilience is knowing their family stories.[10] These narratives help children establish a robust framework of internal resources. When confronted with new challenges, they have a ready-made tale from a respected adult to orient and guide them as though they are referencing their personal store of life experiences. If thrown into a situation filled with unknowns, all they need do is recall a story that their parents told them when they faced similar circumstances. Just the thought *My parents got through a similar situation when they were younger* reinforces a young person's belief in their resourcefulness.

There are other notable effects of parental reminiscing. Mothers who discuss emotional experiences, especially highly stressful ones, facilitate their children's understanding of negative emotions and how to manage them.[11] Moreover, mothers who elaborate more when reminiscing help their children "construct a more elaborated and coherent sense of self."[12]

Finally, reminiscing with your children can help them develop a more profound sense of security within themselves and with others, leading to their ability to form more loving and trustworthy relationships. It's especially true when parents deploy this form of reminiscing about stressful events. When absent, though, children are at risk for a whole host of developmental and interpersonal challenges compared to children who can better manage negative affect.

It's interesting to compare our culture to that of more traditional, storied cultures. In these settings, parents and adults regularly expose children to their personal stories and heroic legends and tales embodying life lessons. These cultures endow youngsters with a historical treasure trove embodying the cultural memory of how generations going back hundreds if not thousands of years traversed difficulty and survived. As you recall in the previous chapter, Paula Underwood's father told her stories about her people spanning back in time for ten thousand years. While there are exceptions, we dare say most of us today can't recall or tell stories spanning back in time more than a century, much less a generation ago.

In contrast, when confronted with dangerous levels of confusion and stress, children who do not know their family stories or the societal stories extolling perseverance and hope in the face of trials are left with little to stand on. It's long been our contention this lack of narrative scaffolding helps to explain the high incidence of teen suicide. Suppose you are a victim of cultural destorification and don't have a story about weathering a dark night of the soul. From your limited world view, it might seem to be an unendurable, never-changing reality. When faced with such a painful conclusion, is it any wonder children and young adults make ill-informed, self-destructive choices?

Not all of life is filled with such stark realities. I once had a student in a college-level course on storytelling whose parents had divorced when he was relatively young. He was living within a void of stories about his family and their past. His dad was out of the picture, and his mother, who had shouldered the responsibilities of raising him and his siblings, was hardly ever home. His first name was Alex, and his last name had Irish derivations. I sent him on a scavenger hunt to fill this void to find out everything he could about his name. When the next class came around, his whole persona had changed. With a face lit up with excitement, he recounted how he had discovered the town in Ireland where his family originated. He knew intimate details about this place, almost as though he had firsthand experience. These were his people. Then, he detailed all he had uncovered about his namesake, Alexander the Great. Just the act of learning about this hero from the past had somehow magically transferred to him a sense of strength and spirit lacking just the week before. Out of nothing, he built a platform of stories to begin creating a life of meaning, relevance, and belonging.

The Value of Autobiographical Reasoning

Two research psychologists, Habermas and Bluck, contend that our ability to link our life events together is what endows it with meaning. They call it "autobiographical reasoning."[13] It's how we develop our sense of identity. As they put it, "Only the ability for autobiographical reasoning allows individuals to understand what it means when they are asked for self-defining memories."[14]

This capacity to biographically weave our life's salient events into a whole fabric leads to four kinds of global coherence. The first of these has to do with the cultural context in which normative life events are sequentially structured. For example, we develop an unconscious expectation as children that we'll go to school. Then, we'll find a life partner, perhaps concurrently with finding a vocation. Next in line, you'd expect to raise a family. At the end of your work life, you'd retire. You might even have a fuzzy notion about dying peacefully after having lived a long life.

When these normative events don't occur, there is a kind of psychic disruption of our narrative. For example, if it came time to raise a family but you can't get pregnant, suddenly your life story and the flow of meaning you'd expect to derive from having children is abruptly stopped in its tracks. Like tectonic plates grinding against each other, this creates immense psychic friction because you have grown up with a template with a built-in expectation that you will have children. A similar process occurs when we come down with a life-changing disease like cancer. Getting seriously sick is not part of our anticipated narrative. It requires a reappraisal of every other aspect of our life, playing havoc with all kinds of expectations of how things should look.

If you have bought the retirement myth about leading a life of luxury and endless play, you may be in for a rude awakening in your sixties. You may discover it feels empty and find yourself asking the iconic question from the Peggy Lee hit, "Is that all there is?" Years ago, I got to know a businessman who retired to Boca Raton and lived in an exclusive gated community along with lots of other successful, retired businessmen. One day they were heads of multinational corporations, the next day, the highlight of their morning was taking out the trash. They sought meaning by going to the club for a round of golf, followed by lunch with their buddies. After a few months of this, they were restless, feeling lost and empty. When reality meets a cultural lie, the human spirit suffers.

Secondly, we organize our lives chronologically to provide a sense of order to everything. We find comfort in knowing where to place a particular memory along this timeline. It becomes particularly important when relating our personal life story to events of the time, like where you were when the planes flew into the Twin Towers on 9/11, when the Berlin Wall came down, or when Martin Luther King Jr. was assassinated. Placing our life events sequentially from past to present provides us with a sense of coherence and meaning by connecting our personal experience to landmark events. The disruption of this timeline is perhaps most apparent if you have known anyone who has dementia. They have lost time markers for placing their personal stories. As a result, they have, in a fundamental sense, lost themselves and no longer can say with confidence who they are.

Thirdly, we tend to attribute more meaning to those events where we had some agency. We need the world we have constructed to reflect our inner motivations, values, and our sense of life purpose. If we see our world as one predominantly structured by others, where we had little or no say in how things unfolded, we'll tend to have a discordant view of our experience. The result is a sense of incompleteness. If our world reflects our personality, our desires, and wishes, then the outcome of our actions will seem logical. Our life story will make sense, reflecting a feeling of wholeness.

Finally, we develop what Habermas and Bluck call "global thematic coherence." As we reflect on our life in our later years, we're able to see continuities running through the decades-long span of our experiences. Suddenly, something that occurred while we were young has relevance for things arising in our marriage. We see our desire to pursue a line of employment connected to our childhood fascination with how things work and the time we spent taking apart and putting together old watches. Our kindness has its origins in a relationship we had with a compassionate grandparent. These through-lines, threads of connection, and themes bring order to what otherwise might look like a disconnected list of choices, activities, and behaviors. They become the warp and the weft of the rich tapestry of our life story.

The range of how our stories embody the notion of change and growth is also defining. Some people may tell stories explaining how they have remained the same for years on end with a stable personality. Their narrative emphasizes how they are tried and true friends to others, consistent and unchanging across multiple settings and myriad relationships. Others' stories may highlight how they have radically changed with time and even the differential ways those changes show up in the various contexts of their life. The interesting question is, which came first? The stable personality, or the story the person chose to tell omitting any evidence of instability? In the case of the adventurous soul, was it their nature to always seek new possibilities to stretch and grow, or did their parents tell them stories about them coming from a family accustomed to exploring and taking risks? As a result, did they unconsciously choose to make these stories the scaffold for the unfolding of their life biography?

Autobiographical reasoning in this context is akin to bringing a third-person perspective to our own life. It's easy to see the thematic evolution of another's life when reading their biography, but we often can't discern it when reflecting on our own. With some psychic distance, though, we're able to see how things connect and make sense. In this way, we're able to grasp how painful experiences led to particular choices. Comprehend the ways circumstances early on were formative. Understand the crucial impact of a life lesson and how it became the basis for every decision from then on. Or appreciate the many ways cherished relationships amplified an aspect of ourselves that otherwise might have remained dormant. This is how we construct a dynamic, durable personal narrative over time. It's also how we reveal to others who we are and what makes us tick. Likewise, listening to others' tales enables us to discover what is most relevant and intimate about their unique journey, perhaps finding in their story a bit of our humanity.

Reminisce to Make Meaning

Whenever we gather informally, the conversation often turns to the past, especially as we grow older. Some venues are more conducive than others. Sitting around a potbelly stove on a winter's day or relaxing on a porch on a spring evening seems to catalyze reminiscence. Or, musing about days gone by can bring comfort to a loved one who's facing a health challenge in a hospital. There's an old saying. Around age fifty, it becomes more important to look back than to look forward. In all probability, we have more life behind us than ahead of us. Telling stories to make sense of what this journey has been all about is baked into our constitution. This kind of storytelling has a whole lot to do with our psychological health and sense of well-being.[15]

There are different kinds of reminiscence, each of which has a particular value and place. This section will examine in greater depth four types and provide you enough background to deploy each in your life.

Simple Reminiscence is the stuff of our daily routines. It's the stories we tell when we gather with our family for dinner after a hard day's work or get together with friends over a glass of wine to joke about earlier times. Most of the tall tales we discussed earlier are first cousins of this type of storytelling. We tell stories for no other reason than to have fun, share our life experiences, and remember the good times. Someone recounts an event when they were a young woman. That tale spurs our memory. We play tag team as we add our story into the communal stew. There is no ulterior reason for telling these kinds of stories other than enjoying each other's company and entertaining ourselves.

Interestingly, though, sharing positive memories does have some hidden psychological and physiological benefits. The field of psychoimmunology has taught us the body strangely doesn't know the difference between a real event and an imagined one. When we share our fond memories of good times, we are fundamentally reimagining that experience. As far as our body is concerned, telling the story tricks it into believing it is occurring in the present moment. It's bathed in the biochemistry associated with positive emotions. Our work with the LivingStories program described in the following section demonstrates how merely encouraging patients to share positive memories lowers their anxiety and, frequently, their need for pain medication. That's profound for something relegated to the "simple" bin in a taxonomy.

Instrumental Reminiscence is a pragmatic form of looking back. In addition to getting us unstuck personally, this kind of reflection can also be critical and powerful for organizations facing seemingly intractable problems. Years ago, Lucasfilm was working on one of the prequels to the Star Wars trilogy. The team was struggling with how to pull off a tricky effect. After several hours considering their options, they had reached a dead end. One team member had been involved with a similar but distinctive challenge years earlier during the filming of *The Empire Strikes Back*. He shared the story of how they solved that problem. Something in this tale about the past got them thinking again, reflecting, seeing their current issue through a new lens. A problem whose solution seemed as far away as a distant star in another galaxy suddenly felt manageable. Within a few minutes, someone had a breakthrough idea leading them down a fruitful path.

Instrumental reminiscence can also have remarkable health

benefits. In the LivingStories project that we initiated with Novant Health in North Carolina, we trained volunteers to elicit patients' stories of times they successfully met a challenge. The early research by Bruce Rybarczyk and Albert Bellg showed how the very act of recalling a time when you faced a problem or overcame a difficulty can empower you to meet a current health challenge. They need not be earth-shattering events. Examples could be times when you mastered a challenging subject in school, landed your first job after a long search, or even learned to ride a bike. The goal is to "heighten the participants' awareness of positive strengths and resources they have used to meet challenges. Patients' increased awareness of their coping resources presumably minimizes the perception that the medical stress they are facing is overwhelming."[16] Rybarczyk and Bellg found that individuals who participate in this form of reminiscence have a higher degree of confidence in their coping skills. Presumably, they'll fare better when recuperating from their surgery or illness.

The research supporting this approach is extensive. When healthy, older adults just participate in an instrumental reminiscence session, it increased their problem-solving coping levels.[17] The effects of this kind of reminiscence were still apparent three months later. In another study[18] where elders participated in eight instrumental reminiscence sessions, the intervention improved their overall quality of life. Plus, it proved to be a much better alternative to antidepressants for those who needed them.

Interestingly, we need not draw strength from our own life experiences to deploy instrumental reminiscence. In a recent conversation with a friend recovering from cancer, he shared one of the most important sources of strength for him was not his own stories of perseverance. Instead, his spirits were buoyed by stories he knew about his parents and close relatives who made it through horrific conditions during the Holocaust. He figured if they could deal with all of those dreadful challenges, he could face his cancer with resilience.

The good news is we need not wait until our elder years to make instrumental reminiscence a daily life practice. Anxiety disorders affect forty million people in the United States, and these people are three times more likely to go to the doctor and be medicated.[19] We, as a society, must find better ways to cope with the complexities of modern life. Instrumental reminiscence may be the cheapest cure available, one with no adverse side effects as far as we know.

Integrative Reminiscence addresses an entirely different life challenge. It's about making a whole of the fragmented and often discounted and disconnected aspects of our past. If we think of our life as a book, are all the chapters included? For some of us who have experienced trauma, betrayal, or a destructive conflict with someone we loved, we tend to omit those details when telling our life story. Other times we exclude vital pieces of our life narrative because some chapters from our lives simply don't match our expectations for ourselves.

Elders whom we have known who lived through the Great Depression, survived oppressive political regimes, and suffered through war are more likely to balk when asked about their earlier life. They tend to see these previous times as painful and prefer forgetting or deleting these experiences from their narrative. They often rationalize this avoidance of the past by saying things like, "Why recall bad times when so much good has happened since we escaped that awful place? There are things there I don't want to remember."

Attempts to avoid remembering because of a fear of reigniting feelings of pain are understandable. But if we're willing to break through this initial obstacle, something valuable and productive can emerge. We can begin seeing how everything that occurred since that event is attributable to the fact that we courageously went through that trying fire. We may even be able to come to a place of gratitude toward our oppressors for the lessons we were able to learn, or the strengths and internal resources we developed as a result. What's ironic is that the things we discounted and minimized in the past may grow to be seen as hugely valuable if given room to breathe. In the next chapter, we'll examine how we can take painful events and transform them, making what the poet Antonio Machado characterizes as taking our old wounds and failures and turning them into "white combs and sweet honey."[20]

The psychological benefits of this kind of personal reckoning are significant. Integrative reminiscence sessions reduce people's mild to severe depression.[21] It's also important to note that well-adjusted and physically healthy elders regularly engage in integrative and instrumental reminiscence.[22]

On the other side of the coin, depressed people tend to omit many positive facets of their life experience from their narratives. Integrative reminiscence becomes, then, a way of balancing the picture we have of ourselves. It provides a fuller, perhaps more authentic and truthful appraisal, admitting into the chapters of our experience events and qualities emphasizing what is both good and bad about the past.

To this end, we once worked with a group of adult children of alcoholics. We invited them to participate in a reminiscence exercise and draw the floorplan of their childhood house, including the footprint of various furnishings in each room. We encouraged them not to draw rooms if they preferred not to visit them. This kind of exercise is a potent stimulator of forgotten memories. What came out of the process for many was something surprising. Before the activity, they painted their childhoods with a broad brush, sounding something like, "My father was an alcoholic, and we were always on high alert. We never knew when he'd explode and become violent." As a result of drawing their floorplans, they recalled times when their dad wasn't drunk, when there was a Christmas filled with joy and happiness. Emerging from these recollections was a more nuanced picture of their childhood. Many of the overwhelming, awful times were tempered now by positive memories. Including these stories in their overall narrative brought to it a richness. A sense of compassion and forgiveness seeped into their earlier tale of growing up. As Hollon and Garber, experts in cognitive therapy, put it, "Individuals may thus disconfirm global, negative evaluations of the self that are associated with depression and begin to develop a realistic, adaptive view of the self that incorporates both positive and negative attributes."[23]

Interestingly, telling stories about adverse events in the past lessens the emotional charge, helps us make meaning, and increases our sense of well-being. The research on this does provide a caution, though. Merely thinking about an adverse event without telling another about it decreases our sense of well-being.[24]

Transmissive Reminiscence is especially relevant for those of us who have rounded the bend of midlife and wonder what our legacy will be. What would we like to leave behind that hopefully outlives us? How we answer this can take many forms. Perhaps the most fundamental approach is telling stories embodying what we have learned about living a meaningful life. You're engaging in transmissive reminiscence if you have ever found yourself telling a child or grandchild about things you wish you had known at their age. Or mentoring a younger person at work and sharing some of the mistakes you made early in your career, hoping these tales will be instructive and shorten her learning curve.

Over the centuries, a unique Jewish tradition has evolved, elevating this practice to a ritualized art form. It's known as an ethical will. Unlike a traditional will conveying to another your property and other physical assets, an ethical will is all about sharing one's values, ethics, stories, and most prominent lessons. The beauty of this kind of document is you need not wait until you die to pass on what may be dearer and more precious to you than any material possession.

Referring to this kind of wisdom preservation, Rabbi Zalman

Schachter-Shalomi, a modern Jewish mystic and founder of the Jewish Renewal movement, used to ask, "Are you saved?" But he wasn't describing a religious conversion in the contemporary Christian context. Instead, being a fan of computer metaphors, he was referring to the whimsical notion of a hard drive in the sky. Have you hit the save button to ensure everything you have learned in this life has been recorded for posterity to benefit future generations? The ethical will is one way of preserving all that is precious and valuable and passing it on to younger generations as a useful map.

There are no rules or prescriptions when writing an ethical will. Sometimes writing a short statement can be more impactful than a lengthy discourse. You should also tailor it to your audience. You can direct it narrowly to one child or grandchild or all of them. What would you want them to know about you that could be valuable in their life journey? Are there decisions you made along the way you'd like them to understand? Would you want them to appreciate the context for your career choices? Are there material possessions you intend to bequeath to them having little or no monetary value, but their backstory is precious and significant? Your hope is they, too, will cherish the object as much as you do. Is there an important lesson you learned that could be valuable to them as they make a start in life, from finding a spouse to pursuing a rewarding vocation?

Almost anything can be the subject of an ethical will. But many writers in this field caution against using this document to manipulate others or attempt to bend them to your will. The ethical will is a sacred text documenting what has been central to you with the recognition the reader is a distinct human being, perhaps on a path entirely separate from yours. It's pernicious when we attempt to impose our values, will, or world view on others through guilt or shame in an attempt to get them to do our bidding. To do so will leave a lasting impression, probably filled with resentment. You'll find a wealth of resources to guide you in creating your ethical will at the end of this chapter.

Developing a MasterStory:
A Means to Finding
Enduring Significance

In the eighteenth century, there lived a great scholar, Rabbi Zusya. As he lay dying, his disciples gathered around him and saw tears in his eyes. Naturally, they attempted to comfort him. "Don't be sad. Certainly, you have led a good life, and there will be a revered place for you in the world to come. You were almost as wise as Moses and certainly as kind as Abraham."

Rabbi Zusya shook his head. "I am not sad, but rather afraid."

"Afraid of what?" they asked.

"I am afraid," he said, "that when I arrive in the world to come, God will not ask me how come I was not more like Moses or Abraham. I am afraid that God will ask me, 'Zusya, why were you not more like Zusya? Why didn't you follow the path that was yours alone to follow?' And I won't know what to say. That's why I am crying."[25]

A central task for all of us is to become more of who we inherently are and harness that knowledge to fulfill our most profound potential. We have discovered that you will not realize more of your potential than your narrative or story accommodates and animates. The stories you adopt, consciously or unconsciously, set a range and trajectory of possibilities. They define how you'll experience the world, whether it will be dominated by limits, doubts, and fears or filled with wonder, possibilities, and miracles.

Ultimately, to become your authentic self and fulfill your highest potential, you must discover the story that aligns you with the path that reveals and nurtures your unique calling. We call this your MasterStory. It's all about learning to assume full authority over the trajectory of your life. Instead of living a story conditioned by familial or cultural forces, you can consciously become the master of your story in all of its dimensions.

While we have focused most of our discussion so far on

enhancing personal coherence by exploring your past, developing your MasterStory can help you cultivate the last two legs of the stool of meaning—an abiding sense of purpose and significance. There are some essential components of the MasterStory we'll elucidate in the following pages.

Discerning Your Core Values

If we know the things we value and hold dear, we have an invaluable road map for our lives, not conditioned by others' opinions. It can stand up to forces at work inexorably attempting to influence us to behave in ways out of step with our authentic selves. It can also resist the immense power of societal and cultural pressures to conform. Anchored in our values, we have a well-defined reference for every decision, guiding our choices to ensure they are congruent with who we are. While we may seek outside counsel to help us see all sides of an issue better, we can rely on our inner sense of what is right for us when we have a clearly articulated set of values.

Most of us, though, have rarely excavated our values or articulated them into an explicit statement. There are plenty of tools and programs available, including assessments proffering you a definitive list. While these approaches are undoubtedly useful, we'll introduce you to a more organic approach grounded in story at this chapter's conclusion. This method will reveal both the source of your values and provide you story-based guidance to inform all of your choices and actions.

Discovering Your Gifts and Talents

Another facet of your MasterStory is discerning your unique gifts and talents, then integrating them into the daily focus of your life. To better understand this, we make a vital distinction. First, you possess an inherent, unique set of gifts that can lead you to deep satisfaction, gratification, and the experience of feeling fully alive. You may also be very talented in certain realms, but we don't see gifts and talents as the same. We contend that an unfathomable mystery enshrouds the source of our gifts. We're born with them.

In contrast, we must nurture and develop our talents. In this sense, talents are the expression or activation of your gifts. For example, you may be gifted musically. Yet, the way that gift finds expression in your life is through the talent of playing the violin. Only through hard work and countless hours of training can that musical gift be fully expressed through your playing.

Here are a few more examples. You may be athletically gifted with excellent hand-eye coordination. While you could have been relatively good at almost any sport you played in high school, you decided to make tennis your game of choice. That's when you began the hard work of conditioning and practice to develop a world-class topspin backhand and a monster serve. In turn, the thousands of hours of training enabled you to become a top-ranked player. Your athleticism was indispensable to your success, but without the continual practice and development of your physical and mental gifts, you would never have fully realized the potential of this gift. Players like Roger Federer and Rafael Nadal are great examples. There is something unique and special about their capabilities. Still, they are also incredibly dedicated, spending more time in the gym and on the court practicing than most any other player.

Another example: you might have the gift of nurturance and could have gone into teaching children or practicing as a psycho-therapist. Instead, you decided to work with the elderly and have used your gift to develop your talent as an exceptional, compassionate social worker.

If you're in doubt about your gifts and talents, we provide you some concrete approaches to discerning them at the end of the chapter.

Finding Your Deepest Purpose: The Transcendent Force to Creating a Life of Significance

We have explored many different avenues for finding and creating meaning in our lives. One center of reference transcends all of these, empowering us to move beyond our past and freeing us in immeasurable ways to continually rejuvenate our personal story. It's the discovery of our highest purpose—what we like to refer to as our calling in the world. This is the heart of your MasterStory.

To better understand our calling's relationship to the rest of our existence, let us tell you a brief story that illustrates how our purpose is often hidden from view and elusive. In 1957, the Thailand government planned a new highway to cut through the remains of a temple. Amid the ruins was a giant plaster statue of the Buddha with inlaid pieces of colored glass. The plan was to move this icon a few hundred yards to a new temple under construction. They brought in a large crane and secured the statue with straps. As they were lifting it, cracks began appearing, and the crew immediately lowered it to the ground. What to do? Calls went out to experts for advice.

Meanwhile, one of the monks in charge had a tarp placed over the Buddha to protect it from rain. That evening he went out to check on the tarp with a flashlight and saw something reflecting at him. In closer inspection, the reflection was coming from one of the cracks. The next morning, he and the rest of the monks inspected the crack and deduced the stucco was covering up something far more valuable—gold. They began carefully chipping away at the plaster to reveal a brilliant Golden Buddha.

How it got covered up was a bit of a mystery. Most probably in the late 1700s, the Burmese invaded Thailand and were pillaging everything. The monks undoubtedly got wind of their impending arrival and decided to avert the plundering of their most precious possession—the Golden Buddha. They hatched a desperate plan, quickly covering the Buddha with stucco. It worked. The army ignored what they thought was a worthless statue and moved on after slaughtering most of the monks. With them died the secret of this hidden treasure.

We like to think of the Golden Buddha as a powerful metaphor for our calling. We come into this life with a clear direction. But soon, we're socialized and taught to adapt to the ways of our family and society. Others tell us how to feel, what to pursue in our work, and what to value. Very quickly, that deep, creative impulse we're born with is covered over and forgotten. But it's still there waiting to be rediscovered. We believe the unearthing of our calling is the path to living the most authentic, meaningful life possible.

If you're like many people we know, though, this may seem to be an elusive quest. You may have been waiting for years for your higher purpose or calling to hit you over the head, trying dozens of different jobs and myriad volunteer opportunities. It has been elusive finding something more meaningful and enlivening. We hope by the conclusion of this chapter, you have dramatically altered this story.

What do we mean by this term? Parker Palmer, an American author and educator who focuses on leadership and spirituality issues, puts it this way:

> "Let your life speak" means something different to me now. Vocation, I've learned, doesn't come from willfulness. It comes from listening. To understand this insight, we must understand the word *vocation* rooted in the Latin for "voice." Before I tell my life what I want to do with it, I must listen to what my being wants to do with me. I've come to understand vocation not as a goal to be achieved but as a gift to be received—the treasure of true self I already possess. Vocation doesn't come from a voice "out there" calling me to become something I'm not. It comes from a voice "in here" calling me to be the person I was born to be.[26]

People who discover their calling often experience life from the viewpoint of a mission that may have various vocational expressions throughout their lives. It will likely evolve as you grow in knowledge and experience. Or, it may surface as a compelling, almost irresistible urge to pursue a path with deep personal resonance and meaning.

Your calling is distinct from a job in which you trade your time for money. On the other hand, a vocation can become a role and a platform bringing your calling to life by focusing and sincerely tapping your gifts and talents. If we were to diagram it, it would look like a series of concentric circles as in this illustration.

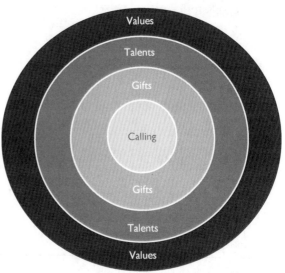

Every action emanating from your purpose harnesses your unique gifts, is expressed through your talents, and is congruent with your values. For some of you, your calling may have been apparent for many years, almost blaring like a loudspeaker, instilling in you a profound passion for doing something significant with your life. For others, it may be barely audible, just a whisper, a faint impulse registering in your consciousness.

Interestingly, Robert Vallerand[27] and his colleagues have identified two distinct kinds of callings and the incumbent passion people feel while pursuing them. He characterizes one as obsessive and the other as harmonious. If your calling keeps you up half the night, producing anxiety and frequently leading to burnout, Vallerand would characterize this as obsessive and deems it destructive in the long run, no matter how energetic it makes you feel. In contrast, he'd describe it as harmonious if your calling has the quality of a slow-burning wood stove. This kind of calling infuses your life with vitality, leading to consistently improved performance and positive emotions in whatever you're pursuing.

If you're uncertain about your calling, we'll give you a simple process to identify and clarify it at the end of the chapter.

Journey Deeper

House Tour

We first learned this technique from Sam Keen, an American philosopher and colleague of the mythologist Joseph Campbell. Start by drawing the floorplan of the house or apartment you grew up in. If you moved a lot while growing up, go back in time to the home you remember best. Sketch in the footprint of the furniture as well. Don't worry if it's not exact—this is not an art contest. If there were significant features outside of the house, sketch those in as well. As you're drawing, you'll discover you'll remember events from various rooms you may have long forgotten. Make shorthand notes of these off to the side. When finished, sit with a friend or spouse and give them a tour of your home and tell them stories of significant things that occurred there. What insights did you have as you share? If you journal, write about the experience and what you learned.

For a variant of this exercise, draw the neighborhood of your youth. What were the outer limits of your universe? Which places defined your childhood?

Storyboard Your Life

Using the technique we described in the first chapter, direct the process at your own life to see how things fit together and connect. Begin by considering what have been the significant issues or events in your life. Write them down individually on a sticky note and adhere them to a surface. Don't worry about how you order them. Once you have the big things out, you can rearrange them according to a prescribed order, either along a timeline or thematically. You may decide to merge a couple of ideas or discard those already implied in another one.

Then, take each one of these big ideas and begin fleshing out details for it using the same method of writing events or experiences on a card or sticky note and adhering it to the surface under this heading. Initially, don't be concerned about these items' order—just get them out to be viewed. Once you have exhausted everything you can think of under a particular header, step back and begin rearranging the sub-items. Once again, thematic or time-related criteria often prove to be most effective. Repeat this process for each primary header. What you'll discover is you can map out your entire life in a relatively short time. This an excellent method for life review and engaging in integrative reminiscence.

Seeing Your Life Flash before Your Eyes

Some suggest that we see our life replay before our eyes at the moment of death, like watching a film sped up tenfold. It's an interesting metaphor, but you need not wait until you die to see your life flash before your eyes. This exercise we learned from Sam Keen accomplishes this. Take a piece of adding machine tape, approximately four to five feet in length. Label one side of the tape "Personal Life." Label the other side "Professional Life." Now divide each side into increments of seven years.

Using the following Themes for Reflection section, write in the relevant time frames a short description of a related story. For example, if you felt alienated from your friends as a teenager because of something they said or did, you would write in the 14–21 segment on Side 1—Personal Life the word "Alienation" with a brief description of what occurred. If you also felt alienated in your first job when you were in your midtwenties, on Side 2—

Professional Life, write "Alienation" and a description of the events that occurred at work between the twenty-one- and twenty-eight-year segments. Do so for each of the themes, and for all of the times the subject arose. If there is a theme for which you can't think of anything relevant, skip it and move on to the next one.

When finished take the two ends of the machine tape and give one end a half-turn, then tape the ends together to create a Möbius strip. You may remember making one of these in elementary school. Strangely, what you end up with is a tape with only one side. As you slide it between your hands, you will seamlessly move from your personal life to your professional life back again to the personal. It's a beautiful way to take in your life in its entirety in one sitting. To see a short video demonstrating this exercise, go to www.storyintelligence.com/resources.

Themes for Reflection

Alienation – A time when you felt alienated and what you did to attempt to remedy this.

Ambition – A time you got what you wanted or were thwarted in getting what you wanted.

Betrayal – A time a friend or love betrayed you, causing you pain; or a time when you betrayed someone close to you.

Celebration – Favorite memories of family or community celebrations.

Coming of Age – A time when you lost your innocence physically, emotionally, or spiritually.

Courage – A time when you found the courage to deal with conflict; or a time when you felt you lacked courage; or a time when you developed courage when you had none; or a time when you conquered your fears.

Death – A time when you had to face and deal with the death of someone significant in your life.

Deception – A time when you felt deceived; or a time when you cheated others that you may or may not regret.

Discovery – A time when you discovered new places, inner meaning, and strengths you didn't think you had.

Dreams – A time when you had big goals for your life or saw your dreams fulfilled, or were disappointed.

Escape – A time when you escaped from life, routine, family pressures, or even a dangerous situation.

Faith or Hope – Either a time when you found it or a time when you lost it.

Fear – A time when your fear was driving you, you had to confront your fears, or you conquered your fears.

Freedom – A time when you lost your freedom, or had to handle new freedom, or had to fight for your freedom.

Isolation – A time when you felt physically or emotionally isolated.

Jealousy – A time jealousy caused you trouble.

Justice – A time when you felt the need to fight for justice or confront injustice.

Loneliness – A time when you felt incredibly lonely.

Loss – Of life, innocence, love, friends, or a time when you attempted to avoid it.

Love – A time when you fell in love or fell out of love; or a time when love helped you overcome obstacles.

Power – A time when you searched for lost power and what you were willing to exchange for it.

Prejudice – A time when you experienced or dealt with racism, bigotry, snobbery, or bullying.

Sacrifice – A time when you had to give up something for something more substantial.

Security – A time when you felt the loss of security, felt the need for it, or how you acted when your security was shattered.

Spirituality and God – A time when you struggled with your relationship with God or when you discovered a deeper sense of spirituality in yourself and the world.

Survival – A time when you felt you were in survival physically or emotionally.

Tough Decisions – A time when you had to make a tough choice.

Triumph – A time when you triumphed.

Change the Metaphor, Change Your Life Story

Whether or not you were an English major, you no doubt know what a metaphor is. Our language is laced with them. These figures of speech often shed light and meaning on our experiences in descriptive language by applying the qualities of one object to something seemingly discontinuous or not so obvious. For example, if a colleague at work is on a fast track to getting a promotion, you might refer to him as *a shining star*. If you know of a family of children who grew up in a sterile environment, yet they flourished regardless, you might say they were *flowers grown in a concrete garden*. If you're a student of contemporary lyrics, perhaps you know this one from Bob Dylan: *Chaos is a friend of mine*.

What metaphor would you use to describe your life? The journey you have been on? The ups and downs you have experienced? Has it been characterized by triumphs or failures? Have you always taken the high road, or have you settled for a more pedestrian path? Whatever metaphor you choose, to what extent does it adequately describe your life? In what ways does it fall short?

Now, consider seeing your life through the lens of a metaphor you wouldn't typically choose for yourself. Here are a few examples to consider. Choose one even though you may not currently feel it to be accurate. What insight would it open up for you about your life? What light would it shed on the choices you have made, your significant relationships, and the meaning you ascribe to your journey so far?

- My life is a garden filled with roses and thorns.
- I live my life on the battlefront.
- My life has been a crooked, winding road.
- I'm a bamboo house in a storm.

- My emotional life is a roller coaster.
- My life is a mountain trail.
- My life is nothing but a rat race.
- Every failure has been a stepping-stone for me to something better.
- Life is a box of chocolates, because you never know what you're going to get (Forrest Gump).
- I always take the high road.
- Life is not an easy street.
- Always take the straight and narrow path.
- I'm on the downward slope.

My Life Has Meaning If . . .

One way to shed light on things that enrich you is by completing over and over the phrase, "My life has meaning if . . ." Keep writing until you have exhausted all of your feelings and thoughts on the subject. A variant is "My life has meaning when . . ." See what doors and unexpected revelations arise when experimenting with this avenue into the heart of meaning.

Tools for Developing Your MasterStory

Identify Your Angels and Heroes to Elucidate Your Values

To start, take a piece of blank paper and draw a line on it, dividing it up into seven-year increments, as illustrated here. For the sake of this illustration, we went to fifty-six, but your map may be somewhat shorter or longer, depending on your age.

| 0 | 7 | 14 | 21 | 28 | 35 | 42 | 49 | 56 |

There is nothing magical about seven-year increments, but it's interesting to note these age breaks correspond nicely with natural life stages. Around fourteen, we leave childhood and become an adolescent. At twenty-one, most of us are on our way to establishing independence and perhaps even starting a family. At forty-nine, many go through a classic midlife crisis. Around sixty-three or seventy, we're often transitioning away from a vocation and into retirement.

Identify in each time increment someone who was an angel or hero. Even though you may have had a great relationship with your parents, avoid using them more than once in any of the segments. Instead, attempt to identify others who played a significant role in your life. You might include an aunt or uncle who took you under their wing and gave you excellent guidance. Perhaps your neighbor next door always had a welcoming ear, offering you cookies and milk when you needed to get something off your chest. One of your heroes or angels might not even be someone you knew personally. They can also be fictional characters. A person in one of our programs put Dr. Spock from *Star Trek* in an earlier segment of his life. Many of the things he values to this day can be traced back to emulating Spock in difficult, stressful situations.

As you identify an individual in each time frame, write down everything you admire about this person. Especially elucidate the valuable things this person modeled. If there's a time frame where you simply can't think of someone, don't fret over it. Just move on to the next time segment.

When done, create two columns on the reverse side of the page. At the top of the first column, write, "My Angel or Hero"; at the top of the next column, write, "The Things I Value because of Them." Here's an example from my life. When I (Richard) was in college, I had a philosophy professor named Charles Scott. Charles was a beloved teacher, and his door was always open. He was keenly interested in engaging in meaningful conversations with his students. I would drop in, and Charles truly cared to hear about the things I was thinking about and feeling. Until then, none of the adults in my life were curious about what was circulating in my head and heart. From Charles, I learned the value of deep listening. So, if I were doing this exercise, I'd put Charles' name in the left-hand column, and "deep listening" in the right-hand column.

Another example: When I (Richard) was very young, my great-aunt Faye came to live in Tampa. Faye was a colorful character, uninhibited by the social rules governing my grandmother. I'd spend weekends sleeping over at her house, go on all kinds of adventures with her, and she would gladly take me to a double-feature film on Saturday afternoons. From her, I learned the value of fun and laughter.

Finally, another example from Richard's life: My first real boss in the work world was Dave Chapman. Dave gave me my first job in the advertising business. I knocked on his door after finishing my master's in psychology and dropping out of a PhD program to do a stint at the Art Institute of Chicago. Desperate to find a job, I was sure I wanted to do something creative. Dave asked me if I could write. "Sure," I said, "I just finished writing a master's thesis." He wasn't interested in that kind of writing. What he wanted to know was if I could write creatively. They were considering representing a product called City Farmer. It was a five-gallon container of mulch you could grow vegetables in on the porch of your apartment. Dave challenged me to draft some TV commercials. The only problem was I had no idea of how to write a commercial, never having taken any advertising classes in college. Luckily, I had an interview that afternoon at a TV station for a position in sales. As I was departing after being told they didn't have any kind of entry-level positions available, I asked, "How do you write a TV commercial?"

The sales manager said it was simple. "Just draw a line down the middle of a piece of paper to create two columns. On the left is a description of the video and action. On the right, the dialogue."

With this limited knowledge, I departed, wrote about ten

commercials, and had twenty more ideas. Two days later, I walked in and presented them. The scripts were imaginative, and I got the job.

So, here's the beginning of my values list:

My Angel or Hero	*The Things I Value because of Them*
Charles Scott	Deep listening
Great-Aunt Faye	Fun and play
Dave Chapman	Being creative

Now, it's your turn. Compile your list, then look at each of the things you deduced from your admiration of these individuals. Which of these have you been able to integrate into your life successfully? Which do you aspire to but still have a lot of work to make them real every day? These are uniquely your values, built out of the story of your life.

Share this exercise with people who are close to you. Together you'll discover insights about what motivates you, what brings resonance and fulfillment to your work, and what is an essential bedrock of your identity.

Discern Your Gifts and Talents

So, how do we ascertain our gifts? The approach we have found most useful is to identify times we found terrific pleasure in doing something. As you look back over your life, write in a notebook or share with a friend stories about things you love to do, including hobbies, pastimes, and fulfilling activities at work. They may be things you used to do at an earlier stage of your life, but for whatever reason, you put them aside; or they're things that energize you while doing them, that come easily, where you might lose track of time because they're so engaging. When done, see if you can deduce the gifts these things might point to. Make a list. To help you, we have included a list of possible gifts. It is by no means exhaustive. Examining the list, see if you can identify additional gift clues you think you may have missed. Check up to ten items.

Gift Clues

- ☐ Ability to Compartmentalize
- ☐ Ability to Handle Change
- ☐ Adaptability
- ☐ Aesthetic Sensibility
- ☐ Athleticism
- ☐ Choreographer
- ☐ Cognitive Intelligence
- ☐ Compassion
- ☐ Critical Thinking
- ☐ Dance
- ☐ Determination
- ☐ Discernment
- ☐ Eloquence
- ☐ Empathy
- ☐ Forward-Looking
- ☐ Good with Animals
- ☐ Handiness
- ☐ Ingenuity
- ☐ Intuition
- ☐ Mathematics
- ☐ Multitasking
- ☐ Negotiating
- ☐ Nurturing
- ☐ Organization
- ☐ Peacemaking
- ☐ Perseverance
- ☐ Problem-Solving
- ☐ Resolve Conflict
- ☐ Seeing All Sides of a Situation
- ☐ Selflessness
- ☐ Social Intelligence
- ☐ Words
- ☐ Ability to Conceptualize
- ☐ Academics
- ☐ Advocate
- ☐ Asking Questions
- ☐ Caregiver
- ☐ Clear Thinking
- ☐ Collaborator
- ☐ Contemplation
- ☐ Curiosity
- ☐ Decision-Making
- ☐ Diagnosis
- ☐ Dreamer
- ☐ Emotional Intelligence
- ☐ Fixing Things
- ☐ Generosity
- ☐ Green Thumb
- ☐ Humor
- ☐ Innovative
- ☐ Learner
- ☐ Multilingual
- ☐ Musicality
- ☐ Numbers
- ☐ Optimism
- ☐ Patience
- ☐ Perceptivity
- ☐ Pragmatic
- ☐ Public Speaking
- ☐ Runner
- ☐ Seeing the Big Picture
- ☐ Singing
- ☐ Storytelling
- ☐ Visualization
- ☐ Writing
- ☐ Understanding the World Narratively

Look back at the gifts you identified and the stories of things that brought you tremendous pleasure. Now, make a list like the following one of what you think are your top five gifts. Every gift we have may have associated talents that bring the gift to life. Can you identify the talents you have developed as a result, even if they still need to be nurtured and honed? Are there gifts you have listed you've neglected over the years? What would it look like if you were to devote more energy to developing their expression? How can you better use your gifts and talents to improve your life and work? Here are a couple examples.

My Top Gifts	Related Talents
Storytelling	Writing fiction, performing stories, public speaking, video production
Aesthetics	Painting, photography, graphic design
Seeing All Sides of a Situation	Mediator of conflict, synthesizer of ideas

Discover Your Calling

The following exercise can lead you much closer to this inner truth. Here is a list of some of those impulses, what we call "calling clues," which we adapted from the work of Richard Leider.[28] They may elicit an *aha* moment and shed light on your deepest calling.

Step 1: Start by putting a check mark beside all of the clues most like you.

Step 2: Reduce the "most like you" to ten items by circling the ten most core to who you are.

Step 3: Reduce the list to the five most essential items. Next to each one, reflect on what it is about it that resonates with you. Is there an item more primary among the five you have chosen? Put a check mark beside it. Then transfer this to a table you have created on a blank sheet looking like the one following with examples from my preliminary list. Beside each item, spell out what resonates with you about this particular clue. As an example, see the following table.

☐ To Cultivate
☐ To Design
☐ To Elevate Possibilities
☐ To Envision
☐ To Evaluate
☐ To Explore
☐ To Heal
☐ To Help
☐ To Inspire
☐ To Invent
☐ To Lead
☐ To Learn
☐ To Make Connections
☐ To Make Peace
☐ To Mentor
☐ To Minister
☐ To Nurture
☐ To Achieve/Realize Potential
☐ To Account
☐ To Advocate (for)
☐ To Analyze
☐ To Awaken Spirit
☐ To Build
☐ To Coach
☐ To Communicate

☐ To Compete
☐ To Compose
☐ To Construct
☐ To Convene
☐ To Counsel
☐ To Craft
☐ To Create
☐ To (Give) Care
☐ To Create Order
☐ To Orchestrate
☐ To Perform
☐ To Persuade
☐ To Plan/Organize
☐ To Promote
☐ To Protect/Defend
☐ To Repair/Mend
☐ To Restore
☐ To Research
☐ To Seek Justice
☐ To Sell
☐ To Serve
☐ To Support
☐ To Teach
☐ To Unite
☐ To Write

Calling Clues	What Resonates with Me about This Clue
To Create	I have spent my entire life joyfully devoted to creative pursuits.
To Teach	I love sharing with others what I have learned about the power of story.
To Envision	I like to imagine what's possible and see how things could be different and better.
To Communicate	Writing has always been a passion and joy for me.
To Explore	For me, painting and photography have always been a process of exploration and invention.

Now it's time to integrate everything you have discovered about your calling. Write the first draft of your calling. Use the clues you identified previously where you identified experiences that resonated with you. If possible, try to frame it as succinctly as you can, hopefully in one sentence. Make the one item you checked of the five the central tenet of your draft, perhaps considering the other four more like a supporting cast.

Here's a current formulation: *To creatively elevate human potential and spirit.* As you can see, it's concise and to the point. As we see it, this statement informs activities such as writing this book—it's our hope what you learn here will elevate your spirit and expand your potential. But it also cuts across many of Richard's other creative pursuits, from painting to a personal performance entitled *The Maggid,* which celebrates the human spirit through the stories of the Jewish mystic known as the Baal Shem Tov, who lived in the 1700s.

When writing your first draft, just write. Then, see if you can pare it down to its core elements once you have an initial draft. I printed mine out on a small card and keep it on my desk. Consider where you can place yours as a reminder as you create your life story from here on.

Here are some questions and ideas to consider now that you have your draft of your calling:

- How does your draft statement make you feel?
- Imagine what it would be like to use this statement to guide you when making important decisions.
- Consider how your calling can inform the story of the next chapters of your life when activated through your gifts, talents, and values.
- What do you wish to create in the future, given what you now know about your calling?
- How could the world you want to live in be different if you were pursuing your calling in every facet of your life? What new course might you chart?
- What impact do you want to have in the world?
- What preliminary commitments would you like to make to activate your calling and best use your gifts and talents in line with your deepest values?
- How do these goals intersect with the needs of the world? Where can you make the most impact?
- What internal and external dragons do you need to slay to succeed? How do you think you can best achieve this?
- Who are (or can be) your allies personally and professionally as you move to make an impact in your world?
- How would you like to enlist their help? To whom can you reach out for direction and guidance along the way?

A word of caution—once you know your calling, the consequences may be grave if you fail to follow it. Research psychologists Michele Gazica and Paul Spector[29] surveyed nearly four hundred academicians looking at a wide range of factors, including calling. They asked them to rate their work engagement, job involvement, career commitment, life and job satisfaction, and physical and emotional well-being. Not surprisingly, those with a calling fared better on these measures than colleagues who had no calling at all.

But those who identified that they had an unmet calling reported worse physical and mental health than those in the other two groups. It would seem once you let the genie out of the bottle, there is no putting him back in there. There's a price to be paid for denying it.

This notion fits with Joseph Campbell's work on the Hero's Journey. In this archetypal model, an ordinary person is living a safe, perhaps even uneventful life. Then one day, there is either a faint whisper or a clarion call in their head beckoning them out of the safety of the known. Regardless of the call's amplitude, our protagonist must make a choice—accept the call or refuse it and return to the ordinary world. Perhaps fear overtakes her. Or second guesses. Or a doubting voice. It would be unreasonable and foolish to leave what is known and safe for what it is unknown and perhaps physically or psychically hazardous. Hopefully, she overcomes her reluctance. If she doesn't, she will live the rest of her life wondering what she sacrificed to remain in the confines of her small nest of a world, living in the illusion this would make her feel secure and fulfilled. Such a dream can be incredibly powerful and seductive. It can also deaden the soul.

Know Your Metastories

Albert Einstein once said, "There are only two ways to live your life. One is as though nothing is a miracle. The other is as though everything is a miracle." This familiar quote is an excellent example of a metastory that can shape our fundamental world view and our place in it.

As we see it, there are two pairs of metastories. Consciously or unconsciously, you have adopted one from each set. The first is your relationship with the universe. Either you believe that there's a creator or some higher power with a hand in all human affairs, or you don't.

The second pair has to do with your relationship with the world we live in. Either you believe that everything is interconnected or that we live life as a solipsistic existence, separate and alone.

The two choices you have adopted together form your metastory, and it shapes your relationship with others and the world as a whole. In no way do we intend to make a judgment or advocate for a particular metastory. We endorse that everyone should first make a deeply-thought-out and informed decision on what and why you have opted for those stories. Secondly, you must understand that the stories you adopt will profoundly affect the trajectory of your life experience. The depth to which you are committed to your metastory also matters. Deep commitment increases the magnitude of its power in your life.

Do You Know?

We earlier discussed the work of Robyn Fivush and Marshall Duke, in which children who know about their family's stories experience higher self-esteem and resilience. The more positive answers a child gives to the twenty items in the *Do You Know?* Questionnaire, the more likely they'll have high self-esteem and resilience. For a downloadable version of the questionnaire, go to www.storyintelligence.com/resources.

Oprah on Calling

Oprah has been one of the most prominent contemporary proponents of people following their calling. Here are some of her best videos on the topic:

- Oprah Explains the Difference between a Career and a Calling (www.youtube.com/watch?v=opNxqO70smA)
- Can You Miss the Clues for Your Calling? (www.youtube.com/watch?v=LPT-WY3SD8w)
- 4 Questions to Help You Find Your Calling (www.youtube.com/watch?v=4Rl0N2W7arw)

Books We Recommend

There is a wealth of resources available on how to create an ethical will. Here are a few that have been particularly useful to us:

Ethical Wills: Putting Your Values on Paper by **Barry K. Baines**

Ethical Wills & How to Prepare Them (2nd Edition): A Guide to Sharing Your Values from Generation to Generation by **Rabbi Jack Riemer, Dr. Nathaniel Stampfer, et al.**

Your Legacy Matters: A Multi-generational Guide for Writing Your Ethical Will by **Rachael A. Freed**

While this chapter is focused more on how we as adults can discover our life calling, **Bill Damon in *The Path to Purpose: How Young People Find Their Calling in Life*** has forged new understanding and tools to help younger people make that journey and find greater meaning in their lives.

If there was ever a classic on what it means to live a meaningful life, it's *Man's Search for Meaning* by **Viktor Frankl**. If you're going to read just one book, put this one at the top of your list.

There are few books that have influenced us more than *Sensemaking in Organizations* by **Karl E. Weick**. Weick will take you on a journey into the subconscious of your organization and illuminate how powerfully stories inform the construction of organizational meaning and provide the lifeblood of vibrant business cultures.

5

The Power of Story to Transform

The ability to transform seemingly intractable problems into enlivening possibilities and create new life trajectories.

What happens is of little significance compared with the stories we tell ourselves about what happens. Events matter little, only stories of events affect us.

— Rabih Alameddine

One of the most critical questions we humans must face is whether we can change our story. Are our past actions and those of others set in stone for all eternity? Is the story we've been telling about events the only one possible, or even the true one? What if the past is just a construct, an idea that we have the power and authority to alter and rewrite?

While these questions may seem rhetorical, they have important practical implications. If we are story masters with the capacity to influence the past, present, and future, then we can sharpen our SQ to unlock immense power in our lives. The fact that we have evolved as creatures imbued with story powers may just be our salvation and ticket out of a "past" that often imprisons us.

How We Preserve the "Past"

What occurred five minutes ago, yesterday, or even thirty years ago, resides in what we all refer to as the "past." In this sense, the past no longer exists. As far as we can see, the only way things in the past can be kept alive is through the stories we tell about them. Essentially, the past is re-presented to our consciousness each time we tell a story about it, allowing us to reexperience it imaginally as a facsimile in the present.

If I were amnesic, I'd forget anything you or others did by the next moment. There would be no story to tell. The past would evaporate as an idea. All that exists would be the present moving into the future. If you offended me, it wouldn't matter. Within an instant, I'd forget everything you said. There would be no need to ask for forgiveness. Incapable of recalling your actions, I would be clueless about assessing your worthiness as a friend. You would mostly be a stranger to me, from moment to moment, day to day. Unfortunately, this is the reality for many who are suffering from dementia or Alzheimer's.

But this isn't the case for most of us with relatively intact memories. If we're physically injured or emotionally hurt by another, that memory becomes indelibly imprinted in our minds. Imagine you insulted my wife over dinner last week. If someone were to ask me about my appraisal of you, I'd likely retell that story creating an anchor for a broader generalization. From that one egregious act, I might conclude you have a severe character flaw, perhaps even attributing to you all kinds of evil traits and faults. In effect, I'd weave together a story about an event in the past with a characterological description of who you are in the present. By implication, it's who you'll be in the future. If this behavior occurred on more than one occasion, it's more fuel for the fire, no doubt fanning the flames of my story about you as a nasty piece of work. Once I tell that story repeatedly, it gets physically wired into my brain, even somaticized. These stories aren't just abstract ideas swirling around between my ears. They live as much in my gut, chest, and throat as they do in my head. In a real sense, I become shackled to this story and its fixed points of view. Even if I witness times you are kind and generous, those experiences most likely will be deflected like a nonstick pan. Once a story about the past finds its grooves and is regularly repeated, it becomes relatively impermeable to new, contradictory information.

Not only is this true for the stories we tell about others, but it also applies to the stories we tell about whole peoples and nations. It often takes just one person from an ethnic group to violate our cultural norms and expectations. Usually, with religious and political leaders' encouragement, stories soon begin circulating, implying all people from this group are not trustworthy. Worse yet, they are heinous, inhuman beings, maybe even killers and rapists. From the particulars of one story, we make broad generalizations in the service of making sense of our experiences. It's all done to bring coherence and certainty to a world filled with ambiguity and unknowns.

It's even more challenging to see with any objectivity the stories we have repeatedly told ourselves about ourselves. What we fail to recognize is that these are mere inventions as well. They are acts of fiction masquerading as reality. Is it possible these stories are just one version of what may be a multitude of takes on the past? That we could have as quickly chosen a different story to tell about the same "facts"? More importantly, can we today fundamentally change the past by selecting an alternate account?

Seeing Life's
Difficulties in a New Light

Alexander Graham Bell once said, "When one door closes, another door opens." Most people don't know the rest of the quote, though, which is even more significant: "But we often look so long and so regretfully upon the closed door that we do not see the one which has opened for us." Let's face it—we become attached to the story we've been living. It's familiar, comfortable, and provides a vital organizing function in our lives, regardless of its harmful components. Even if it does little to nourish our souls, it's our story, and we're prone to hang on to it, no matter the cost.

Why do we cling so to such unattractive realities? Perhaps the thing we loathe more than a painful story is not having a story at all. We define ourselves by these narratives. Without them, we experience a vacuum that feels like it may consume and destroy us. It's better to continue to stare at the closed door, pining for its familiar ways, than to experience the anxiety of starting anew, opening a door shrouded in dark shadows. In all likelihood, we'll fill this void with stories too. In our fear, we'll imagine dangerous creatures lurking behind that new door, ready to consume and destroy us. No wonder we want to cling to the monsters we know. They may be stressful and unfulfilling, but we have learned to live with them.

How could we adopt a different attitude toward the changes inevitably arising in life? Is there a more freeing, exhilarating story we could tell about the events besetting us? There is a brilliant Chinese tale that demonstrates this alternative approach to change, gains, and loss.

The Remarkable Horse[1]

Long ago, an old, sickly man and his son lived in an impoverished village. Luckily for the older man, his son was healthy and robust; otherwise, they would have surely perished. One day while they were working in their barn, a magnificent wild horse unexpectedly rode into their stable. The father motioned to the son to quickly close the gate. For such a poor farmer, this was an incredible stroke of good luck. No one in the village had ever seen such a brilliant animal, and it would fetch a very high price at the market. A neighbor stopped by to visit, remarking to his elderly friend how fortunate this was. Yes, the gods were smiling with favor on him this day. The older man's response surprised him. Stroking his beard, he said, "Perhaps this is good fortune. Perhaps it is not. Only time will tell."

Sure enough, three days later, the horse jumped over the fence and was gone. The neighbor stopped by to commiserate with his friend and commented on how unlucky it was the horse had escaped. But the old man just echoed his words of a few days earlier, "Perhaps this is bad fortune. Perhaps it is not. Only time will tell."

A week passed. While the older man and his son were repairing their house, they heard what sounded like thunder. It was a whole herd of wild horses led by the magnificent horse that escaped only a few days before. He led the others into the corral, and the older man's son quickly closed the gate. When the neighbor heard of this miraculous event, he stopped by and commented to his friend on his good fortune. The old man just shook his head, muttering, "Perhaps this is good fortune. Perhaps it is not. Only time will tell."

The next day his son was attempting to break one of the new horses and was thrown, his leg shattered in two places. The village doctor was hopeful in his diagnosis, saying the young man would walk again after fitting a tight brace around his thigh and shin. But he warned it would require many months of healing and rest. Given his arthritis and fragile back, this was terrible news for the older man. He depended on his son for help with many of the more arduous chores on the farm. What was he to do now? As you might expect, the neighbor visited to express his regret about the accident and to declare what an unfortunate turn of events this had been. But the old man patiently replied, "Perhaps this is bad fortune. Perhaps it is not. Only time will tell."

Two weeks later, a regiment of soldiers rode into the village. A war was brewing with a northern province, and they conscripted every young man to fight, except, of course, the older man's son who was convalescing. Not one of those men returned alive from the war. The older man's son eventually healed and was once again able to help his father. And, as the wise father often said after his son was *spared the fate of so many other young men, "We never know whether a thing is good or bad until the story is finished."*

This story beautifully illustrates how readily we ascribe a valence to the encounters we have in the world. Often, we base these judgments on past experiences. An unexpected windfall can lead us to shout for joy, but is it, in fact, a good thing? Maybe yes, maybe no. Look at the history of people who win the lottery. The winners' stories sound more like a litany of nightmares—failed marriages, siblings hiring hitmen, disastrous investments, bankruptcy, all ending in tragedy with winners destitute and penniless. Was it good or bad?

On the negative side, we might view a child's loss to an unexpected injury as a tragedy from which we could never recover. Still, even amidst heartbreak, there are seeds of possibility if we're willing to look up from our grief. When Bob and Lisa Gfeller lost their son in a football accident years ago, they found themselves embarking on a journey to improve all young athletes' safety. At the time of Matthew's death, the national conversation about concussions was just beginning. As they describe it, the tragedy swept them along in unimagined ways. A couple of weeks after Matthew died, they got a call from the Winston-Salem Foundation. Unbeknownst to them, people throughout the community were contributing money to the foundation in Matthew's name. Through these generous donations, they decided to endow a scholarship in honor of Matthew. A story shared with them by one of Matthew's friends and fellow football players inspired the scholarship's criterion. After the quarterback called every play in the huddle, Matthew would look at his teammates and say, "I won't let you down." Now, every year, a student is selected who embodies this spirit and is awarded $2,000 a year for college. The many young men and women who have received scholarships have gone on to have outstanding collegiate careers. Now they're graduating and making significant contributions in their communities.

Another way the Gfellers were carried and supported by their community was in the creation of the Matthew Gfeller Foundation. Matthew's best friends approached Bob and Lisa, wanting to do something to remember Matthew and make a difference so future athletes can avoid catastrophic injuries. The result was an annual donut run. They raised hundreds of thousands of dollars to support the Childress Institute for Pediatric Trauma at Wake Forest Baptist Medical Center and the newly created Matthew Gfeller Sport-Related Traumatic Brain Injury Research Center at UNC-Chapel Hill. Now, UNC is actively pursuing studies designed to reduce concussion risk for all youths playing sports. Research at the Childress Center continues to raise the quality of care for severely injured kids in the Piedmont region of North Carolina and across the country.

Perhaps of most significance was a psychic shift Lisa had. When a tragic event occurs, our first and natural response is to ask, "Why?" After many weeks of grieving, Lisa woke one day and recognized this question was not helping her or her family heal. A different question came to her: "What now?" Shifting from "Why?" to "What now?" allowed Bob and Lisa to use the pain of this event to create something that has touched the lives of thousands of young athletes and children.[2]

We must train our minds to manage life experiences flexibly, so we don't become fixated on the door that closes, creating a rigid, confining story. Instead, we must learn to reorient our perspective to the presenting possibilities, even amid intense difficulty. That means practicing the art of seeing our stories without adding a conclusion. No event is necessarily a bad thing or a good thing. It becomes such only in terms of the story we choose to tell about it and the meaning we ascribe to it. In a strong sense, conclusions are a projection of a future storyline onto a set of facts. Matthew died tragically, but what it meant was ultimately up to Bob and Lisa Gfeller. They chose to live without appending a dire conclusion onto the story of what happened that fateful Friday night on a football field. That's not to say they don't still dearly miss him or feel unbearable sadness about his absence from time to time.

If we do the same, life can become fascinating and curious. In reality, no story is ever finished. With time everything changes. When we can approach life suspending conclusions, we open ourselves to seeing possibilities where none existed. Returning to Bell's metaphor, we inquisitively see the doors opening even as one we dearly value closes.

The Need to Learn to Self-Distance

Many years ago, J.R.R. Tolkien, the author of *The Hobbit* and *The Lord of the Rings*, coined the term "eucatastrophe."[3] He constructed the word by combining the Greek prefix *eu*, meaning good, with catastrophe, which in literary works refers to the unraveling of characters' lives. A eucatastrophe is a device Tolkien used to propel his mythic stories. When bad things happen, they often transmute into something good or useful. The immense forces mobilized to capture Sauron's magical ring from Frodo lead to an onslaught of tragedies and reversals. Then, like the phoenix rising from the ashes, forces of good appear to save the day.

The eucatastrophe concept is akin to the Hebrew phrase *gam zeh l'tovah*, meaning "even this is toward or for good." If you adopt a perspective that life is filled with challenges and hardship but is always changing, even a bad thing has within it the seeds for something good to grow. This insight can change the way you view your life. By suspending judgment, even in the grimmest of circumstances, we can grow to expect something good always evolving out of the mire we're in. Hence, we return to the notion of placing a modicum of psychic distance between ourselves, the events of our lives, and their ultimate meaning. It's what we described previously as "seeing our life from the other side of the street."

Researchers have been looking at this topic through several different lenses. Igor Grossmann and Ethan Kross observed that we generally can distance ourselves from others' stories. Still, we tend to struggle with distancing when it comes to emotionally charged issues in our own lives. They refer to this as the Solomon paradox.[4] King Solomon was sought out by citizens and leaders from around Judaea to mediate their disputes, gaining a reputation for astute discernment. But when running his affairs and those of the state, it was as though his ability to direct the wise counsel to himself evaporated, leading to the kingdom's downfall.

Isn't this the case for most of us? When it comes to others' dilemmas, we can often clearly see the forest for the trees. But when it comes to our own, we have difficulty gaining psychic distance from our troubles. Immersed in the emotional components of the problem, we simply can't get any perspective. These authors point out that "people's attempts to reflect adaptively on their negative feelings often fail because they focus on their experiences from a psychologically immersed perspective, making it difficult for people to reason objectively without getting caught up in the emotionally arousing details of what happened to them."[5]

So, how can we take a proverbial step back and see emotionally challenging events with more perspective and wisdom? Is it possible to view our problem through the eyes of a trusted friend who is psychologically removed from the situation?

Over the last few decades, many in the psychological field have explored this idea. One of the cofounders of cognitive therapy, Aaron Beck, saw that the therapeutic encounter's goal is to build this capacity for self-distance. People seek out therapeutic help because they're too embroiled in their problems. But with time, they learn how to do this on their own.[6]

In more recent times, the proliferation of mindfulness practices has attempted to use this contemplative format to engender self-distancing. If you're familiar with the practice of meditation, a simple instruction is to become the observer of your thoughts and feelings. See them as though you were lying on your back, watching clouds pass overhead. Note and observe them, knowing they will change. New thoughts and feelings will emerge to be replaced by others. This practice of not identifying with your thoughts, feelings, and stories soon becomes second nature. From this perspective, enlightenment is not the absence of thoughts or emotions. Instead, it's the ability to observe them and recognize who you are is *not* them.

A teacher of ours, Richard Moss, illustrates this with a liter bottle filled with water and sand. He first shakes the container, leading to a cloudy, swirling mixture. Once the shaking stops, the sand quickly settles, and the water returns to its original, transparent state. He likens this liter bottle to enlightened consciousness. Yes, strong emotions can cloud the mind. But enlightened individuals have trained their minds to clear their thoughts and feelings quickly. They shift into a different mode of consciousness with ease, allowing them to see their experiences with a modicum of distance. This awareness mode is devoid of the drama, often accompanying us unenlightened folks' reactions to life events. For most of us, the liter bottle can remain cloudy for days, weeks, and even years. We begin to believe the muddy mixture is who we are, whereas we are actually the crystal-clear water.

If you're not up for years of meditation practice, there may be more straightforward strategies for achieving much the same outcome. According to research psychologists Ethan Kross and Ozlem Ayduk, merely seeing life from a different vantage point can do the trick. The results are impressive. Participants reported lower levels of negative emotional reactivity and an ability to focus more on reconstruing the experience, leading to less short-term distress.[7]

The benefits of this approach may also extend beyond just the emotional dimension of life. Researchers have found people experience more stable blood pressure if they can effectively self-distance. When aroused, self-distancing returns their blood pressure quickly to healthy levels.[8] Maybe our anecdotes can be the antidotes to stress, leading to quicker recoveries.

To conclude, let's return to the theory that "neurons that fire together wire together." Researchers are exploring whether this strategy of self-distancing rewires the brain. Sure enough, people who deployed self-distancing and reported lower negative affect also saw a reduction in activity in the brain region that plays a crucial role in depression and excessive rumination.[9] It just may be that the most important task of modern education is the training of our minds to be more flexible and nimbler when it comes to the stories we tell.

Recontextualizing: The Most Powerful Form of Self-Distancing

While past experiences play a central role in our narrative construction, they need not exclusively determine that narrative's shape. Often, we forget that we create the stories we tell about the past, abandoning awareness of our authorship with tacit and unconscious automaticity. Forgetting our responsibility in the matter, we then live inside these stories as though we had no hand in their creation. The truth is that the story we tell about our lives is ultimately an act differing little from any author's craft. This capacity for invention allows us to examine and rewrite our stories in a manner that better serves our deep fulfillment in the world. It can also support the narrative arc we wish to pursue.

Perhaps better than any other contemporary author, Viktor Frankl captures our capacity and freedom to reframe the story in every moment, even amid horrific experiences like being imprisoned in a concentration camp. Humor was one of his go-to strategies for recontextualizing present suffering, seeing it as a means of rising above the situation's misery. Frankl sums it up this way: "Everything can be taken from a man but one thing: the last of the human freedoms—to choose one's attitude in any given set of circumstances, to choose one's own way . . . It is this spiritual freedom—which cannot be taken away—that makes life meaningful and purposeful."[10]

We believe what Frankl was extolling was our capacity for authorship. Sam Keen[11] points out the word "author" has its roots in the word "authority." Until we embrace and take responsibility for our life's authorship, we relegate our power to parents, peers, and society. To assume real authority over the trajectory of our lives, we must examine the stories we tell. If they don't nurture our souls, then we must be prepared to re-author them.

To better understand this concept, we turn to the world of performance storytelling. There is an old saying: the best-known storyteller is less well known than the least-known soap opera star. Storytellers walking through the airport don't attract crowds of autograph seekers or the paparazzi. Nevertheless, Donald Davis is in the echelon of truly gifted performers in our lifetime. If you have never seen him perform, you need to. Growing up in Waynesville, North Carolina, Donald weaves a panoply of unique characters throughout his tales. There is one story he shared recently at a Tedx Talk that's integral to our discussion of transformation.[12] It was told to him over fifty years ago by his father.

When growing up, Donald's dad, Joe, headed up Waynesville's only bank. It was a small operation, and he was the sole employee. There were three Joe Davises in town, so each had a nickname to avoid confusion. Donald's dad was "Banker Joe."

One day young Donald was visiting his dad in the bank. As his father was closing up, the gentleman who owned the town's furniture store across the street was closing up as well. The two men greeted each other. What deeply disturbed Donald was the furniture store owner greeted his dad in a demeaning fashion. "Have a good evening, Cripple Joe."

When they got into the car, Donald said, "I didn't like that." His dad was a bit miffed and asked what he didn't like. He told him being called Cripple Joe was disrespectful. His dad turned off the engine and proceeded to tell him this story.

When he was five years old growing up on a farm outside of Waynesville in the early 1900s, against his dad's instructions, Donald's father played one day with a small hatchet used to clean splinters off shake shingles. When he attempted to stick the hatchet back into the log, it bounced off the wood and ricocheted back, its blade burying in his knee.

When his parents found him, they wrapped the wound as best as they could. Joe's dad got on his horse with him on his lap and rode to the doctor's house. This country doctor had never seen an injury so severe and recommended they amputate. Luckily, Joe's dad decided to seek a second opinion. He got Joe back on the horse and rode into Waynesville. He discovered they had just missed the train to Asheville at the train station, but the train to Murphy would be coming soon, and he could switch trains there for Atlanta. The train trip spanned nearly two hundred miles. Lucky for Joe, Atlanta's Grady Hospital had just opened. Their gifted surgeons were able to save his leg, but they had to remove the kneecap. He'd walk with a limp for the remainder of his life.

Unable to do "men's work" in the field, Donald's dad took up spinning flax and making socks. More importantly, he had a lot of time on his hands to read. In his early teens, his dad died, and soon he had responsibility for supporting his mother, his younger siblings, and a widowed aunt. Joe recognized he would never be able to manage farmwork like his brothers. So, he spent all of his savings to enroll in a business school in Charlotte. Upon returning to Waynesville, two men who ran a wholesale grocery hired him as manager. Years went by until the man who owned the only bank in Waynesville wanted to retire and approached Joe to see if he wanted to buy it. That's how he became Banker Joe.

While they sat in his dad's Plymouth as the sun began to set, his dad explained to him how he embraced the nickname Cripple Joe. "Can't you see, son? If I hadn't been Cripple Joe, I never would have been able to become Banker Joe. I would still be out in the country plowing up fields, and your mother would never have paid any attention to me." From then on, Donald didn't mind if folks called his dad Banker Joe. But he relished the times his closest friends referred to him as Cripple Joe.

On a visit to his dad years later, Donald asked him how many times he had told that story.

"Probably over two hundred times."

Donald was stunned. His dad explained when he returned from Atlanta, he was depressed. His mother said to him, "Now it's time for you to tell the story."

Young Joe objected. "I don't want to tell the story. Telling the story wouldn't change anything. I'm a cripple."

His mother, in an act of supreme wisdom, said, "You're not telling the story to change what happened. You're telling the story to change you."

Over the coming days and weeks, she made Joe tell the story repeatedly, each time from a different point of view. First, she'd say, "Tell the story and tell what you learned by living through that." On another day, she'd ask him to see it through the eyes of other characters. "Now tell the story and tell what you think your daddy and I learned from living through that." Then she'd have him tell the story from the perspective of what the Waynesville doctor learned, followed by the station master, the doctors at Grady Hospital, and each of the nurses who cared for him. On and on, she'd have him retell the story over the following weeks and months.

One day she said, "Joe, if you don't tell this story enough, when you're fifty years old and look at your leg, you'll be five again, and you'll be pitiful. Because when something happens to you, it sits on top of you like a rock, and if you never tell the story, it sits on you forever. But as you begin to tell the story, you climb out from under that rock, and eventually, you sit on top of it."

Days went by. One morning, she said, "Now Joe, tell the story and tell it from the point of view of what you get to do that your brothers don't get to do."

Joe began telling the story and suddenly found himself

smiling. "I get to stay in the house and read while they work on the farm." Joe realized chopping his leg was maybe the best thing he had ever done in his life. He finally appreciated that his mother had been right all those months previously when she insisted on him telling the story. "The story doesn't change what happened, but the story has the remarkable power to change our whole relationship to what happens."

We have learned from Donald Davis that it's possible to take any challenging and dire situation and transform it by seeing it through all the critical players' eyes. From this point of view, everything is open to reinterpretation if seen through a different lens. To do this requires discipline, and perhaps facilitation by others. It takes perseverance to see multiple storylines in every life experience rather than settling in on one and letting that point of view stultify us. This may be the ultimate form of self-distancing. If only we all had someone in our lives with the depth of wisdom of Donald's grandmother. We could all benefit by introducing playfulness into our stories and injecting vitalizing nuance and possibility into every life scenario, no matter how tragic and painful.

This implied technology requires telling the story often. With time, its hold on our existence loosens, and its emotional valence weakens. It becomes just a story about something that occurred in the past. No longer is it a story that defines us or predicts what will happen forever in the future. We must enter into our narratives as an explorer and architect, willing to see events from alternative perspectives. Herein lies freedom. No longer can the story negatively bind us.

The Power of Story
to Heal Old Wounds

It's commonly believed in the world of psychotherapy that we become stuck because of maladaptive responses to trauma and familial behavior patterns. Therapy becomes all about changing those behaviors.

Michael White, the creator of narrative therapy,[13] suggests none of us suffers because of the psychological wounds we've endured. Instead, we suffer because of the story we continually tell about those events. That's what keeps us stuck in misery. The problem is that we carry those stories like badges of honor. Is it possible that simply changing the story, as Cripple Joe did, can change the way we feel and act?

This approach doesn't minimize the destructive nature of abuse or deny that people inflict grievous harm on children. Instead, the act of telling the story of those abuses is what harms us in the present.

Narrative therapy takes a relatively straightforward path by identifying the problem as the story, not the decades-old event. Once again, this is a self-distancing strategy. If you accept this premise, what ways can we deconstruct that story and reconstruct a new one that better serves us? The story we have been telling ourselves and others all these years is not the only possible one we could construct out of these events. It is freeing to recognize we are the ones who created that story. Therefore, we can emphasize particular features of the experience and deemphasize others, choosing to tell an alternative tale with the same facts.

The first step to transformation sees our problems in our relationships and our work as grounded simply in a limiting narrative. Now comes the challenging task of reimagining our lives rooted in a completely different narrative. The old story will have a gravitational pull, enticing us back into its fold. Once something is told, repeated frequently, believed, and hardwired into our brains, it becomes what appears to be an ironclad version of the way things truly happened. It also implies that things will continue to occur in the same manner. The story becomes our reality. These beliefs take up residence and expand their foothold in all the rooms of our psychic and spiritual house. Moreover, they inform all of our choices for decoration and landscaping. In this field of action, our beliefs become corporal manifestations, taking root and growing, with the potential to imprison us.

As with any evolving habit, we must craft the new story and commit to telling and retelling it, if not to others, at least to ourselves, over and over again for weeks and maybe months. Slowly it will take root, growing tall within our psychic landscape. Soon it will overshadow the old story as it slowly recedes into the ground to become compost. This is what self-authorship is all about.

Become a Master of Your Storylines

In every moment and every interaction, we have a choice to make. It can be in response to someone else's behavior, political events in the world, natural disasters, or a confluence of forces resulting in personal tragedies. While we can't change external circumstances or others' behavior, we can choose what storyline we'd like to inhabit about these events. Recognizing this can have long-lasting consequences for every facet of our lives and, most importantly, our sense of well-being. Here's an example.

Let's say you're in sales at a nationwide bakery. You've been working for months to get a major grocery chain to pick up your line of specialty cookies, only to discover the buyer decided to go with a competitor's products. What kind of story are you going to tell in response to this disappointing outcome? You could say, "This guy's a real jerk. The other company's rep must be bribing him. It wouldn't have mattered what I did. This sale was doomed from the beginning." You'd subsequently write him off, choose never to pay another visit, and bitterly move on to other prospects. It's a relatively limiting storyline, holding little to no potential for redemption or turnaround in the future.

Alternatively, you could say, "Can't win every sale. I wonder if there's something I could have done with my presentation to make it stronger. Let me go back to work and plan to make a more persuasive argument next quarter." Whether you succeed in the future becomes irrelevant in this scenario. This storyline is introspective, takes responsibility for what you have control over, elevates your possibilities, and leaves the door open for things to change. With this comes growth, optimism, and often a self-fulfilling prophecy of success.

What self-limiting storylines have you adopted in your life? Which ones elevate your potential? By committing to note the storylines you automatically select without giving it a second thought, you can choose more uplifting ones. This, in turn, empowers you always to elevate your possibilities in every moment of every day.

Stories Transform More Than the Inner Landscape

Focusing on the past to heal old wounds and challenges with others is just one of the many story-mastery benefits. Writing can also directly impact how we behave in the future. It all depends on the lens through which we gaze.

Adam Grant and Jane Dutton were interested in whether writing stories could improve university call-center fundraisers' performance. To test this hypothesis, they had one group of fundraisers reflect on and write about a time one of their colleagues generously did something for them. They asked a second group to write about a time they contributed to others at work. The question was whether the differences in the objectives of this simple writing task could produce more prosocial, helping behavior. Could it influence the zeal with which the fundraisers engaged donors to give?

By simply monitoring the number of calls they made, they discovered the second group, who wrote about helping others, made a whopping 30 percent more calls than the first group. The second group was also more than twice as likely to donate money to an earthquake relief fund when asked weeks later to describe three recent giving experiences. As the authors put it, "When it comes to motivating prosocial behavior, it may be true it is better to confer benefits than to receive them."[14]

Timothy Wilson, using an approach he calls "story prompting," studied first-year college students at risk of flunking out. As you might imagine, the stories they were telling themselves and ingraining in their self-concept were self-deprecating. They simply concluded they weren't college material based on their less-than-stellar performance to date.

Wilson's intervention was novel. All his team did was provide them stories normalizing their experiences. They suggested that many people struggle in their first year and then have successful academic careers once they get the hang of things. They showed them video interviews of upper-class students discussing their first-year challenges.[15] From our perspective, they nudged them toward a more positive interpretation of the meaning of their difficulties, thereby creating a self-fulfilling prophecy. Simply put, they were encouraging the students to see failure not as evidence of a fixed limitation, but rather as a step along the journey to success.

Another approach to changing one's story is story editing. Using this technique, when something painful or disappointing occurs, Wilson asked subjects to consider the situation's silver lining. In effect, he asked them to edit the story they are telling themselves. Just this tiny shift in one's narrative perspective from "the sky is falling" to considering unexpected good coming from the adverse event shifts one's sense of what's possible. Is this not what Donald Davis' grandmother did? Suddenly his dad saw having to stay home due to his injury allowed him to read, something his other siblings would never have time to do. Donald's grandmother gently invited his dad to edit the story of what happened and what it meant.

Wilson also experimented with an inverse approach that simply encouraged people to adopt a new behavior, which led to the adoption of a new story. As he puts it, "People's behavior shapes the personal narratives they develop. If they act kindly toward others, they begin to see themselves as having kind dispositions, and the more they view themselves as kind, the more likely they are to help others—thereby strengthening their new narrative."[16] With this notion of "do good to be good" as a backdrop, they addressed issues such as early teenage pregnancy by getting teens involved in volunteering in their community. Hypothesizing that their alienation contributes significantly to their unhealthy choices, they found this experience shifted their story of themselves and decreased risky sexual behavior. This technique also reduces teenage violence and lowers the use of alcohol and drugs.

By becoming the authors of our life story, the possibilities for change, healing, and transformation open up exponentially. This small shift in consciousness may be the secret to a significant difference in our life trajectory as we grapple with immense challenges like climate change. We need today to develop a new generation of actively engaged young people who are equipped with the resilience and narrative skills to transform our organizations and societies to make this a better world.

How a Simple Story Transformed the Trajectory of an Institution

When he was at the World Bank in the 1990s, our colleague Stephen Denning[17] was abruptly called back to Washington from his responsibilities overseeing the Bank's work in Africa. A new president had taken over and wanted to install his team in leadership positions. Steve had become interested in the burgeoning field of knowledge management (KM) and believed the World Bank could better serve its international clients if it shared its knowledge with them. It made perfect sense, at least to Steve. You see, they had teams of professionals with lots of credentials who would be paired up with other experts to solve significant problems in the developing world. These professionals consulted with governmental ministries on agricultural practices, road and infrastructure development, water management, health and nutrition, technology, and economic policy. When their work concluded, they'd disband and be reassigned to a new group addressing similar problems in a different region. The challenge was they carried their learning with them.

There's an old saying: knowledge is sticky. It's difficult for us to sum up what we have learned and pass it on to another person. Most of what we know is tacit. If you can ride a bicycle, it's a challenging proposition to make explicit to a young person wanting to ride for the first time all of the subtle steps and actions required to keep your balance while traveling down the road at twenty miles per hour. We learn to do something and quickly forget all of the things we had to go through to get there. The journey from tacit knowledge to making it explicit requires considerable thought and time. Just try breaking down all the steps for creating a peanut butter and jelly sandwich for an alien visiting this planet who knows next to nothing about any of the ingredients and the required utensils.

Imagine how challenging this journey is for experts in water hydrology, for example. Even if someone wanted to share their know-how at the Bank, there simply wasn't a scalable approach for making insights and breakthroughs available to colleagues, much less accessible to their clients around the globe.

Steve thought if the Bank could harness many of the new sharing technologies quickly evolving because of the explosion of the internet, the Bank and the world would be better off. The only problem was all of the new president's close advisors and handlers thought this was a bad idea. In their minds, the Bank had one primary purpose—to lend money. Period. The sharing of expertise was viewed as a secondary service at best. In their mental frames, there wasn't any room for the Bank to pivot in this manner.

Steve had one major communication challenge. He knew if a colleague had an hour or two to sit with him, he could convince him of the many benefits of pursuing a knowledge-sharing strategy. Here's the rub. There are over ten thousand people who work for the Bank, many of them in Washington, DC. Many more work all over the world. Steve simply didn't have the time to talk with enough players to build a groundswell of support.

One day a colleague who just returned from Africa joined Steve for lunch in his office. After listening to Steve's tale of woe, he offhandedly said this knowledge-management thing sounded a lot like something that happened in Kamana, Zambia, just a few months previously. There are a few things you need to know to appreciate this tale fully. Zambia is one of the poorest countries in the world. Nearly 60 percent of its population lives below the poverty line, going up to over 80 percent in rural communities where Kamana is almost four hundred kilometers from the capital Lusaka. Here's the tale:

> The World Health Organization gave a health worker in 1995 a computer. There was an outbreak of malaria in his community, and he was able to get on the Center for Disease Control's website in Atlanta, Georgia, to find a solution to the problem, thereby averting a major health disaster.

It's a short story totaling a mere fifty words. Steve's colleague asked him if this was an example of knowledge management. He was a bit circumspect but agreed the tale contained all of the fundamental elements. A person in one locale has a problem and uses technology to find a solution halfway across the world.

Steve began retelling the Zambia story and found to his surprise that people suddenly "got" the idea of sharing knowledge. He could immediately see that the story resonated. So, he kept telling it, which led to invitations to staff meetings to make presentations on knowledge sharing, and the Zambia story was always central.

This groundswell of support continued over the weeks as he made his presentations, followed by the health worker's story in Kamana. He continued to enhance his slide presentation, growing increasingly pleased with the combination of the Zambia story and his graphic expertise. Meanwhile, the senior managers were trying to find ways to close the whole thing down.

This story of knowledge management at the World Bank reached a turning point when Steve was serendipitously sitting in a VP office in charge of strategic planning. This gentleman was a convert to Steve's cause, and they were discussing the next steps when the phone rang. It was James Wolfensohn, the president of the Bank. He was sitting in a cab in New York City caught in traffic, reading a speech this VP had written for him to be delivered to the finance ministers of the world in two weeks. Wolfensohn complained there was nothing new in the speech. Didn't this VP have something exciting they could announce? The VP said he had Steve Denning sitting in the office, and he had something innovative. Handing the receiver to Steve, he recounted the health worker's tale in Kamana and asked Wolfensohn to imagine what it could mean if they organized the Bank to share its knowledge with its clients effectively. Wolfensohn immediately grasped the implications and asked the VP and Steve to rewrite the speech. To the horror of his handlers and diehard traditionalists within the Bank, Wolfensohn announced two weeks later the Bank was going to become "the knowledge bank" and share its expertise with the world. Who did they appoint to head up this initiative? Steve, of course. Three years later, leaders in the field recognized the World Bank as one of the world's leading knowledge-sharing organizations, all because of a simple story.

Steve has spent considerable time reflecting on how this small story accomplished so much. The first insight was to recognize at any one moment when we're communicating information, facts, data, or a story to others, listeners already have a story running in their heads. When information confronts us that doesn't mesh well with that story, we tend to reject it.

Moreover, information and data invite analysis. Any academically trained mind geared to question inevitably found something to object to in Steve's presentation chock-full of facts. We have all heard the saying "analysis leads to paralysis." It's no wonder very few people approached Steve.

In the World Bank leaders' case, their story was the Bank's sole focus is as a lending institution. There was no room in this story to change the Bank's mission to include knowledge sharing. Serendipitously, Steve discovered the only way to decrease their propensity to analyze an innovative idea to death was to invite them stealthily into a story containing its own logic and belief structure. In the health worker's story, the idea of using technology to find the solution to a problem made perfect sense. It was a wise tactic any highly educated person would consider in the circumstances. When listening to the story, Steve suggests the critical voice in the audience's minds, for the briefest of moments, quieted, becoming more receptive to an alternative reality, however contradictory it was to their current mindset. When Steve then invited them to imagine what their work could look like if they could organize and access their knowledge in this way, there was ample mental bandwidth to go on a mental journey where they benefitted from just such a solution. Because of this capacity, Steve dubbed this a "springboard" story because it triggered new thinking leading to innovative action.

Steve has a few additional caveats about why he thinks this story worked. First, these stories can't be foreign or extracted from worlds the listener isn't familiar with. The story of the health worker in Kamana was, in many respects, a story they were all familiar with. Everyone at the Bank had worked with nongovernmental organizations (NGOs) and staff like this person. Plus, they had all faced intractable problems in the third world, given the scarcity of resources.

Steve also thinks the story has to be based on real events. If he made up a story that hadn't yet occurred, their analytic minds would likely have reared their ugly heads and dismissed the whole idea as a piece of unrealistic science fiction. Whether this is the case is debatable, given what we have learned about how fictional stories have as much power to transport a listener as real ones.

He also suggests the story must have a degree of strangeness to work its magic. Think about it. What's odd about this story, given it occurred in 1995? We're so accustomed to the ubiquity of the world wide web today, it's hard to imagine that just a short twenty-five years ago, it was a clunky experience and robust search capabilities were several years off. Also, imagine an NGO worker in this backwater town in Zambia. How did she get a reliable online connection with a phone dial-in? Did she have dependable electricity? Just how searchable was the CDC website at the time? All of these barriers made it a minor miracle that she found a solution.

A couple of last notes. Once Steve had succeeded in creating a near revolution at the Bank, where change moves at a glacier pace, few people recognized or appreciated how he did it. He openly shared how he used a story to accomplish what no one thought possible.

Finally, once Steve awoke to the power of story, he decided to experiment with other delivery methods. Would printed springboard stories spur innovation? To his disappointment, the answer was no. While we have little data to help us understand why, one hypothesis is there is something unique occurring in the oral delivery of a story and how, in the right settings, it quiets listeners' critical functions and opens them up to consider alternative action. While written stories may transport people and even open them to changing their beliefs, they may not possess adequate power to incite significant innovation.

How Stories Can Transform Health Outcomes

Researchers from the University of Southern California are exploring how they can use story-based communication technology to improve health communication. The prevalent model is to focus on equipping patients with adequate information provided by recognized experts. The assumption has been that information leads patients to make better choices for their care. These researchers wanted to see if they could reduce cervical cancer, especially among Latinas in this country. Globally, this form of cancer is the third most common among women in general. Among Latinas, the incidence rate is remarkably higher when compared with non-Hispanic whites. Could a narrative intervention increase cervical-cancer screening via a Pap test and expand prevention via the use of the human papillomavirus vaccine?

To test this proposition, they created a short film entitled *The Tamale Lesson*. It portrays a multigenerational family of Latinas preparing food for a quinceañera, the traditional celebration of a Catholic girl's fifteenth birthday. The film opens with an older daughter in her twenties making tamales with her younger sister. She tells her sibling that she had taken a Pap test and discovered that she had contracted the human papillomavirus because of unsafe sex. While discussing this unwelcome news, she casually weaves into their conversation the facts and dangers of not getting screened. When the mother and their grandmother enter the scene and want to know what they're talking about, the conversation expands, and the older daughter encourages her skeptical grandmother to get tested. Comically the daughter demonstrates the exam procedure, using the chicken they're preparing! You can watch the video if you're up for the graphic of a chicken spreading its legs for a cervical exam. However, you may never be able to look at a chicken in the same way ever again.[18]

The researchers contrasted this entertaining story's effective-ness with a non-narrative film informing the audience about the importance of getting tested, laced with essential facts. It's the tra-ditional approach featuring a professional in a white lab coat delivering the message. As we'd expect, after watching the tamale story, a more significant percentage made an appointment to get a Pap test versus those who viewed the informational film.

Imagine if we brought this storied approach to health education to other issues that impact morbidity and mortality worldwide. Is it possible we could significantly impact the quality of life for billions of people?

Using Story to Transform Entire Societies

In the late 1960s, a weekly telenovela ran on Peruvian television entitled *Simplemente María*. It was a touching story watched by thousands of Peruvians. This made-for-TV drama forever changed what is now known as social and behavior change communication (SBCC). First, we'll briefly describe the storyline. We'll then tell you the story of what happened when a Mexican TV producer, Miguel Sabido, became curious about how this show impacted poor Peruvians' behavior. We'll conclude with an example of how one organization we're familiar with uses insights and theories developed by Sabido. They're taking them into the field to change the behavior and attitudes of entire communities and countries.

In the telenovela, Maria was an eighteen-year-old peasant working in the kitchen of a wealthy aristocratic family. The son of the family took a fancy to her. When she got pregnant, he revealed this news to his parents. Not surprisingly, they had no interest in this young woman becoming their future daughter-in-law. They drove her from the house, pregnant, penniless, and desperate.

Serendipitously, she found an old, used Singer sewing machine. To survive, she taught herself how to use it and began taking in clothing needing mending. Harboring aspirations to do something more with her life, she decided to enroll at a local school to learn to read. As the show progressed over the weeks, months, and years, she developed a knack for designing dresses and began selling them to her clients. By the end of the show's run, models displayed her haute couture on the runways of Paris. Maria had become a consummate success.

In the next-to-last episode, she accepted her literacy coach's proposal of marriage. When word got out they'd be filming the wedding at a local church, five thousand people showed up with presents. The producers weren't expecting this kind of outpouring, especially for a make-believe wedding. To appease the crowd of well-wishers, they rented a nearby soccer stadium. As their admirers filed by, the stars of the show received each gift. Interestingly, the show was re-produced throughout Central and South America and even was a hit in Russia.

As a result of this show, a more critical, less glitzy story was unfolding in Peruvian society. Singer sold over thirty thousand sewing machines to women wishing to improve their financial status. Something else even more momentous occurred. Over thirty thousand women signed up for literacy classes all over the country.[19]

Miguel Sabido became very curious about how this show impacted behavior. How could a mere story motivate women to uplift their economic fortunes? Meticulously, he deconstructed each episode, frame by frame, mapping out the storyline's ebb and flow and the characters' development. Sabido began formulating a methodology for using serial dramas on radio and TV to impart prosocial values. He combined this analysis with Carl Jung's theory of archetypes and Albert Bandura's social learning theory. He recognized the importance of what happens in communities when people listen to or watch these melodramas. As people begin to talk and reflect on culturally accepted beliefs, their attitudes and behavior can change.

He coined this form of story communication "edutainment." A key to its success is grounded in Bandura's understanding of how people change through stories by vicariously walking in the story's characters' shoes. Whether characters are rewarded for their actions or suffer adverse consequences provides the listeners powerful role models to emulate or reject. In this context, Sabido found *Simplemente María* contained three kinds of characters—a positive role model, a negative role model, and a transitional character who is attempting to decide which path to follow. The "good" characters embrace prosocial behavior or belief changes, whereas the "evil" or wicked characters resist and reject them. The transitional character is conflicted, trying to make up his or her mind.

At about the same time that Sabido was formulating his theories, a seminal book came out entitled *The Population Bomb*[20] by Paul and Anne Ehrlich. They proclaimed we were on the verge of a worldwide catastrophe and mass starvation was sure to wipe out hundreds of millions because of the lack of food. Enormous social upheaval would result, destabilizing societies across the globe. Many who read this book were alarmed. The founders of PCI Media, an organization in New York City, became proponents of the Ehrlichs' work and had, by chance, read about Sabido's scholarship. They put two and two together, seeing edutainment as the perfect antidote to people in developing countries having a dozen or more children. If they could use serial radio dramas to convince them to use effective birth control, perhaps they could prevent the end of the world as we knew it.

Adapting the methodology, PCI Media began working in developing countries around the world. The organization also expanded its portfolio to address health issues (such as the AIDS crisis), the environment, and social justice. It's a powerful model resulting in substantial results. For example, in partnership with UNICEF and local NGOs in Mozambique, PCI Media has produced over 250 radio episodes of *Ouro Negro* (*Black Gold*) addressing a whole host of health issues such as reproductive rights, gender equality, child nutrition, hygiene, and malaria prevention. It has become the most popular show in the country, playing on more than seventy radio stations, touching up to four million listeners per show.

One secret of PCI's success lies not in the actual storylines, but in what occurs when the show ends. Each radio station runs a call-in show to discuss the themes covered in the episode. The host invites listeners to tell their stories and discuss their reactions to the show's plot and characters. To enhance the messaging, local theater groups take the radio dramas' scripts and translate them into fourteen different languages. They then perform them in rural communities. These performances are, in turn, recorded and rebroadcast on local stations.

On another front, PCI Media is partnering with hair salons to bring products and information to the place many Mozambicans like to socialize and have trusted conversations. Hairdressers are trained on key messages and provide access to birth control and other resources. It's a multilayered model for engagement and change, and the monitoring of outcomes shows it works.

Can this approach be the key to transforming attitudes and behaviors essential to our planet's survival? PCI Media is currently expanding its work to address climate change issues, the global pandemic, and building a more sustainable world. As they say, the story isn't yet finished. There's still hope.

For us, it's heartening to see how story is powerfully impacting the lives of people around the globe. It's an antidote to the discouraging narratives dominating the 24-7 news cycle. Imagine if every nonprofit in the world could use lessons from *Simplemente María* to engage their constituencies to improve their lives. How could our city and state governments apply these insights to their work to enhance their citizens' quality of life? How could we better engage people to improve their health? The knowledge to change the world is available. It's now up to us to expand our SQ and deploy it responsibly and effectively.

Journey Deeper

There are several approaches and tools available to hone and transform your stories, whether told or written. To propel your transformation, give these a try.

Writing as a Path to Transformation

Over the last decades, many researchers have examined the transformative power of writing about old wounds and current difficulties. The literature suggests people continue to suffer from past wounding not because of the events that occurred, but rather because they could never make sense of these events. Hence, these past unresolved memories tend to hover in orbit, continuing to exert a gravitational pull on their daily lives. They have dubbed this the "writing cure." Writing about the events over several days gives the writer a chance to sort out what occurred and create a more cohesive story to make sense of and learn from it.

Remarkably, writing daily for just twenty minutes about a topic over four days has significant effects, psychically and physically. Immune function and sleep habits improve,[21, 22] better joint mobility lessens symptoms of rheumatoid arthritis,[23] college students' academic performance goes up, systolic and diastolic blood pressure improves, heart rate variability and skin conductance all change for the better, and physical symptoms caused by stress[24] are lessened, with the effects often lasting up to four months.[25] Writing even improves the health and well-being of cancer patients.[26]

To benefit from writing doesn't require prodigious literary skills or academic training. Nor do you have to have experienced profound trauma in your life. James Pennebaker,[27] a leader in this research, suggests you simply need to pick a topic where you have experienced conflict or stress, then write about it. Nothing is off limits. It only must matter to you, and you must have a personal investment in resolving or improving it.

The key to this method's effectiveness is to write continuously for the allotted time. Whatever comes to mind, write it down. Don't be concerned with style, grammar, correct spelling—you won't be turning this in for critique. It's for your eyes only.

Pennebaker provides one caveat. If there is an issue so charged you fear you can't handle writing about it, then don't. It's that simple. He calls this the "Flip-Out Rule." He also forewarns people that powerful feelings may arise for a short while after the writing, including sadness. It's perfectly natural. Just observe it, and it should quickly evaporate within an hour or two.[28]

If you follow the regime for twenty minutes on four successive days, you can explore the same topic over those days. Or, if you wrote everything you can about a particular problem on the first day, devote your time to other issues on successive days. In each case, explore not only what you feel or think about this issue, but consider how it connects to those who are close to you. What do you think they think or feel about what occurred? As in the case of Donald Davis's dad, Pennebaker and his colleagues found it helpful to see a situation from different perspectives. Have you been able to discern what caused people to act as they did? What insights are you gleaning? What do you understand better now having written about it? In subsequent days, explore how this trauma impacted all facets of your life and what you think or feel about that. Write about what you have been learning as you delve deeper and deeper into your experiences.

Upon completing this exercise, participants experience more positive emotions, feel more lighthearted, fall asleep more quickly, and think a lot less about the trauma. Their loved ones also find them more agreeable. As a result, you'll discover more meaning in your life. Most importantly, you'll develop greater self-understanding and feel more compassion toward yourself and the struggles you have gone through. Perhaps of utmost importance, people writing about past traumas can see positive sides of the negative experience and find it much easier to cope with whatever life serves up.

A Host of Other Writing and Story Activities to Transform Your Life

Adopt the Third-Person Perspective When Writing about Emotionally Charged Experiences. What gets in our way of moving through painful, emotionally charged experiences is overidentifying with the feelings. When writing in the first person about "my feelings" or saying, "I feel," we reinforce the identification with the feelings, keeping us stuck even more. Try switching to the third person and see how this distancing technique provides you a degree of perspective that will loosen the hold the emotions have on you.

Write from the Perspective of Your Ideal, Future Self. Imagine it's five years from today and you are your ideal self. Write a letter from the future to yourself in the present filled with encouragement and affirmation about how you achieved your goals, enriched your life, and deepened your friendships and significant relationships.

See Your Story from a New Vantage Point. First, write a brief description of a problematic situation or troubling relationship. Second, rewrite the story from a different character's viewpoint who's involved in the story. Now, take the story and retell it from other characters' points of view. This can give you empathy for the other's perspective and insight into how we can be a catalyst for possibility rather than a proponent of limitations. Reflect on what you learned from this process.

See Challenges through the Storyline Lens

- Describe a significant, specific challenge or stressful event that evoked a strong emotional reaction within you.
- How does the story you are currently telling yourself and perhaps others about this situation open possibilities or dampen the potential for you and all concerned?

- What would be an alternative, more positive, possibility-creating story you could tell about these same circumstances? How does this story feel in comparison to the previous account?
- What internal or external obstacles stand in the way of your adopting the more possibility-creating storyline?
- What can you learn from this experience when it comes to facing challenges?

How to Develop a Springboard Story

Have you ever had the experience where you share a story about an idea you'd like to pursue in the organization, and a few weeks later, your colleague or boss tells the same story in a meeting as though it was his or her original idea? In many respects, this is what the springboard story does. Here are some straightforward tips for constructing and delivering a springboard story and using it to "infect" the minds of others and get them moving on innovative new approaches to solving problems.[29]

1 What is the specific change in the organization or community or group you hope to spark with the story? What actions would you want people to take?

2 Think of an incident either inside or outside your organization, community, or group where the change was in whole or in part successfully implemented. Describe it briefly.

3 Who is the single protagonist of the story?

4 Is the single protagonist prototypical for your particular audience? If not, can the story be told from the point of view of such a protagonist?

5 When did the incident happen? Give the date.

6 Where did the story happen? State the place.

7 How fully does the story embody the change idea? Are there hidden aspects of the story?

8 Can the story be extrapolated to embody more fully the change idea?

9   Does the story make clear what would have happened without the change idea?

10 Has the story been stripped of any unnecessary detail? Are there any scenes with more than two characters?

11 Does the story have an authentically happy ending? Can it be told so it has such a conclusion?

12 Does the story link to the purpose to be achieved in telling it?

13 What is the incisive question you can link with the story to spark action? It would usually be formulated like this: "If we could [refer to the protagonist and the change idea], imagine with me what it could mean . . ."

Other Resources

- Edutainment and Social Behavior Change Communication: www.pcimedia.org
- Using Story to Change the World: www.thegoodmancenter.com and www.frameworksinstitute.org
- Transforming Your Corporate Story: Microsoft has been actively studying how to deploy storytelling in their corporate setting and have now shared their insights in a handbook available for free online at news.microsoft.com/handbook.

Books We Recommend

As we have detailed, writing about illnesses and injuries or troubling emotions can have profound therapeutic effects. *Writing Out the Storm: Reading and Writing Your Way through Serious Illness or Injury* by **Barbara Abercrombie** may be one of the best guides for this personal journey. You'll also find *Writing as a Way of Healing: How Telling Our Stories Transforms Our Lives* by **Louise Desalvo** and *Expressive Writing: Words That Heal* by James W. Pennebaker and John F. Evans terrific resources as well.

If there was ever a master of the spoken tale, it's Donald Davis. His insights, wisdom, and delightful tales will be not only instructive, but also healing. Here are some of our favorite books and online resources that Donald has created:

Telling Your Own Stories: For Family and Classroom Storytelling, Public Speaking, and Personal Journaling **by Donald Davis**

Cripple Joe: Stories from My Daddy **by Donald Davis**

Writing as a Second Language **by Donald Davis**

Story of Cripple Joe **by Donald Davis** (on YouTube: www.youtube.com/watch?v=wgeh4xhSA2Q)

One of the great insights of narrative therapy is that our suffering is not the result of some hidden mental disease, but rather that it's our stories that we keep telling ourselves that inflict so much of the pain we feel. *Story Re-Visions: Narrative Therapy in the Postmodern World* **by Alan Parry and Robert E. Doan** will be a great introduction to this invaluable approach to healing. *Retelling the Stories of Our Lives: Everyday Narrative Therapy to Draw Inspiration and Transform Experience* **by David Denborough** will provide you some of the nuts and bolts tools to use these valuable insights in your own transformation and healing.

The Springboard: How Storytelling Ignites Action in Knowledge-Era Organizations **by Steve Denning** details his journey into using storytelling to transform an organization. The fact that he was able to use this approach with an organization like the World Bank, where change has historically moved at a glacial pace, is testament to the power of his approach.

6

The Power of Story to Unite

The ability to listen to and tell compelling narratives that help people transcend divisive or misinformed beliefs.

Social engagement begins when we share our stories . . .
Social change happens when we agree together to change the ending.

—The Needmore Fund

We're engulfed today in a crisis of disconnection and conflict. Heightened levels of political polarization are threatening the very bedrock of our notion of civil society. Racial divides still plague us. The wounds of slavery and social inequality are still years, if not generations, away from being healed. Millions of desperate people are looking for a haven free of war, persecution, and climate change.

Moreover, many people continue to play out centuries-old dramas of hate and recrimination. Israelis and Palestinians still consider the other mortal enemies. Sectarian violence among Sunni and Shiite Muslims in the Middle East looks more and more like a powder keg ready to ignite. Is this inevitable?

Pat Speight once said, "A story is the shortest distance between people."[1] While developing Story Intelligence is not the panacea for all of the challenges mentioned, we believe story has an influential role in mitigating them to bring people together. In this chapter, we'll explore the many ways our conscious efforts to increase our SQ enables us to be catalysts for meaningful change. If practiced robustly, we envision a different story emerging. Humans can learn to accommodate differences and develop their consciousness to a level where they replace the automaticity of hate and prejudice with kindness and understanding in our communities and on the world stage.

Conflict and Hatred Start at Home

We don't have to look far to appreciate how we humans have such a difficult time getting along. All we need to do is look at ourselves in the mirror. In our own lives, we have seen what would appear to be a silly dispute in our communities blossom into bitter recriminations bringing out the worst in our neighbors and us. If you have ever been a member of a homeowner's association, you no doubt can anticipate where this tale is leading. Several years ago, we agreed to be on the board. There was a vigorous debate about assessing each household a few hundred dollars to add extra lighting along the sidewalks. It seemed like the commonsense thing to do. But a few people saw additional light as a scourge on the night's beauty. We suspect their real objections were grounded in the idea of the added expense. The eighteen-month conflict led to one family selling their home in protest. We had to endure numerous board meetings filled with shouting and expletives. When our local power company finally installed the lighting, they shouldered the lion's share of the cost. Folks could only scratch their heads, wondering what the brouhahas were all about.

In reflecting on this curious incident, is there some latent human impulse inclining us to be oppositional for opposition's sake? These kinds of conflicts also seem to incite a level of self-righteousness rarely evident in our day-to-day interactions with our neighbors. Perhaps there's a lot more than we realize to the saying that "a man's home is his castle." Regardless of the fallout, any perceived threat catalyzes our desire to mount our horses with spears and swords and ride into battle.

This kind of warfare can become even more brutal and painful in the context of familial disputes. Any violation of family norms can come with recriminations and even expulsion from the family system. In the early 1970s, during the OPEC oil embargo, a friend's father, Charles, turned to his two brothers to keep a hotel he had built afloat and out of the hands of his creditors. Luckily, he turned the situation around and eventually sold the property and paid them back.

After the sale, Charles fancied himself to be a wheeler-dealer and found a piece of property on the outskirts of town that looked like a steal. Lacking the resources to buy it, he turned to his brother James. With a handshake, James put up the money and gave Charles a third of the deal.

Many years passed with no buyers. Finally, an offer came in, and James was happy to unload what had turned out to be a dud of an investment. That's when the trouble began. James thought they should split the proceeds to compensate him for what would have been a reasonable rate of return if he had just stuck his money in a conservative investment. Moreover, Charles had mismanaged the taxes, and there was additional money due. Charles balked. A deal, after all, was a deal in his mind. The dispute escalated. Attorneys were engaged. During discovery, Charles learned James had used the property as collateral for a business loan. He then found case law suggesting James should compensate him a third of all the money James made in his business during the loan period. So began the longest-running lawsuit in their town's history, consuming millions of dollars in legal fees, which, ironically, far exceeded the property's worth.

Both men, tragically, died having exhausted all of their wealth attempting to destroy the other. Ironically, when James died first, Charles wept when he called his son with the news. His son was surprised at this reaction. He commented that he thought Charles hated his brother. Why else would he have doggedly pursued such a case? Charles' response was surprising and tragic. "He's my little brother. I never meant for this thing to become personal. It was just business." Maybe James had stolen Charles' baseball mitt when they were kids, which in turn festered into this tragic affair. That explanation was as good as any for what was irrationality verging on insanity.

Throughout this ordeal, all of their family made attempts to mediate the dispute, but to no avail. The repercussions rippled like a tidal wave throughout the family constellation. If two brothers can fight in this manner over something as inconsequential as a few dollars left on the table, what does this mean for peoples who have even more at stake and have been at it for centuries?

The Origins of Hatred, Mistrust, and Persistent Bias

Perhaps better than any other polemic on the topic, the biblical treatment of the problem of the stranger sets the stage for understanding just how difficult it is for us to transcend differences with others. Undoubtedly, distrust of the stranger is hardwired into our biology and has roots in our tribal beginnings. People from afar could be hostile, rapacious, murderous, and wanting our lands. Differences in dress, skin color, or cultural mores were enough to set off our fight-or-flight mechanism. This little spark would quickly cascade into a massive bonfire of hate-filled action.

It's easy to see this as an adaptive survival mechanism and why peoples have always found their most insulting language to describe outsiders. The Greeks referred to strangers as barbarians because they likened the sound of their spoken word to grunting farm animals. It also provided them a self-deceiving rationale for murder. While there were prohibitions in their culture against killing humans, slaughtering a farm animal, well, that was another kettle of fish. Distrusting strangers' intentions and presence in our midst became a biological survival imperative reinforced by compelling narratives reducing others to animal status. This, in turn, gave dominant cultures collective moral cover for genocide. If strangers are just vermin or roaches, why should we feel any remorse in exterminating them?

Recent history is littered with examples of this kind of hatred. In the late 1700s, at the height of the French Revolution, which extolled human beings' innate rights, riots broke out in Alsace targeting the Jewish community. In 1881 crowds went on a killing spree against Italian immigrants living in Marseilles. A mere half-century later, virulent antisemitism reemerged in neighboring Germany, resulting in the slaughter of six million Jews. Today, antisemitism and anti-Muslim sentiments are on the rise again throughout the world.

Often these heinous acts are reinforced, if not encouraged, by institutional authority. For example, it's no secret that both the Catholic and Protestant churches actively promoted the narrative that Jews were less than human and deserving of punishment because they supposedly were responsible for the crucifixion of Jesus. Other times they simply turned a blind eye as the slaughter of innocents was carried out right under their noses.

Proponents of these practices often cloak them in the pseudorationality of science. Twisted interpretations of Darwin's famous theory regarding "the survival of the fittest" have, at times, become a justification for exterminating minorities. While most of the scientific community has thoroughly debunked the many threads of scientific racism, there are still vestiges of "scientific" work being pushed out by hate groups under the guise of "legitimate" academic journals. Going strong today is the *Mankind Quarterly*, touting itself as "a peer-reviewed academic journal" covering physical and cultural anthropology, human evolution, intelligence, ethnography, linguistics, mythology, and archaeology with the "aim of unifying anthropology with biology."[2] This journal presents all the trappings of an authentic scientific endeavor and even has individuals on its editorial board with advanced degrees from prestigious universities. In reality, though, it is presided over by the psychologist Richard Lynn, a known racist. While experts have widely panned his research methodologies, pseudoscience like this readily reinforces narratives of hate groups in this country and Europe.

Jews aren't the only targets of hate-filled narratives. To this day, natives from Central America are characterized as murderers and rapists by the president. But Donald Trump didn't invent belittling language to demean others. Peoples from around the world disparage strangers with all kinds of colorful, emotionally charged language. Many Europeans vilify Muslims fleeing the civil war in Syria. Some whites, especially in Florida, still refer to black children as "alligator bait." But people of color are not exclusively derided. The terms "cracker" and "white trash" denoting poor white Southerners are still part of the everyday American lexicon.

Other countries have liberally partaken in demonizing others who aren't part of the mainstream. Australians refer to Aborigines as "boongs," meaning dead, infected, or dysfunctional. At the time of the Rwandan genocide, Hutus went on a rampage, slaughtering over a million Tutsis. They characterized the Tutsis as "inyenzi," meaning cockroaches.

Given the ways we're wired, it's incredibly difficult to change mental paradigms on any subject, much less one so emotionally charged. People who hold racially or ethnically biased perspectives don't even recognize they're living in an inherited paradigm. For them, it's a concrete reality. In rural America, where people rarely have a chance to interact with people different from themselves, when confronted with strangers who don't look and behave like them, it's understandable they react by seeing these outsiders as a threat. When our world becomes increasingly uncertain, and we perceive our autonomy and way of life disappearing, we're likely to feel this more acutely. A case in point is the mistaken belief Muslims are forcing Shariah law on American communities, a myth relentlessly sold as gospel truth by alt-right hate groups. The fact that our economic system is rapidly changing around us due to globalization and robotization is conveniently shuttled aside by politicians. In its place, they stress a story that immigrants are here to take your jobs. It's no surprise they want to shut the door to strangers.

In his seminal book *Don't Think of an Elephant!*,[3] George Lakoff demonstrates why it's hard to move people toward a more tolerant position. He suggests our mental structures are frames tied up with a lot more than just our views of immigrants. They condition the way we see ourselves and our place in society. Challenging a person's frame threatens their reason for being. The more those frames are questioned, the more people dig in their heels and double down on what they believe.

According to Lakoff, if we want to encourage people who are afraid of immigrants and people of color to become more tolerant, we must learn to speak differently. Instead of directly confronting their views, we must craft an alternative language built on other things they believe. In these circumstances, it's futile to provide facts and information to people holding flawed and uninformed perspectives. To make sense of alternative facts contradicting what we believe, they "have to fit what is already in the synapses of the brain. You can only understand what the frames in your brain allow you to understand. If the facts don't fit the frames in your brain, the frames in your brain stay, and the facts are ignored or challenged or belittled."[4] When confronted with the idea that immigrants are responsible for less crime than white Americans, that they are generous contributors to the life of a community, racists are not going to hear or believe this information. It's more likely they'll write it off as progressive propaganda or fake news.

Psychologists refer to this as confirmation bias. We are predisposed to naturally find information, evidence, and facts confirming what we already believe. Then we discount anything contradictory. We'll always give evidence conforming with our world view extra weight, regardless of where we stand on the political spectrum. The left is as guilty as the right when it comes to this. And the political abyss between different political ideologies appears to be growing wider.

Whether it's due to inflexible mental frames, confirmation bias, neurobiology, or just thousands of years of socialization, the problem of the stranger, as in days of old, continues to challenge us to find an alternative approach to being with our neighbors who are distinctly different. While we can't change millennia of social conditioning to distrust strangers, we must find a better way to come together as a world population to address the grave trials confronting us collectively. We have to become smarter, more aware, and more adept at using our SQ to override the automaticity of distrust and herd behavior. What's needed is a new story allowing us to feel a modicum of safety and security while also accommodating others whose cultural mores, values, and appearance are distinct. At the very least, we must find a way to respect the stranger. At best, we need to learn to love them.

Alternative Approaches to the Creation of a New Story

Religious traditions have addressed the issue of the stranger by taking a moral stand. The Abrahamic faiths (Judaism, Christianity, and Islam) have tackled this problem head on through the exhortation to "love the stranger." Building off a vital tenet of these faiths to "love your neighbor as yourself," the commandment to love the stranger appears no fewer than thirty-six times in Hebrew biblical texts. The sages responsible for writing these texts understood the challenge quite clearly. Accepting strangers into our midst needed buttressing from a Higher Authority to overcome our natural predilections to distrust the other. It wasn't enough to simply adopt an enlightened philosophy about the dignity of every human life. Failing to follow the commandment to love the stranger needed a big stick endorsed by God.

Perhaps empathy for the "other" was borne out of the Jewish experience of enslavement. In the eighth century BC, the Assyrians subjugated the Israelites. Two centuries later, the Babylonians conquered and exiled them again. The antecedent of all these exiles was the Jews' experience of forced labor to build the Egyptian pyramids. The annual Passover ritual of retelling the story of Moses memorializes this event. The story has many layers. First, Pharaoh ordered the killing of all the Hebrews' male children. The Jews were becoming too populous, and he feared their numbers, especially if an enemy were to invade. Where would their loyalties lie? Then Moses fled Egypt after he killed a taskmaster who was beating a defenseless Jew. In Midian, he was a stranger, yet welcomed with open arms. His wife was also Midian. Perhaps this lesson in acceptance made a more significant impact on him than biblical scholars tend to recognize, and he built into the Torah these lessons he "received" years later on Mt. Sinai.

In the retelling of the story during the Passover meal, foods on a specially prepared plate are arrayed to symbolize different facets of the experience of slavery and oppression. Jewish children from an early age partake in this perennial reenactment. No doubt, the story becomes firmly wired into their consciousness. The Passover tale asks us to stand in the shoes of the stranger. In the telling, we reexperience what it must have been like to be an oppressed minority, an outcast treated by the dominant culture as less than human. Jews' cultural character was forged in identifying with the oppressed stranger, leading them to have the empathic capacity to step out of their everyday comfort to see the world through others' eyes. It makes sense why so many Jews readily embraced the struggles of Black Americans during the fight for civil rights in the 1950s and 1960s. They put their lives on the line at a time when the dominant national narrative saw Black Americans as second-class, inferior citizens.

Another source for this empathic capacity comes from the Holocaust, when for no other reason than being Jewish, the Nazis marched six million to their deaths. There had never been a xeno-phobic event carried out so mechanically and with so much mal-ice until this time. Indeed, Jews had experienced tremendous oppression and injustice over the centuries. It started with the Crusaders as they marched across Europe to liberate Israel's land from "infidels," slaughtering Jews all along their route. Then came the Spanish Inquisition and Church-sanctioned genocide. In the centuries that followed, pogroms were a regular occurrence leading up to the Holocaust. But in Germany, Jews had labored to assimilate into society. Who could have predicted they would become the scapegoat for all the misery of the German people fol-lowing World War I? Collectively, these experiences of being a minority and a stranger in a strange land sensitized the Jews to this issue in a way no other group can fully comprehend. It pre-pared them to stand up to a dominant narrative robbing the humanity of a group that had been unjustly exiled and enslaved in the Americas. As Rabbi Jonathan Sacks so eloquently states, "There is only one reply strong enough to answer the question: Why should I not hate the stranger? Because the stranger is me."[5]

In *Civility*,[6] Stephen Carter tells a story supporting this thesis. It was 1966. Carter's parents, both highly educated Black American professionals, decided to move into an all-white neigh-borhood in Washington, DC. As Carter and his siblings sat on the front porch that first day, they felt as though white passersby were watching them in a fishbowl. Nothing was welcoming in their gazes. Carter's trepidation was there would be no friends, no allies, no safety here. Then something unexpected occurred. A white woman who lived across the street was returning from work and saw them sitting there. She smiled and shouted, "Welcome!" A few minutes later, she emerged from her house with a platter of cream cheese and jelly sandwiches and introduced herself. For Carter, this one moment changed everything. He went from being a stranger to becoming a cherished friend. For years to come, Sara Kestenbaum would warmly welcome him and his siblings into her home. Yes, she was Jewish, and most probably grew up immersed in the moral imperative to welcome the stranger. As Carter frames it, her Jewish tradition, steeped in the idea of *chesed*, Hebrew for performing acts of kindness, is "derived from the understanding that human beings are made in the image of God." *Chesed* informed Sara Kestenbaum's life down to the core of her being. For her, welcoming them was a fulsome expression of her faith and convictions. For Carter, "Civility itself may be seen as part of *chesed*: it does indeed require kindnesses toward our fellow citizens, including the ones who are strangers, and even when it is hard."[7]

Does this mean that all Jews act with the utmost integrity when it comes to welcoming the stranger? Obviously, no. Given the complex history of Jews and blacks since the civil rights movement of the '50s and '60s, it's clear even the weight of a commandment from on high is insufficient. Even a mutual history of oppression has been inadequate to forge a lasting partnership. We must all recognize that maintaining tolerant and accepting attitudes and behavior can never be taken for granted. Today, most Jews are not particularly religious and have become more like their secular brothers and sisters in the Christian faiths. If they know the stories and the commandment to love the stranger, they have chosen to ignore this cultural heritage, embracing a kind of mutual isolation instead. Conveniently out of sight and out of mind are the plights of the poor and oppressed. Refugees who arrive on our shores with nothing are invisible as well. Sans moral imperative or a compelling narrative to reinforce it, what is left?

What Science Can Teach Us about Changing Minds and Hearts

As we have seen, holding a strong belief about ethnic groups' unworthiness to receive fair and equal treatment makes you more likely to accept evidence confirming your biases. Within this mindset, you would rarely be highly critical of any information disconfirming your beliefs. If the evidence is mixed, you'll likely become more ensconced in the way you see things. Unfortunately, most of us are oblivious to how we process information and how it profoundly influences our judgment. Our point of view invariably becomes intertwined with our identity.

The recent upheaval in Great Britain around the question of Brexit is powerfully illustrative of this issue. In the run-up to the decisive vote on whether to remain in or leave the European Union, stories were spun on each side of the debate painting a gloomy picture for the British people if they chose the alternative option. While each side undoubtedly propagated a host of persuasive arguments, the "Leave" group laced their statements with subtle emotional appeals to nativist nationalism. They advocated a return to being able to make decisions best for Britain without the meddling of foreigners. Laced within these arguments were subtle racial undertones, referring no doubt to the open borders EU membership allowed. They suggested Britain's very character may be permanently changed in the years to come if they continued to admit without restrictions people with different religious and cultural heritages. It didn't hurt their cause by embedding in their communication a load of misinformation about the actual cost of the move to the British people.

Is it any surprise the Leavers garnered more of their support from conservative regions of the country where fewer foreigners lived? The "Remain" group had on their side a lot of reasons for staying, mostly economic. But they did an anemic job of creating a story to motivate and engage the general public's hearts and minds, especially those who leaned toward leaving. Nor did their statements do anything to assuage conservatives' fears about the perceived scourge of foreign influence. To complicate matters, large swaths of the younger electorate who preferred to stay and appreciated the flexibility of open travel simply didn't participate in the election. When it came down to the final vote, they naïvely believed it was going to be defeated.

While negative economic consequences for leaving are now fairly apparent, why do so many people still fervently adhere to the Leaver position? The best explanation is it's about identity. Once you have identified with the Leaver camp, you will forever be a Leaver come hell, high water, or unbearable duties on imported goods. To abandon the Leavers and become a Remainer would require an act of courage, humility, self-effacement, and a clearheadedness about what is best and right. Yet, as we have seen through the research on confirmation bias, jumping ship to attach your identity to a different story is challenging to do.

Is there a way, though, to break through this cycle? Can we get people to open up to another perspective that diametrically opposes their deep-seated assumptions? Charles Lord[8] set out to test this by asking subjects who were either supportive or opposed to the death penalty to examine the evidence about this form of extreme punishment's deterrent effect. One experimental group was encouraged simply to be as objective and unbiased as possible when evaluating the evidence by assuming the role of an impartial judge who evenhandedly weighs all the evidence. They directed the second group to look at the evidence through an entirely different lens, calling this the "consider-the-opposite" condition. This group's directions were, "Ask yourself at each step whether you would have made the same high or low evaluations had exactly the same study produced results on the other side of the issue."

In his broader discussion, Lord points to the concept of psychological "anchoring," which leads us to make faulty conclusions about people's behavior. If we see someone behave in a particular manner, that action becomes the basis for a host of generalizations about their character and intentions. We then ignore all of the situational reasons a person behaved as they did. Could the act of imagining the same individual acting quite differently under different circumstances loosen the hold of the original assumptions anchored in our thinking? Would it act as a filter for all future assessments?

He found it did indeed accomplish this feat. The strategy exhorting subjects to be unbiased did little to change their perspective regardless of the actual weight of the evidence disproving their stance on the death penalty. In fact, in some instances, the contrary evidence hardened their attitude, making them even more resistant to considering evidence disconfirming their fundamental beliefs. This occurred regardless of whether they were for or against the death penalty as a crime deterrent.

The "consider-the-opposite" strategy, on the other hand, actually helped to overcome their biases. This thinking strategy allowed them to see things they were utterly incapable of comprehending any other way.

The implications are enormous. We must abandon attempts to bombard groups who have hardened and perhaps misguided perspectives with more and more information contradicting their way of seeing things. Instead, we must first enter into a dialog, building trust. Secondly, we must invite them to consider the opposite as an exercise in looking at the "facts." Using the "consider-the-opposite" strategy, ask people to look at an issue not from where they are standing, but from where the other is standing. If only for a few brief moments, it's akin to asking them to be willing to walk in another's shoes. This shift requires an act of imagination, not intellect.

Molly Andrews, the co-director of the Centre for Narrative Research at the University of East London, calls it "compassionate citizenship," building on philosopher Martha Nussbaum's belief that we must become "intelligent readers of [a] person's story and understand [their] emotions and wishes and desires."[9] But it's not only an alternative strategy for looking at the "facts" and reconsidering their veracity and relevance. It's a shift in many dimensions of identity. If you move from distrusting strangers with darker skin than yours to abruptly seeing them as humans like you, you will find yourself in a new camp. Most probably, you'll have to jettison relationships with people who shared your previous prejudices either implicitly or explicitly. You may even become a traitor to a cause if you leave your affiliation with a group like the KKK or the John Birch Society. You will have a changed heart. In some fundamental ways, you'll never be the same person again. Windows and doors will suddenly open, letting in a life-changing, fresh light.

How Story Can Change Prejudice and Hate

How can the power of story bring people together? Let's begin by examining what enables a diverse group to act with some level of cohesion amidst a level of disagreement.

When people organize themselves for a shared purpose, whether it's a family, a neighborhood, a city, or even a nation, what binds them together to a large extent is a familiar story. Such a narrative is the basis for a collective identity and action for the common good. Sometimes it's a story about a sinister outside force, as was the case in World War II, where everyone came together, despite their differences, to make sacrifices to defeat Hitler's Germany. Other times it's a story about what it means to be neighborly, as in the case of barn raisings when everyone puts their needs aside for a day to help a fellow farmer. For some groups, it's a story built on a religious heritage, like when all Jews came together to contribute to Israel's survival in the early years following its founding, even if they disagreed substantively with internal Israeli politics. For other groups like the Army, stories become the backbone for unity and communal purpose in combat times. Storytelling thus becomes central to recruit indoctrination. It revolves around stories of how individuals performed heroic deeds in the face of impossible odds, often sacrificing their lives for their fellow soldiers and our country's ideals. When the fighting starts, this makes it more likely platoons will persevere and cohere even in the most stressful conditions. Through the fires of boot camp, the Army takes ordinary people and transforms them into heroic actors in a story bigger than themselves. Is this not the stuff of the hero's journey that Joseph Campbell eloquently wrote about some fifty years ago?

These stories provide groups a common reference point and the ability to understand each other's intentions and actions. They also offer a level of structure and predictability about the future. Without a story, a common purpose would be inconceivable. Army units would turn and run when they confronted the first enemy fire. Communities would become fractured and divisive, incapable of mobilizing to help those in need, a phenomenon we're witnessing today. And nations would splinter and polarize, a spectacle currently playing out worldwide. If storytelling is the thread binding groups together, finding ways to use this "technology" effectively must be the first step toward unifying those at odds and disconnected.

Counterintuitively, to build a compelling story "technology," the opening step is not storytelling. Instead, it's story-listening. In earlier chapters, we discussed a variety of Native American story traditions. One of those is the Tulalip from the American Northwest. A storyteller I know from this tradition is Johnny Moses. Johnny's traditional name is *Whis.stem.men.knee*, or Walking Medicine Robe. As a carrier of the *Si.Si.Wiss* (sacred breath, sacred life) medicine teachings and healing ceremonies of his Northwest Coast Tulalip people, he understands that there can be no community without listening. Johnny introduces audiences to the importance of listening by alerting them that he will pause from time to time. Not until the audience shouts out "hamikawich," which means "we are listening," will he resume the telling of his story. After commencing the tale, in midsentence, Johnny occasionally looks to the ground and falls silent. When the audience responds "hamikawich," he resumes the story. He does this periodically throughout the telling, thereby weaving together telling and the audience's affirmation "we are listening" with a response like a chorus in a Greek tragedy.

In a world where there is a shortage of listening, we believe this is the place to begin. Nowhere does this show up better than in the debates about climate change. A recent op-ed in the *New York Times* by Katherine Hayhow[10] takes on climate change deniers. She's a professor at the Climate Center at Texas Tech University. It's important to note that she's also a self-identified theological evangelical "who takes the Bible seriously." Hayhow contrasts her scientific position with "today's political evangelicals. Their statement of faith is written first by their politics and only a distant second by the Bible. If the two conflict, they will prioritize their political ideology over theology." What surprises her are the attacks from people who identify themselves as conservative Christians, accusing her of spreading satanic lies and consorting with "those people." As a Christian herself, this was at first baffling given the first victims of climate change are the poor and dispossessed, seemingly a strong priority for those who believe in the Gospel of Jesus. She also found this to be perplexing because God gives us responsibility for every living thing in Genesis. It would seem if we're harming God's Kingdom in irreversible ways, we should pause, reconsider, and chart a new course.

From her perspective, the disconnect between some Christians and the environment results from a marriage of conservative politics with conservative theology. There is also an interesting phenomenon emerging from this strange union in which prominent politicians like Ted Cruz and Lindsey Graham have deemed climate science a religion that's attempting to upstage its Christian rival. As you can imagine, to some, this would put the climate and its spokespeople, the scientists, in direct opposition to the Gospel. If you're a true believer, there's nothing worse than a false prophet.

Where is the potential for building bridges with this as a backdrop? It would seem these positions and beliefs are irreconcilable at first blush. So how does Hayhow manage conversations with people on the other side of this divide when they approach her at church with this opening salvo: "Do you believe in climate change?" Her first response is often disarming—"No, I don't," befuddling her accusers. This opens the door to a more thoughtful conversation where they can stand on common ground. She begins by explaining, "Climate change is not a belief system. 'We know the earth's climate is changing thanks to observations, facts, and data about God's creation we can see with our eyes and test with the sound minds God has given us.' And still more fundamentally, I [go] on to explain why it matters: because real people are being affected today, and we believe God's love has been poured in our hearts to share with our brothers and sisters here and around the world who are suffering."

In a subtle yet powerful way, she reframes the conversation in terms that makes sense to her accusers, undercutting the mounds of misinformation and false claims they conflate with science and caring for the environment. She doesn't begin the discussion with all of the evidence for how we're harming our world. Instead, she begins by identifying things she shares in common with the person standing in front of her:

For some, this could be the well-being of our community; for others, our children; and for fellow Christians, it's often our faith. By beginning with what we share and then connecting the dots between this value and a changing climate, it becomes clear how caring about this planet, and every living thing on it is not somehow antithetical to who we are as Christians, but rather central to it. Being concerned about climate change is a genuine expression of our faith, bringing our attitudes and actions more closely into line with who we already are and what we most want to be.

What undergirds the dominant narrative among conservatives that denies the human impact on the environment? Hayhow suggests it's our fear of needing to change our way of life. People dread that addressing climate change will somehow diminish them. It's unsettling to come to grips with the idea that the things we have grown accustomed to might be the root cause of our future extinction. Perhaps most troubling to Christians and conservatives is their anxiety that their articles of faith will be extinguished if they side with science. Hayhow has been willing to listen and identify with their concerns while at the same time reminding them of their deepest beliefs. In this way, she helps them shift from polarization and conflict to reconciliation.

Arriving at this understanding might not change a climate denier into someone who embraces science and becomes an activist for the environment, but it does build a bridge. Most importantly, it opens communication lines and thinking between people who are seemingly on two sides of a vast divide reinforced by conflicting narratives. Sharing stories, empathizing, and listening seem to be the key to finding common ground between these narratives.

Knowing the Other's Story Creates Empathy and Tolerance

The isolation of modern living not only cuts us off from others, fundamentally it cuts us off from the chance to hear and know their stories. Where everyone knows everyone in smaller communities, egregious, and perhaps even asocial, behavior is more easily tolerated at times. By understanding the person's backstory, we're less likely to draw incorrect generalizations from one action to condemn their character. Perhaps we know the person just lost two siblings to cancer in the past month. She's got good reason to be cranky. Or, she has had a lifetime filled with disappointments and setbacks, giving the recipient of their wrath enough pause to consider, *I, too, might be cantankerous if I had gone through everything she has.*

But in larger cities, we interact daily with strangers we most likely will never see again. When they misbehave, it becomes much easier to write them off as a jerk or cretin or attribute some racial stereotype to them to explain why they behave the way they do.

Stephen Carter, whose story we shared earlier, traced the roots of incivility to the atomization of our lives. We leave our single-family households and get into our car alone for a lengthy commute to work. Given the many ways work has evolved over the last years, we may spend hours alone staring at a computer screen. At 5:00 p.m., we get back in our cars to return to our family for a night, not of sharing, but isolation as each person retreats to their private space to peer at a bright screen for entertainment. The COVID-19 pandemic has put a strange twist on this story. Now, loneliness has become practically institutionalized.

Contrast this with our earlier history when we lived in close quarters with people different from ourselves as we traveled great distances on trains. Being in such proximity for such a long time forced people from different social and ethnic backgrounds to get to know strangers unlike themselves and discover their stories. Those stories revealed their mutual humanity. Listening in this way made it possible for them to recognize they were no different than the stranger sitting across from them, even if he or she had a different dialect, a darker skin, or a foreign religion.

Today, it's much easier not to know the stranger's story and settle into prepackaged stories diminishing their humanity. We don't know their story, nor are we predisposed to try. It's much easier to fall back on family relationships or connections with our identified clan. By doing so, we block out any inkling of awareness of others' tales of suffering or difficulties.

Yet knowing another's story elicits in us an empathic response. Earlier, we saw how our brain patterns mirror each other when listening to a story. This emotional and physiological response connects us and is the bodily counterpart to what it means to walk in another's shoes. That's why first-person narratives can be so compelling in changing the way we see others. There is a growing body of evidence demonstrating how this works.

Antonya Gonzalez[11] wanted to find ways to combat racial prejudice in older children. A host of data suggests racial bias starts at an early age and is most influential in ethnically homogenous communities. The question Gonzalez asked was whether there is a way to reduce bias. To test her hypothesis, she recruited nearly four hundred white and Asian children between ages five and twelve in Vancouver. The children heard four fictional short stories. One-third of the children heard stories depicting black individuals contributing positively to their community with an accompanying photo. Here's an example: "This is James. James lives in North Vancouver, where he is a firefighter. James is an excellent firefighter and is working hard to become a fire chief." For two of the sketches, participants learned about a male exemplar, and for the other two, they learned about a female exemplar. Another third heard the same fictional stories but with white characters and white photos. A control group consisting of the remaining children heard stories about flowers. Afterward, they administered to the children a test measuring unconscious racial bias by seeing how quickly they paired pictures of black and white people with positive versus negative words.

These results have important implications for educational initiatives to combat racism. Whereas the younger children's perceptions of blacks remained unchanged by the story intervention, the stories significantly impacted older children, eliminating implicit racial bias. This difference probably can be attributed to the fact that younger children have less cognitive flexibility than older children. Older adults are also flexible. Research shows that exposing them to admired black and disliked white exemplars can reduce their hidden racial prejudices as well.[12] The idea of telling people stories contradicting their prejudices can go a long way to building greater empathy and tolerance for minorities.

In a related study, Dan Johnson demonstrated you could change your biases by just the act of reading fiction about characters you might have viewed stereotypically. This is especially true if the characters represented are counterstereotypical. In the case of this study, the characters in the fictions were Muslim.[13]

Healing the Rwandan Genocide

Suppose we take these insights up a level of magnitude. Would it be possible to use the power of story to resolve significant conflicts between peoples with a long history of hostility? The Rwandan genocide provides a compelling case study of how the right kind of narrative can be a potent tool for healing.

In 1994, horrifying forces of hatred and brutality descended upon Rwanda, resulting in a genocidal fury leaving nearly a million dead. Members of the Tutsi minority woke one day to discover their Hutu neighbors had been incited into an irrational frenzy egged on by political leaders' rhetoric. The result was a hundred days of mayhem perpetrated by thousands of men wielding machetes. Their target was their Tutsi government opponents and their families. Even Hutu husbands inexplicably were incited to murder their Tutsi wives. Ironically, for years the vast majority of Hutus had lived and worked peacefully alongside their Tutsi neighbors, even counting many of them as friends. This all changed when hateful propaganda was broadcast over radio stations urging all Hutus to weed out the Tutsis from their midst, referring to them as cockroaches. No one was immune from the insanity stoked by this malicious narrative. Even priests and nuns actively participated in the slaughter.

During this tragedy, the world watched from the sidelines, refusing to intervene. Not until the Rwandan Patriotic Front (RPF) marshaled its forces, invaded the capital, and asserted control over the country did the wholesale slaughter end. Millions of Hutus, many of whom had participated in the genocide, fled to neighboring Zaire, now known as the Democratic Republic of Congo. Many of the remaining Hutus were indiscriminately slaughtered by the invading RPF, which then launched an invasion of the Congo to pursue and kill those who had fled.

In 2002, the UN Security Council established the International Criminal Tribunal for Rwanda in the Tanzanian town of Arusha to prosecute the ringleaders. They convicted over ninety Hutus who had leadership positions. In local villages across Rwanda, community courts, known as *gacaca*, were created to prosecute the thousands of genocide suspects. For a decade until 2012, twelve thousand *gacaca* courts met weekly and tried more than 1.2 million cases. They jailed over three hundred thousand men, with over fifteen thousand receiving life sentences.[14]

Fast-forward to today. Many of those tried and found guilty are being released from prison and returning home. What's occurring in villages all across Rwanda can only be viewed as a minor miracle. Hollie Nyseth Brehm and Laura C. Frizzell[15] have chronicled how these men are returning to their communities to live among neighbors whose relatives they killed.

Preparing to be released, most of the prisoners expected the worst. Many feared for their lives. What they encountered, though, was bewildering. Instead of facing hate and recrimination, many of their neighbors, Tutsis among them, welcomed them home. In the years since their imprisonment, Rwanda has undergone an economic renaissance. People have changed as well. They have forgiven these men for the madness enveloping their world, greeting them with gifts and money to get restarted with their lives. Many Tutsis have been providing them food to sustain them as they transition back into society. How is it they have been able to find a way to forgive?

After the trials concluded, a variety of leaders spun a unique narrative. School curricula and public monuments to the killing painted a nuanced picture to explain how the Hutus could perpetrate such atrocious acts. In a brilliant reframing, they traced the roots of their egregious behavior back to the colonial era. They blamed the Belgians for exacerbating latent yet inert divisions between Hutus and Tutsis. This reformulated narrative also pointed at the Hutu government's corrupt practices and the many ways its leaders encouraged discrimination and violence against the Tutsis. Displacing blame away from individuals to larger historical forces and governmental actions changed the way survivors viewed those who perpetrated the crimes. The wrongdoers were portrayed as victims and represented as ignorant people fearing the confiscation of their lands. After all, they were simply following government orders. If they didn't, they, too, might have suffered a violent end.

As the authors of this paper report, this does not remove them from blame—they did, after all, serve prison sentences. And many have felt ostracized by their families upon their return home. Moreover, it doesn't minimize the ongoing psychological suffering of survivors.

While this is a story filled with painful tragedy and redemption, it's essential to consider how the narrative crafted following the event made a transformation possible. It created a nuanced picture of what creates behavior. None of us is an isolated island making choices and acting in a vacuum. Each of us has a past. Strong environmental influences buffet all of us. It recognized we each have a backstory that's complicit in all we do. Within this narrative structure, there is suddenly room for victims to see their assailants with a modicum of compassion. While they could have made different choices, it's also understandable how the government's rhetoric influenced them to make bad ones, ones any of us could potentially have made if we were in their shoes. They paid the price for what they did, and this narrative made it possible for everyone to come together to move forward. What good would be done by continuing to punish them by ostracizing them or making their broken lives worse? Certainly, governmental leadership within Rwanda played a role in this redemptive narrative. But it was the steps of everyday people who courageously transcended their loss and pain to see the humanity in those returning.

When considering the high levels of incarceration in the US for violent and nonviolent crimes, we are left to reconsider how historical and social factors contribute to individuals making terrible choices. What stories could help us understand their decisions better, opening us to seeing them not as convicts, but as human beings deserving of our compassion and forgiveness? Now, imagine widening our lens to look at broader conflicts between nations and peoples around the globe. How could this more nuanced, complex story process help us adopt new approaches to conflict resolution that rely on compassionate understanding? What would it be like if we could humanize perpetrators rather than reduce their stories to stereotypical punchlines demanding retribution and blame?

Can the Power of Story Create the Conditions for World Peace?

In the 1980s, we became involved with the Foundation for Mideast Communication (FMC). Through facilitated workshops, we attempted to deploy the power of hearing the other's story to diffuse the deep mistrust and hostility Arabs and Jews had traditionally held for each other.

There are many levels to the storytelling and story-listening. First, Jews and Arabs, and most particularly Palestinians, each have distinct narratives about the history of this sliver of land currently called Palestine and Israel. Even facts each group thinks are incontrovertible are open to widely different interpretations. For example, in 1917, the British government announced its support for the Balfour Declaration, which advocated for a national home for the Jewish people. While the document itself is a historical fact, its legitimacy as a basis for Israel's creation is an entirely different matter. Jews and Arabs look upon it with altogether different explanations.

Jews and Arabs also saw other historical events through dissimilar lenses. For example, as a Jew, I grew up hearing "historical facts" of how surrounding Arab countries told the Arabs living in Palestine to leave their homes in advance of their invasion in 1948. The surrounding Arab nations promised they could return when the hostilities concluded. Many departed, but the Israelis defeated the Arab countries. Those who fled were shuttled into refugee camps in the neighboring Arab lands and prevented from assimilating into the host countries' societies. According to the Jewish rendition of this story, they safeguarded those Arabs who didn't flee and subsequently gave them citizenship in Israel with equal rights. In this narrative, the Jews were painted as being blameless, portrayed as victims of Arab aggression.

The Palestinian storyline describes a very different picture. While some Arabs did voluntarily leave at the urging of Arab armies' leaders, many were brutally driven from their homes by the Haganah and the Irgun, two Jewish paramilitary forces. Each narrative holds elements of truth. Both sides committed atrocities, and it's no surprise each side claims their massacres were the exception, not the rule.

This history is complicated. The purpose of the FMC was not to engage the two sides with a heated, unwinnable debate. Instead, it was to provide a safe space to meet the other. As the workshop evolved, we gave participants the chance to share their refugee stories, whether it was due to World War II or the battles fought during Israel's quest for independence. Many Jewish participants recounted tales of harrowing escapes from the Nazis or how their parents survived the Nazi death camps. Many had lost entire branches of their families. Palestinians told stories of losing all of their lands and businesses, of extraordinary hardships living in refugee camps in Gaza, Jordan, or Lebanon, and of the continual persecution and humiliation they and their families experience who still live in Israel or the West Bank. For many in the room, this was the first time they had encountered first-person accounts from people they previously discounted as worthy of empathy or compassion.

One of the most profound yet painful experiences was an exercise in which we asked each group to make a public list of the stereotypical properties they had grown up hearing and believing about the other. Many of these attributions were at best derogatory. At their worst, they were inflammatory. It was excruciating to make public what had only been shared in the privacy of their homes or among close friends. There were two remarkable things about these lists. First, they were practically identical. The second was that few could name the source of these beliefs when pressed. Most could remember these epithets being bantered about freely in their homes for as long as they could recall. They had never questioned or examined them but held them to be gospel truth. Some even had shreds of evidence to support the claims, but they were often second- or third-hand. As difficult as it was to see this ugly representation of each other, in some mysterious way, it cleared the air for people to begin seeing each other as unique human beings, not monikers attributed to "those people."

The goals of the Foundation for Mideast Communication were lofty. It held a vision if enough people could participate in this experience, there could be a tidal shift in Jewish-Arab relations. Unfortunately, realities on the ground overshadowed its work. Prime Minister Rabin was assassinated by a right-wing Jew who believed peace with the Palestinians violated God's plans. The

Intifada broke out on the West Bank and in Gaza. Terrorist bombings of buses and cafés resulted in brutal countermeasures. Israel built a wall often bisecting Palestinian communities and destroying countless farmlands. Groups of Palestinians and Israelis who had been meeting regularly in Israel and the West Bank were no longer able to travel to visit each other. This environment wasn't conducive to peace, but instead promulgated distrust and anger on both sides.

Perhaps of even greater importance was that the FMC lacked any way to anchor its work in the day-to-day lives of Palestinians and Israelis. No collaborative projects emerged from these workshops. Nothing on the ground looked different.

Much has occurred since the 1980s and early 1990s to prevent dialogue and exploration of commonalities. Even so, pockets of work like this continue. Projects like Seeds of Peace make it possible for younger generations to meet and begin the slow process of dispelling the false narratives perpetuating distrust and mutual hatred. More recently, groups like Combatants for Peace are bringing together former fighters from both sides of the conflict to engage in political action using principles of nonviolence. Interestingly, the first step in this journey of unlikely partners started with the telling and listening to each other's stories.

Many Palestinians, jailed because of their opposition to Israeli occupation, emerged from their incarceration experiences with the realization violent resistance was only going to continue to destroy the life and culture they so desperately wanted to preserve. When this group reached out to Israelis, who were publicly beginning to question their government's tactics, the Israelis greeted their invitation at first with suspicion and distrust. As Tuly Flint, a former two-star general in the Israeli Army, described it, when he decided to attend a meeting with his Palestinian counterparts, he saw it as a considerable risk. Ever present in his mind was the thought they would abduct him and turn him over to Hamas. Something in his own experiences and story pushed him forward, though. As a trained social worker, he had seen the devastating, traumatic effects of the conflict on Palestinians and Israelis alike. As the Combatants for Peace website[16] describes it, this shared suffering is "a coherent ethos that places the activists' experience at the center. We all have a story worth listening to. It reflects the horrors of this conflict, but also the potential of breaking out of it. Our personal stories, Palestinians and Israelis, are the stories of life here, of the violence to which we were partners or witnesses but also, the story of choosing a path of nonviolence and partnership, a path to a different future."[17]

This shared pain of loss and trauma makes it possible for enemy combatants to seek an approach that transcends political realities. Their stories are heartbreaking yet provide the fuel for concerted action.

During her stint in the army reserves during the Second Intifada, Mai Hascall witnessed a fellow reservist needlessly gun down a Palestinian who ventured out after curfew to visit a friend's house a few meters from his own. When she discovered the army was covering up her fellow reservist's guilt, it shook her faith in the ethical underpinnings of the Israel Defense Forces (IDF). In her words, she "felt betrayed by my state, but also felt like a traitor for speaking the truth." At her first meeting of Combatants for Peace, for the first time, she was free to tell her story, finding "people who could listen, accept, and forgive."[18]

After being detained for his role in the Intifada at age sixteen, Jamil Qassas returned home and witnessed his younger brother gunned down as he ventured out to visit his uncle. The blow of losing her son devastated his mother. When the Second Intifada erupted years later, they were watching television when a news report came on detailing a bus bombing in Tel Aviv where dozens died. His mother began to weep. Surprised, Jamil asked her, "Why are you crying, Mama? Those are Israelis who were killed, not us."

She looked at him and said, "Those kids who were killed have mothers. And those mothers will have the same feelings and the same pain we went through."

Hearing this was a turning point for Jamil when he recognized, for the first time, "The tears of a Palestinian mother are not different from the tears of an Israeli mother. Blood has only one color."[19]

While the starting place for their work is telling their stories, they use the connections they make to build peaceful coexistence. It has shown up in simple acts like accompanying shepherds to discourage attacks by vigilante Jewish settlers, sitting in to prevent the bulldozing of a Palestinian village, or defying the Israeli government by planting new olive trees on Palestinian lands to replace those destroyed by the IDF.

Will Combatants for Peace succeed? While prospects for resolving this conflict appear to be receding, we must remind ourselves that the end of the story is still not written. These brave people have chosen to be the authors of a distinctly optimistic story that is changing hearts and minds on both sides of the conflict. In their words, "By telling our personal stories to our audiences in countless public talks, we allow people to put themselves in their enemies' shoes, to see reality through their eyes, to make sense of what at first seems senseless, to feel pain and hope instead of numbness. Through encouraging attentive listening, we invite our audiences to care about our stories, Palestinians and Israelis, and to join us in writing their next chapters together."[20]

Perhaps the lesson here is that we can resolve even the most intractable human conflicts if we're willing to start listening to each other's tales. This is the prerequisite for opening the space for the possibility of a new story to emerge. We must always believe transformation can take hold and change the reality when people at war stop and listen heartfully to each other's tale of sorrow.

How to Move from Stories of the Past to Stories of Future Action

Nearly twenty years ago, Paul Costello founded Storywise—The Center for Narrative Studies. He wanted to explore the ways storytelling can impact people in conflict. In a recent discussion with Paul,[21] he shared his circuitous journey to creating new models for peacemaking.

An idea from the writings of Michael White, who developed narrative therapy, proved to be a guiding principle: "People are not sick; they just live inside sick stories. You don't have to heal people; you have to heal their stories."[22] He was primed to try out this idea when a friend from Dumbarton United Methodist Church in Washington, DC, approached him. They had just started a modest program in 1998 to bring to DC Catholic and Protestant college students from Northern Ireland. At first, they hired a mediator to hold spirited debates about the conflict tearing the country apart. It went over like a lead balloon. Paul's friend inquired if he could come up with an alternative approach.

Over the next few years, they recruited more groups of young people to come to DC. Paul dove into their stories. He experimented with them sharing their experiences at the Irish embassy, at the Northern Ireland Bureau, and in front of congressional members. Every student had seven minutes of prime time to get up and tell their story. It was no longer just about the conflict, but about developing young leaders.

One of the first distinctions he helped them make was to see what they were sharing was their story, not their opinion. He knew if it devolved into a political argument pitting Catholic against Protestant, or Northern Island against Britain, or addressing the question of whether the Irish Republican Army (IRA) needed to disarm before peace talks could commence, they would be dead in the water. Instead, they came at it from a personal narrative angle because, as he puts it, "We didn't want to add to the argument, we wanted to add to the understanding and to teach people how to tell a story."

They learned the importance of creating the space for Catholic and Protestant students to work collaboratively, share each other's stories, celebrate them, and hold each other accountable to the stories they tell. As a result, when they returned home to Northern Ireland, they had grown immeasurably and felt perhaps for the first time that their voice mattered, and their story had value. As Paul puts it, "Young people growing up in a conflict zone are recruited in the old stories that are so vividly retold and remembered. But when they come to Washington, they're no longer immersed in the old stories. If the program were being held back in Belfast, they'd still be living as though events that occurred on Bloody Sunday in 1921 had just happened yesterday." On that July day during the Irish War of Independence, sectarian violence broke out in Belfast when the IRA ambushed a police raiding party. Protestant loyalists then attacked Catholic enclaves, burning homes and businesses. Over twenty-five people died in the clashes, hundreds were injured, and two hundred houses were severely damaged or destroyed, leaving over one thousand people homeless. Ever since, this story is regularly told and retold in every Catholic and Protestant pub in Belfast, making its injustices and brutality seem like an ever-present current event.

Taking these young adults out of this environment made it possible for them to begin to entertain a new story of the future, which is far more empowering than the story of the past. Paul likens the process to when we're younger and find a new boyfriend or a new girlfriend who is much more interesting than the person we're currently dating. "You can't just argue people out of the old story, you've got to give them a new, better one."

This philosophy has informed the work Paul is currently undertaking with Israelis and Palestinians. He sums it up by saying, "You've got to jumpstart these young people out of their past and into the possibility of a future, and that's so hard because the political and cultural system is built upon remembrance and the belief that they should never forget. The focus has always been on 'let's make sure this doesn't happen again' rather than 'let's do something never been done before.' It's about the precedent of the past rather than the unprecedented possibility of the future.

That's where you've got to try and make the flip." In this way, Paul emphasizes moving away from dialogue toward getting these young people to do something constructive together.

When he announced he would take the group to the Holocaust Museum, one of his Palestinian participants objected because there wasn't a museum telling the story of his people's suffering. Paul challenged him to raise the money and create one, because that's what the Jews did. Today the museum has a permanent home just off of Dupont Circle.

Instead of recruiting people from different sides of a conflict who want to contest for the space of victimhood and argue about who has suffered the most pain, he now recruits people based on whether they have a vision for a transformative project. He expects them to examine problems in their local community, develop a business plan, and then do a pilot. His strategy is to empower them to become an agent of change rather than a victim. As a result, Palestinians and Israelis have created nine nonprofits to impact their local communities. One Israeli started a program called Madrasa, where he's teaching Arabic to Israelis. A Palestinian who is now a lawyer and grew up boxing wanted to build a gym to train kids in his hometown of Ramallah. His dream? The first Palestine gold medal for boxing in the next Olympic games. Today, after much work and fundraising, the El Barrio Professional Boxing Gym is open and attracting young kids to learn a new skill and hopefully create a new life story.

Paul has aimed to move these stories we are carrying inside of ourselves out into the world. "When it's outside, you can walk around it and ask, so how is that story showing up? Is it working for you? Where do you need to shift it? Or do you need to get rid of it for a better story? Let's reimagine what the future could be and how we can get there, and then go back to the past to pull from it what we need." His goal is to move these young people from the story shaping them to a new stance where they can begin shaping their future stories.

Paul is attempting to infect these young people with his core strength—curiosity about life's possibilities. Once they get it, then anything is achievable. His mantra is, "If you want to change the world, you've got to change the story to be transported to some-place new. It's no longer enough for people to learn how to read and write. They have to learn a new twenty-first-century narrative literacy empowering them to know when a story is nothing but manipulation, when a story invites them to conspire in their self-diminishment, or when stories are mean and demeaning. Know-ing how to read better and interpret a story's intentions allows us to choose and to escape the thrall of media hype, political dema-goguery, and headline news that assumes we cannot ever think for ourselves."[23]

In our terminology, Paul's perspective highlights just how important it is for every citizen of the world to develop their SQ. Only then will we be equipped to resist the allure of the sirens beckoning us to crash on the shores of hatred and distrust. Stories like Paul's, what has occurred in Rwanda, and the bridges being built between former combatants in Israel and Palestine open us to possibility. In contrast, distrust always shuts the door to con-nection and change. Suppose groups with severe, real-world grievances can find a way to connect, forgive, and even cohere. In that case, there's a reason for optimism that groups of people who hold conflicting views or political stances can find common ground. There is still hope when we see the Tutsis embrace the killers of their relatives and extend a helping hand. We feel encouraged when a Palestinian whom the Israeli military has physically and emotionally abused can stand in front of an audi-ence with a former Israeli soldier and call him his friend. It's enlivening to hear accounts of how young people from Northern Ireland steeped in distrust fueled by generations of stories find a way to reach across the divide to build a new story characterized by cooperation and respect. We now know how to enable people worldwide to learn the tools to craft a new narrative, unite, and build a better world for themselves and generations to come. It's now up to us to take the first step.

Journey Deeper

Hone Your Capacity to Listen

Paul Costello shares our emphasis on the crucial role story-listening plays in creating a space where change and trust can flourish. Titles fill popular literature on how to tell your story better, how to influence others through storytelling, or how to sell your ideas using story. But little attention has been paid to what it means to develop our competence as listeners. To this end, Paul asks a simple question: "How do I make it safe for others to speak to me, and how do I win listening rights from others?" To accomplish this, the Center for Narrative Studies has laid out some simple and essential principles for effective listening:[24]

1 **What we think a person has said is not always equal to what they said,** so we need to reflect our understanding in our speaking with phrases such as, "What I heard you say was . . ." rather than "You said . . ." Also, note sometimes what the speaker heard themselves say isn't what they said when you replay the audiotape back to them.

2 **What a person says is presumed to be what they mean, but again this is a false presumption** given we use words to mean what we want them to mean (as we hear them), but not necessarily the way our hearers hear or use them. So, if we acknowledge what you say might not always be what you mean, we need to reflect back to the talker in phrases such as, "What I heard you say was . . ." and "I take that to mean . . . Am I right? Did I get that right? Is that what you meant?"

3 **It is also risky to presume what people mean is what people feel.** A team member can be vociferous on a certain

point, and we suppose she is passionate about it, but we need to check it out because how we detect emotional undertones may not be the way they feel it. We need to reflect this back when using phrases such as, "So I am wondering if you feel as strongly about this as I think you might, going on the tone in your voice?" We need to check out the emotional investment in the exchange to know how to respond.

4   **We also need to guard about reading minds too readily.** Though we may catch what a person says and have reflected back correctly what they mean and what they feel about what they mean, *we also need to check out the point of all that.* In other words, what was the intent behind the sharing? So we might say, "So I am taking it your point here is we need to . . . Am I right in that?" This is related to the idea of communicative intent, so as listeners, we get a broader frame of meaning to situate the message. If someone asks us to interpret it later when the person is absent, we know the spirit behind the message—the story behind the story—if not the way it is explicitly applicable in a new situation. This is also the narrative principle we have called *compassionate intention: to always impute to words and actions a more extensive, broader, positive intentionality than they might seem to betray just by themselves.* It is saying to the speaker, "You make sense in the world; you are on purpose and not an accident."

5   **We also stress there is an economy of attention out there.** Attention deficiency is not just a disorder but part of an exchange and part of what the media trade in image and celebrity. Just because I am speaking does not guarantee I am being heard. Listening is an act of generosity and a gift we donate to the speaker. And it's always within our power to revoke the listening rights we give to the speaker. No one can force us to listen. So, listening

somehow always happens in this glorious field of freedom and grace. To speak to this field of freedom means *we have to earn listening rights,* just like a movie must win our attention or a book must grab us somehow to get us to read on. That does not mean we have to cultivate all sorts of cheap rhetorical tricks exactly. But to be much more aware, listening is about an economy of attention. There are attention deficits and attention surpluses. Note how we say, "We pay attention." We have to pay for attention by the way we invite the listener in, and by what we offer them in return. How much we pay for attention is going to be how much our listeners think we value them. If they feel we are too cheap, they pay us in kind. *The quality of listening will often mirror the quality of the effort to earn attention.*

6   **Listening is a co-created reality and response.** If people are not listening to me, I need to ask, where am I speaking to the listening? Where am I inviting them into the process? Some conversations we hear are never inviting us in, so it is tough to listen. Not to listen is one of the subtle but most potent forms of resistance to authority when we feel we are being taken for granted or not being recognized. We perfected that art, most of us, in twelve years of schooling, the art of "switching off while seeming to be attentive." The problem of not listening, then, is no longer just an individual thing. It is a product of group culture and values as well as a personal act. Listening is the way we create and reward relationships. Non-listening is the way we opt out. We are still listening, mind you, only something else has our attention.

7   **Thinking of listening as a set of rights given and earned also alerts us to the experience of having our listening rights stolen away from us.** We tell a story. Instead of our listeners attending to what we said and following on with

recognition through referencing, e.g. "When you said *x*, I couldn't help thinking *y*," we get the usual switch to their story. We are compelled to surrender our story for theirs, and often it can become a game of who can tell the better story. Once that happens, you know listening is not taking place. And it makes you wonder if listening—active or passive—is a rare experience for many of us. Otherwise, how do we explain how grateful we are when we find a person who can deeply hear us?

8   **We also want to draw attention to the silent listener to our every conversation**, and that is *"ourselves listening to ourselves."* How we hear ourselves has a dramatic effect on the quality of our speaking and listening. We give a presentation, and our inner critic keeps saying, "You stuffed up again; they are laughing at you." That inner listening will make it almost impossible to hear what people say in response, or it will make us only hear the critical comments.

9   **If you do a whispering exercise whereby a story is retold** in a chain of transmission, one can demonstrate how we take words and phrases and make sense of them as best we can. We will not pass on, let alone remember, material that doesn't make any sense. Try and recall a set of unrelated names compared to remembering six different tropical fruits. So, we as listeners need to make the compassionate assumption of communicative ethics, saying, *Even if what you said makes little sense to me as I hear you, I presume it is making some sense to you.* This is where my listening can be directed. I need to ask, "How does that make sense for you, so you can help me understand where you are coming from?"

10 **Listening as a Climate:** In summary, we can consider listening as creating a climate, and whenever we are in groups or working in teams, *this climate will determine the quality of the connection between the members* since the way

we honor people and give them recognition for even existing is how we treat or give credit to their voice. The use of names and referencing others' ideas when we speak our own is not just a smart coalition-building exercise. It is also a way of humanizing the group culture. This is more than just about people meeting to complete a task. This is people meeting people. It is a human encounter. As well as a climate of connection, *listening also speaks to the quality of* **attention.** Who speaks and who gets heard? Sometimes that may be because bosses play favorites, and it also may be some are more articulate and more effective than others. Everyone has a responsibility in the group process for the quality of attention. If the group allows people to drift off into irrelevancies, or pays little attention to preparation and time, it is not exercising appropriate care for the quality of attention. It is never a given; it is always paid for, as in "pay attention." Ironically, it is also a gift, the first we give to another human being when we meet them, and the first we will withdraw if we feel we are not being included. Lastly, we can usefully speak of *listening as a doorway into the climate of intention.* Listening is not a blanket skill covering all. We are listening, yes, but for what exactly? If the goals and processes are unclear, then the listening quality simply will decline because listening is an exercise of focusing, of selective editing in and out. Listening as we have described it will help disclose purpose, and the more purpose becomes more explicit, the better the listening becomes. The bottom line, listening is about granting to others the space for their voice by which they can hear they exist, have brains and feelings, and what they do and say makes some sense. It is how we take others into our space. If listening is a problem in a team or a group, it is about relationships and not just skills.

Choose to See the Sacred in Everything

In his seminal work *I and Thou,* Martin Buber states there are two kinds of relationships we can choose to have with the world of things and people: I-It and I-Thou.[25] If we approach the world with a utilitarian point of view, he characterizes this as an I-It relationship. When walking through the forest on a summer day looking for wood to stoke our winter stoves, the tree we cut down becomes for that moment just an "it" and not a living creature. Its value resides in what it can do for us. In contrast, we could walk through the forest with an entirely different intention — to see each tree as a living being and stand before it as equals, appreciating its beauty, majesty, and presence to enhance and lift our spirits. In these rare moments, we and the tree ascend the spiritual heights to a place of mutual regard. We enter into a shared embrace of sacredness, what Buber calls I-Thou.

We can say the same for our relationship with people, especially those who are different from ourselves. Every time we reduce people to a stereotype, to a series of adjectives preventing us from seeing their humanity, they become an "it" to us. Choosing to see the other as a fully alive, mysterious human being waiting to be seen and understood can arouse in us a deep curiosity precluding generalizations. It forces us to meet the person with the fullness of our humanity, what Buber would characterize as a sacred relationship.

This polar dichotomy permeates every aspect of our daily experience. Unfortunately, most of the time, we dwell in the I-It realm. On occasion, something breaks through the automaticity of objectification. We suddenly see the other's story fully in all of its dimensions. Such a breakthrough can come from deep listening, from eschewing labels and simple explanations, and from choosing to put aside our narrow interests to see the needs of another who is suffering. Ultimately, it's a choice. We challenge you to make it.

Imagine the Reversal Story

Sometimes life can throw us a curve, upending what we thought was a stable order where all is good, predictable, and right in our world. Unfortunately, though, we live within the illusion that our life will always continue on its current trajectory. But then some outside force or agency upends everything. It could be a weather event destroying every possession. Or a health event like cancer leading us on a journey not of our choosing. Or an economic calamity such as COVID-19 stalling people's careers and, for many, short-circuiting their dreams. More often than not, these events give us perspective and make us eternally grateful if we survive them and get back on solid footing. They can also instill in us a sense of appreciation for the travails of others.

Developing empathy, though, does not require we undergo tragedy to deepen our thankfulness for life. We can go to these places and become a better person for it by imagining the reversal of our good fortune and health. When we see someone suffering and in need, instead of turning away, we can choose to consider what it would be like if it were us. Within this awareness is a lesson of humility and, more often than not, sensitivity for what others are experiencing. Deep within is the seed for a new kind of action and being in the world, one making room for those who have less, who have lost everything due to circumstances outside of their control, who simply need our help. Here are the seeds for a new story to change your life and change the world. All you need do is imagine what your life would have been like if you experienced systematic racism, generational poverty, or a debilitating illness. Within this imagining, you can develop a sensitivity for others' stories and experiences, expanding your capacity for compassion.

Share and Listen to Stories of Significance

Many years ago, we were hired by Walt Disney Imagination (WDI) when they were mandated to merge with the Disney

Development Company (DDC). The merger of two organizations within the Walt Disney kingdom would seem an easy task at first blush, but these two groups' cultures were as different as night and day, and they each held the other in low esteem. To facilitate this transition, we designed a storytelling/story-listening workshop for staff at all levels of both organizations. Members from each group were assigned seats at round tables, equally mixed, with all designations from secretaries to Imagineers to mechanical engineers interspersed. The day's focus was first to get to know each other and second to share stories of their work, and what they each felt was their contribution to the mother ship's success. We had secretaries proudly discussing how they introduced a new process for organizing the filing system. Imagineers shared their stories of how they dreamed up Space Mountain; engineers explained how they had a brainchild to reroute a road a few hundred yards to the east to save the company $5 million. Each story was celebrated, appreciated, and deeply heard.

While the merger certainly had its share of hiccups and challenges, we believe this process led to a smoother integration of two teams of professionals with disparate skill sets. The workshop certainly put to rest the constant sniping when each division could smugly stand on its hill, looking down on the other's shortcomings.

If you're bringing disparate groups together, whether it be a merger or just a team-building exercise within your company, create space for people to share and celebrate their unique contributions, big and small. As Konstantin Stanislavski, the famous theater director and innovator in world theatre, once proclaimed, "There are no small parts, only small actors." Every role in every company is vital to the overall success of the business. The more your people appreciate and embrace this truth, the better prepared they will be to collaborate and build the company's success.

Change the Metaphor, Change the Story

Jonathan Sacks, the chief rabbi of England, has been imagining what a world would be like if we were to choose the right metaphor to guide our story-making and relationships with others.[26] Massive migrations of people are rocking societies in Europe and the Americas, challenging all of us. The central question many are asking is how to integrate people from other lands without losing our own identities. How can we maintain a cohesive society amid so much ethnic and religious diversity?

Sacks has identified three essential metaphors that have guided our relationship to immigrants both here in the US and abroad. In Britain and Europe during the nineteenth century, they adopted what he terms the "country house model," in which host countries welcomed foreigners in to reside in their land, but never embraced them. They were seen as guests and outsiders and felt they could be asked at any moment to vacate the premises. The Holocaust perpetrated by the Nazis was an extreme example of what happens when we view people always as outsiders.

The US adopted a different metaphor—the melting pot. Even though people retained their ties to their country of origin or their ethnic background, they were all expected to assimilate and become Americans. But their identities were always hyphen-ated—Irish-Americans, Jewish-Americans, African-Americans, etc. But blatant discrimination persisted, and the notion we were or are one people is more of a myth than a reality.

More recently, in Europe, the hotel metaphor took root. Multiculturalism invited people to come and live in these coun-tries and continue to practice their cultural rituals and maintain their cultural identities. All they asked of them was to pay their fair share of taxes and not be too noisy. Long-term residents and newcomers were seen as all living on the premises with equal rights as long as they did their part to keep the hotel functioning and stayed in their rooms at night. Unfortunately, this model didn't work so well for these countries' residents, nor did it work very well for the visitors. No one truly felt at home, and tensions between these rival communities escalated. Segregation has turned out not to be a viable arrangement.

Sacks believes that in the twenty-first century, we need a new metaphor. He calls it "the home we build together" and describes it this way:

> A hundred immigrants turn up in a town. The leaders of the town say, "Welcome. We're so sorry we don't have a country house or a hotel. But we do have some spare land, and lots of building materials, and some expert architects and electricians. So, let's all build you a house together." The natives and newcomers work together, side by side, and in the course of building, the newcomers learn the ways of the natives, and the natives benefit from the skills of the newcomers. The newcomers keep many of their old customs, but they also bring their unique gifts as contributions to the town, and they feel they belong because, with the help of the natives, they have built their own homes, which merge architecturally with the other houses in the town. The model of society as the home we build together emphasizes responsibilities more than rights. It values differences because they're not used to keep us apart, but rather, they mean we each have something different and special to give to the common good. The town grows because of all the new food and music and fashions the newcomers bring to the town square. And the natives still feel at home because the newcomers respect their way of doing things. That is integrated diversity.[27]

Sacks believes this model will work in ways the old metaphors haven't for one simple reason. When people build something together, they bond together, leading to a more profound sense of belonging for everyone.

So, thinking of stories you'd like to create, what metaphor are you currently living within? What metaphor is dominating the viewpoint of others in your community? Your town? Your country? What would it be like to adopt a more inclusive metaphor, one focused on building something with others rather than, for example, protecting what you currently have? That is the question before us. It's the one Paul Costello asks of his participants. What is the story you wish to create in the future?

Books We Recommend

There are a few philosophy books that have remained on our bookshelf over the years that we continue to refer to, and *I and Thou* **by Martin Buber** is one of them. His simple approach to life and relationships sets the stage for how we can approach all beings as sacred and worthy of our highest regard.

At a time when polarization appears to be worsening, **Stephen Carter's** *Civility* stands out as a must-read and a guide for how we can begin the long journey back to a society built on respect.

Just prior to the release of *Story Intelligence*, the country has experienced an election that feels unlike any other in our lifetime. But when you finish reading **Andrew P. Costello's** *The Presidential Plot*, you'll discover that the forces and themes that we believe are so unique to our time are just replications of archetypal narratives that have been played out through presidential elections since the founding of this country.

If you're interested in dissolving what feels like intractable conflict and restoring goodwill, *Cooperative Wisdom: Bringing People Together When Things Fall Apart* by **Donald Scherer** and **Carolyn Jabs** is filled with approaches and tools that we all need to learn.

We live at a time when more and more people are being displaced through war and climate change with calamitous consequences. *Dignity of Difference: How to Avoid the Clash of Civilizations* by **Rabbi Jonathan Sacks** provides fresh thinking about how we can successfully welcome the stranger into our communities, a task that we are all commanded to undertake if we truly believe in the biblical mandate to love our neighbors as ourselves.

7

The Power of Story to Envision New Possibilities

The ability to think prospectively to enable us to imagine a desired future and the actions required to realize it.

It's a poor sort of memory that only works backwards.

—Lewis Carroll

We began our journey into the power of story gathered around a central fire, showing how people from time immemorial have used storytelling to entertain and enthrall the imaginations of young and old alike. Traditionally, stories have been a window leading back in time beyond the ancestors to the creation of this world. These stories provided listeners a context for understanding their lives and how they fit into the bigger scheme of things. But all of this focus on the past may have had a more important purpose. It may have been preparing us to survive and live more effectively in the future. Sharing accounts of past dangers served as cautionary tales about the potential threats lurking just around the proverbial bend in the road. They trained us to be on the lookout for signs that a current situation is similar to a previous one encountered, conveying helpful lessons to confront life's challenges successfully. In this sense, storytelling serves as more of a prospective than a retrospective tool, essential for planning our life and work.

Our capacity to see and create a potential future is the hallmark of what distinguishes us from other species. The link between what is real and what might become real is our imagination, connecting the past to the future. If imagination is this link, then story is the most potent language of the imagination we know for translating our hopes and dreams into reality. Molly Andrews calls this "narrative imagination" and is the means we use for continually "extending the boundaries of our world."[1] Without it, there is no future, making this final power of story so crucial. People who develop their SQ not only accrue tremendous benefits portrayed in the first six powers of story, they are better poised to adapt to and fashion their world. In turn, this leads to more fulfilling and meaningful outcomes in every facet of their lives.

In this final chapter, we explore the many ways you can expand your prospective Story Intelligence to envision the future you want to create. We'll show you how to deploy narrative to better understand the implications of any decision. Our goal is to distill critical lessons you can use to think about your probable futures, whether you're considering a strategic action for your company or you're charting the next step in your professional career or life.

We'll also examine visualization research, clearly demonstrating we can change our future capabilities by simply imagining an action without ever lifting a finger. While there are many things indeterminate and uncontrollable about the future, the stories we tell ourselves and others can profoundly impact events that haven't yet occurred. We aren't merely passive actors in a play with a foregone conclusion. Instead, we can be actors, scriptwriters, and directors in our lives with far greater power to affect outcomes by merely exercising our imaginations. Our ultimate goal is to assist you through the power of story to expand your capacity to create better opportunities for yourself, your communities, your places of business, and the world.

What Can We Learn from Shooting Basketballs?

Since the 1930s, researchers have been exploring the power of imagination and visualization to improve future performance. It would appear that we can enhance the quality of whatever physical task we undertake before we ever twitch a muscle by just imagining executing an action. Moreover, when we combine mental imagery with physical practice, their synergy leads to much higher efficacy than mental imagery or physical training alone.[2]

Some of the most intriguing work focuses on shooting basketball free throws. It's a simple task whose success you can quickly evaluate—either the ball goes through the hoop, or it doesn't. In one of the first studies by L. V. Clark, a researcher who focuses on the power of visualization to impact behavioral outcomes, he had one group mentally imagine themselves shooting twenty-five shots a day with the ball going in. The other group physically took twenty-five practice shots daily. It turns out mental practice was almost as effective as physical practice when the two groups later tested their performance. There was one caveat, though—mental imagery worked best among accomplished basketball players and was least successful with novices. For imagery to work, it appears we must have established muscle memory for a physical task.[3]

Other researchers have dug deeper into this phenomenon and found some people are simply better at producing imagery than others. They, in turn, performed better on a balancing task.[4] Of course, affecting a simple outcome such as shooting a basketball or balancing on one foot is a far cry from affecting complex situations through the simple act of visualization. A host of much more complicated factors affects outcomes in the real world. Moreover, there's a big difference between imagining a basketball going through the hoop versus imagining, developing, and enacting something as complex as a story about the future that has a complicated plot, characters with convoluted relationships, and conflict often involving macro forces such as the economy or weather events. But what if this capacity to produce imagery about something that has not yet occurred actually improves the likelihood that we can enact that imagined future? It would appear that our minds are prewired to simulate the future to better enable us to be the authors of almost any outcome imaginable.

The Mind:
A Powerful Simulation Machine

Some hypothesize we're equipped to handle the cognitive challenge of imagining the future and making it happen because our minds are powerful simulation machines capable of imagining, replicating, and rehearsing events. Psychologists Daniel Gilbert and Timothy Wilson have been exploring these questions. "Just as retrospection refers to our ability to re-experience the past, prospection refers to our ability to 'pre-experience' the future by simulating it in our minds."[5] This prospective ability uses many of the brain's functional capacities used in recalling the past and telling a story.

Of even greater relevance is what happens when we purposefully engage in prospective thinking and storytelling, repeatedly practicing the new story. Experimental psychologists Szpunar and Schacter discovered the repeated imagining and telling of a prospective story made the future scenario more plausible in participants' minds. They call this "imagination inflation."[6]

There are additional benefits. Repeated imagining of the future story also improves decision-making in the present. For example, the more people imagined reaching their healthy weight, the easier it was for them to make sound eating decisions in the here and now.[7] In a related study, overweight women who engaged in episodic future thinking consumed fewer calories while increasing calories from protein and reducing those from fat.[8]

Seeing future events in rich detail also tends to reduce our anxiety and increase our sense of well-being[9] while also increasing the chances of remembering our intentions and acting on them.[10] People who engage in the rehearsal of future travels and navigating complicated routes perform better when confronted with the trip than those who don't. By just imagining the future, we become better planners.[11]

There also appears to be real value in fantasizing about the future when it comes to improving performance. Researchers such as Dominique Morisano have been exploring ways to help students build greater resilience and meaning in their lives through the act of envisioning. "University students were asked to imagine either the goal of doing well on an upcoming midterm or to focus on imagining the details of the process required to attain a good mark. Students who engaged in process-simulation performed significantly better on the test than those who merely imagined the positive outcome."[12]

Also, the vividness of imagery impacts how we interact and construct our future. Researchers into consumer behavior such as Priyali Rajagopal and Nicole Montgomery exposed research participants to a fictional ad about popcorn replete with rich, descriptive copy and evocative photographs. A week later, those who viewed these ads were as likely to say they had tasted the popcorn as those who sampled the actual product.[13] They refer to this as a "false experience." It points to how profoundly suggestible we are.

Finally, the process of envisioning the future can have a substantive impact on our current health and well-being. Laura King, a psychologist focused on the health benefits of writing, has been experimenting for some time with the power of asking students to write about their life goals. After simply writing about their plans, they reported significantly higher measures of psychological well-being. Interestingly, before the study, there was no difference between the experimental and control groups' use of the school clinic. But after this modest act of writing about their plans, the experimental group's visits were significantly less a full five months after the experiment.[14] The act of prospective thinking may just change us in ways we never imagined possible.

Challenges with Imagining the Future

The question then is, why don't we succeed more often if imagining the future is so simple? Why do we set goals at the beginning of each year to find we haven't even come close to realizing them when December 31 rolls around?

All too often, we act impulsively in the present without considering the impact on our future self, months or years from now. We reach out and take the crème éclair from the server's tray because it looks so tempting. The delectable treat anesthetizes us to the implications for our waistline a month from now when it's swimsuit season. Or, we rashly purchase expensive new cars every three years, strapping us with large monthly payments because we can seemingly afford it. Never does it cross our minds to wonder what the implications of this purchase are for our retirement.

The problem would appear to be a deficiency of imagination. That future self is entirely absent in our decision-making process and does not have legal representation at the table to voice an objection on behalf of the future! Imagine if that were the case as your hand impulsively reached for the calorie-laden dessert. Your future self's representative would dutifully speak up, loudly clearing his or her throat to get your attention. "On behalf of your future self, I'd like to counsel you to cease and desist this abhorrent action which adversely affects you in the future, degrading your health, happiness, and long life, not to speak of your waistline." Who among us would not pause and reconsider what we're doing and whether we would come to regret it?

Another factor is that some of us may be far worse at seeing possibilities in the future because it's difficult for us to recall the past accurately. We have already seen how our memories of the past are malleable and colored by multiple psychological factors. We're likely to substantially miss the mark if we use those memories as the building blocks to simulate what to expect in the future. As Gilbert and Wilson point out, "It seems that everyone remembers their best day, their worst day, and their yesterday. Because unusual events and recent events are so memorable, people tend to use them when constructing simulations of future events."[15] The problem is the best day, worst day, and yesterday often are not necessarily representative of a typical day. That's why we often predict adverse events will be worse than they turn out to be, and inversely why good events frequently aren't as good as we expected them to be. For example, if you just visited your sister who has two fabulous youngsters and you had a great time playing with them, you might likely build a picture of parental bliss far from the day-to-day reality of parenting. Your fantasy most probably won't contain sleepless nights walking a colicky baby, dealing with stinky diapers or temper tantrums in public places, or how your child's sickness would make you incredibly anxious. Instead, it will be colored by yesterday's events that make parenting seem like a frolicking good time.

The more an event is in the distant future, the more inaccurately we'll envision how it could play out. We'll also pay less attention to nonessential elements in our decision-making. Inversely, the nearer the future, the more we give it in-depth thought. In the previously stated example, if you were attempting to get pregnant today, it's more likely you'd weigh collateral issues in your decision-making. You'd anticipate more accurately how getting pregnant would affect your current uncomplicated lifestyle. There would be no time for weekday movies and dinners out, last-minute decisions to take a trip, and leisurely Sunday mornings drinking coffee and reading the paper in bed.

Another variant of this issue is when we imagine something catastrophic happening, like a crippling car accident. Or some incredibly good experience, such as getting that promotion we've been angling for over the past year. As we imagine the future, our minds tend to gravitate to the initial day when all this occurred, when the respective pain or joy was the most intense. We have a much more difficult time building a picture of what life would be like a few months hence, or a year or two down the road.

In the first example, we'd amplify the difficulties of being injured, focusing on the debilitating pain. We wouldn't imagine what it would be like when we're on the road to recovery with our discomfort relatively well managed. In the other example, in our minds, we'd inflate the fantastic benefits of a promotion only to discover a few weeks later the extra money and prestige came with bone-crushing responsibilities. In the end, it might not profoundly change our daily happiness or fulfillment. We simply overestimate the consequences of bad things and good things—a blind spot we must accommodate whenever we engage in any kind of future envisioning.

Other Narrative Blind Spots

Many of us struggle with more complex kinds of imagining or "storying" the future when there's a lot at stake. This is particularly true for the adverse effects of climate change, for example, and the existential threat it poses. A recent study by experimental psychologists Schubert, Caviola, and Faber highlights how our minds have a blind spot when confronting potential catastrophes with far-reaching consequences.[16] They tested this premise by posing three outcomes to research participants concerning climate change: 1) no one dies as a result of the climate crisis; 2) 80 percent of the human race is wiped out, but we go on to regenerate ourselves; or 3) 100 percent of the human race is killed, and we become extinct.

Unfortunately, most of us are not living or acting as though either of the latter two scenarios is possible. We're still merrily row-row-rowing our boat down the stream, denying there's a calamitous waterfall just around the bend. Yet, even those who recognize and embrace the idea that humans are the root cause of the growing climate crisis have difficulty accepting a modicum of sacrifice. We're not alone in this regard. History is peppered with examples where people knew their consumption behavior would lead to devastation and misfortune, but they simply couldn't muster the collective will to do anything about it. In *Collapse*, Jared Diamond recounts numerous instances where communities knowingly exhausted their natural resources to the point where none could survive.[17] A classic case was Easter Island in the eighteenth century. Inhabitants deforested the island in full recognition of the consequences, making it uninhabitable. They basically couldn't or didn't know how to stop themselves from committing what amounted to environmental *harakiri*.

Another facet of our failure to beneficially act to avert cataclysmic disasters is our tendency to discount the problem temporally. It's so far off in the future we choose not to deal with it. Many of us rationalize why we don't need to act through the mistaken belief future generations will be better equipped technologically to solve the problem. Or we believe the problem won't show up for a few centuries, so why fret?

The underlying reason may simply be there is such a long lag perceptually between the causes of the problem and the potential effect. Therefore, we discount it.[18] We come by this blind spot quite naturally. After all, evolutionarily, we had little reason to concern ourselves with consequences one hundred or two hundred years in the future. Things changed very slowly for millennia until the twentieth century. Agriculturally centered societies built their lives around the dependable changing of the seasons. They measured time organically, expecting tomorrow to be much like today, and the coming spring to be much like past springs.

264 | Richard Stone & Scott Livengood

Because of this, humans learned quite understandably to be slow to act when it comes to instituting new policies or laws.

With the advent of the Industrial Revolution, though, the pace of change accelerated geometrically, forcing our sense of time to evolve. In the last years, we've developed a broader horizon for thinking about the future and the impact of our actions. But it still only extends out about fifteen years.[19] It taxes our brains to envision the consequences of using oil-based products and emitting immense amounts of carbon twenty, thirty, forty, or one hundred years from today. To make matters worse, it's relatively invisible to the human eye. As we attempt to get our heads around the issue's enormity, the MEGO effect sets in—My Eyes Glaze Over. Unfortunately, the MEGO effect is indicative of the responses of our current political institutions to a problem overwhelming their capacity to see the danger and act.

A recent poll by the Energy Policy Institute at the University of Chicago reinforces this notion. While a large percentage of people acknowledge there's a problem, a full 29 percent of our population don't buy it. Those who do accept the science seem to be unwilling to make a sacrifice to fix the issue. When asked if they'd pay a small tax on their electric bill to underwrite the costs of addressing the problem, only 57 percent of Americans would support a paltry one-dollar-a-month surcharge. If the monthly tax went up to ten dollars a month, the numbers supporting the idea fall precipitously to 28 percent. The US is not alone in this regard. People in Canada demonstrate a similar noncommittal attitude.[20]

We find ourselves today in this confounding quandary. Understanding and acting on the climate crisis isn't a failure of science and research; it's a shortcoming of our imagining, storytelling, and persuasion skills. Our failure to not see or imagine ourselves as an integral part of this planet may also be at the root of the problem. One thing is certain. If we're going to build a more sustainable future successfully, all of us must learn how to harness our SQ in new and novel ways.

Painting a Better Future
through Strategic Narratives

Starting in the 1990s, many companies began reassessing the effectiveness of their strategic-planning efforts. It required enormous amounts of money and time to research and produce these documents. When organizations like 3M did a postmortem to see the degree to which their strategic plans predicted the future, there were huge disparities. To make matters worse, all too often, these plans took up residence in large binders on dusty bookshelves, rarely ever viewed again.

Why are attempts to predict the future so easily disregarded? And, how can the art and science of narrative thinking help companies and people better prepare for what's coming down the road?

At 3M, they found several serious flaws with both the process and the end product. For starters, strategic plans proved to be too general to make a difference for teams expected to implement their recommendations.[21] Goals like "increase market share by 14 percent" sound terrific on the face of things. But if you scratch beneath the surface, there may be only flimsy reasoning why achieving this goal is doable, much less desirable. Such a target doesn't address why we think we could steal market share from some of our stiffest competitors, how we should think about doing it, what it would take internally to gear up production to meet the added demand, or how we'd train our folks to be more effective at selling. Nor does such a broad proclamation consider the fact our competition would certainly not take our aggressive moves lying down. If you were reading the plan and came across this lofty goal, how would you start operationalizing it? Doing business is complicated, and making significant change requires action across a host of dimensions. Summing it all up in a simple statement like "increase market share by 14 percent" doesn't begin to do justice to the enormity of what leadership is expecting everyone down the line to do to succeed.

Looking more deeply at why strategic plans frequently fail to produce the returns we'd expect, the problem appears to reside in that they all too often rely on bullet formats. Lists of good things to do like decreasing costs, increasing market share, and improving the bottom line sound like wishes uttered at Santa's knee. Are they obtainable business objectives grounded in some kind of shared reality? It's no wonder people hear these goals fervently spoken by their CEO at the annual kickoff meeting and then wander back to their cubicles to pick up where they left off. What are they to do without any significant understanding of what they'd have to do differently in their personal or team domain to get there? A lot of thinking may have gone into the declared goals. And bullets are certainly an economical shorthand for summing up the robust discussions of the leadership team. Unfortunately, they do little to inspire innovative action by those who have to make it happen.

With this recognition, 3M embarked nearly twenty-five years ago to reinvent the planning process, grounding it in story-making.[22] Why? Stories accomplish something bullets don't. They provide a rich context for decision-making, infusing dimensionality into your thinking about the future. Whereas bullets tend to be unidimensional, stories give the reader a three-dimensional, nuanced picture of reality. The added benefit is that storying the future forces us to think more robustly about the environment we're attempting to influence and consider how people will react if we tack in a new direction. Stories force people to consider a more comprehensive array of conditions and trends affecting desired outcomes. In a story, we can consider the ways competitors have behaved in the past to predict better how they might act in the future. Plus, we can foresee how expected changes with environmental degradation, shifts in the global economy, and government policies could affect our strategic moves. A strategic narrative also more fully explores the intricacy of relationships between business partners, suppliers, and even competitors. It can even question whether we should view our competitors as such or imagine what it would be like to develop a cooperative relationship with them. Could we be collaborators and competitors at the same time? Lastly, a good story can reveal critical, invisible assumptions concealed in plans relying heavily on bullets. When these are made explicit, the reader can more fully trust the story's integrity or question its veracity if they disagree with key suppositions.

The most significant benefit of a storied approach to planning is you can map complex, critical functions within a business to provide a more realistic picture of how a small change here can have huge repercussions over there. In this sense, strategic narratives draw upon story-making's inherent structure, what we refer to as "narrative schema." Such descriptions tap into the wiring of employees' brains and provide them with a familiar mental structure to understand the future and their role in it.

For example, in narrative schema terms, our brain is looking to explain the state of affairs. In the business tale, this shows up as a robust analysis of competitors and trends affecting the market's growth or contraction. The story includes not only what they're doing today, but what you expect them to do in the coming months and years ahead.

An initial event drives all stories. While we acknowledge the world's complexities often make it challenging to reduce multiple variables down to a simple cause, it's important to recognize there may be one major factor driving the plot of your future narrative. For example, companies are currently launching communication satellites to blanket the globe. Soon anyone on the ground with a reception device the size of a notebook will be able to get access to the worldwide web at speeds envied by today's businesses. What happens when everyone, all seven-plus billion of us, can connect? That's a question worthy of exploration.

The inquiry then becomes, how should we respond to this anticipated change? Writing this story will force you and your team to delve into the complex relationships between a multiplicity of factors, which leads us to complicating action. Nothing is a straight line in business or life. Now you have the makings for a "strap yourself into the pilot's seat" story filled with twists, turns, and unexpected outcomes. As you'll see in the next discussion, those unexpected turns are the things you need to be on the lookout for because they are so difficult to read and predict.

Finally, the story is never finished. One ending is the beginning of a new episode in a never-ending story, presuming your business can weather all of the changes it must traverse to survive. Embrace the tale with the curiosity of any author. This is the secret to staying engaged with the unfolding world of your life and the life of your business.

What Can We Learn from Scenario Planning?

Fundamentally, we can learn three essential things from scenario planning to inform any of our efforts to envision the future. First, the future is inherently uncertain. There are so many forces at work that can derail any of our attempts to predict accurately what will happen in the next year, much less the next five, ten, or fifty years. Many of these unforeseen dynamics can emerge from the proverbial left field. While many epidemiologists have been predicting a worldwide pandemic for years, COVID-19 caught most business and government leaders flatfooted. The further out we move from the present, the more uncertain things become.

Second, we must attempt to imagine and identify as many factors as possible that affect our future. Whether you're doing this alone or with a team, you no doubt will ascertain a long list of likely forces at play. Some have a strong valence. Others may be a factor but of less import. In all likelihood, you'll find a handful of things you need to zero in on. Here's where Paula Underwood's Rule of Six described in Chapter 3 can be helpful.

Third, when peering into the future, do your best to identify trends rooted in the past that are likely to continue for some time. Ask two questions. First, are they ascendant or descendent? Second, how do they interplay with other trends and forces affecting a situation?

For example, forty years ago, very few people ever considered how their food was grown or whether farmers treated it with pesticides. The only place you could find organic vegetables was at a specialty co-op. Today, organics are a prominent feature in the fresh vegetable and fruit aisles of every grocery store. It's a reasonably good bet interest in organics will continue as people examine the linkages between health and pesticides more and more. If I were a farmer or a grocery chain, gambling on this ascendant trend would be a sensible bet. With that said, are there factors that could limit this growth? Certainly. A momentous economic crash would drive people to tighten their budgets and think twice about paying extra for an organic tomato. During the last recession, we witnessed a downturn impacting disposable incomes, and it would be naïve to assume that another such event won't occur in the coming years. We must also consider the increases in unprecedented warming or drought in some regions while others experience abnormal amounts of rainfall. If you're a grower, planning for the future in this context just became a lot more complicated, even if you buy into the assumption that interest in organic vegetables and fruit will continue to expand.

A related concept is the importance of identifying factors you're dead sure will occur. In the scenario-planning world, each of these is called a TINA—There Is No Alternative. In considering fixing the climate crisis, one TINA is the need to radically reduce carbon-producing forms of energy production. There is a broad consensus we must do this. But still, there are a plethora of possible pathways we can pursue. Should we continue to use gas and coal to generate electricity, but develop better emissions-scrubbing technologies to capture the carbon? Would it be better to double down and undertake the equivalent of the Manhattan Project and build enough solar- and wind-powered alternatives to meet all of our energy needs in the coming ten years? What about outlawing combustion-powered cars in ten years and demand we all drive electric vehicles? Or should we forget about all the previous alternatives and discover new technologies to pull CO_2 from the air in massive quantities? In all probability, any viable solution to quickly fix the problem will require an emphasis on a combination of these and other solutions. But as we have seen, whether the electorate will accede to the changes and sacrifices they may have to make to save our planet is another question altogether.

To interlace all of these possible solutions, we must exercise our capacity to imagine the world as a better place with the solution in force, vividly and persuasively painting this picture for a broad audience. This is true whether it's the electorate or the employees of your company. While there is a wealth of science involved in thinking about issues like climate change, ultimately, it comes down to our artistic gifts to envision and communicate a new, credible story that rings true in the minds of listeners and incites real action and change.

One necessary outgrowth of this kind of prospective imagining is anticipating the unintended consequences of our tale-making. We must have a rich sense of the many subplots contributing to any multifaceted story. How would countries in the Middle East be destabilized if suddenly the market for their oil abruptly dried up? Solving the climate crisis could inadvertently lead to political upheaval and civil war in this region. What would happen to the millions of petroleum workers who would lose their jobs in the transition and be unable to find comparable employment in the green economy? What would we do to support people in communities where the entire economic infrastructure is dependent on oil refining or fracking? Seeing new possibilities is all well and good. Building a cohesive plan to get there requires more than just imagination. In this case, developing your SQ is necessary but not sufficient for the task ahead. We need people in the sciences and engineering, politics, sociology, strategy, business, and education to blend their know-how with the creative power of their narrative imaginations to ensure our children and our planet have a bright future filled with promise.

Notes from the Field: How One Company Is Helping Others Envision a Better Future

Earlier in my career, I (Richard) had the good fortune to work as the StoryAnalytics Master for IDEAS, a brand and experience design firm based in Orlando, Florida.[23] My colleague Bob Allen created IDEAS when he bought his division from Disney. I recently caught up with Bob, the IDEAS Chief Storytelling Officer, to discuss the company's unique process for helping organizations see future possibilities and build bridges for getting there.

In Bob's early career as a Disney Imagineer, they used design charettes to flesh out ideas for theme parks and rides. These sessions had a lot more in common with rugby matches than the typical corporate brainstorming get-together.

> Typically, we'd have a red team, a blue team, and a green team. An idea originating at the Paris Art Institute informed the design of charettes. Artists lived in a U-shaped building with a courtyard in the center. The instructor would have a charette, a cart with a goat harnessed to it, pulled into the courtyard. Without leaving your room, your assignment was to paint the cart and goat. As you'd expect, the charette looked quite different depending on your line of sight and the position of the sun in the sky. Each painter would then render a unique interpretation of the charette.
>
> Our process of StoryJam has its roots in the charette,

rendering different points of view. We soon realized the Disney charettes' competitive nature was not at all conducive to obtaining the best results. So, we engineered a much more collaborative process built around a story's six components— character, plot, setting, conflict, emotion, and voice. We're still using this approach today after over 220 StoryJams.

The idea had a simple premise—let's look at everybody as a designer. They needn't have an artistic or literary background. We've found all of us are natural storytellers if we're put in a safe environment encouraging this latent talent. It's jamming together like a group of musicians. That's how we came up with the name. We've done them in eight countries, even when we were the only people in the room who spoke English. The cool thing is it always works. Adults participating in the process quickly realize you can't make a mistake when making up and telling stories. All we do is light the fuse, and then they take it from there. Perhaps the real key is the process is fun.

It started with the question of how do we encourage clients to iterate on an idea playfully? If we're skillful and organize the play, not around just creative ideas, but around what we see as the six story components, we realized their ideas for creating the future would naturally flow. It didn't depend on whether it was about designing a new theme park, fixing a hotel with below-par occupancy, building somebody's brand, or changing behavior in an organization to better support the company's objectives. The bonus was we found we could take people to places they didn't think they could go.

For one recent client attempting to refresh their brand to become more relevant, when we delivered the experience design plan, they commented there was much more to their brand than they thought. To this typical response, we reply, "Well, you were there. It didn't come from us. That's what you guys said." In this particular case, the story they told about their brand was different from how they were living their brand every day. This is where the rubber meets the road. We said, "You guys need to decide if you want to go there. If you do, then let's start building a pathway to get to that future brand." You see, from our perspective, the StoryJam serves as an innovation engine.

The thing StoryJam gives the organization is not just a future—it's dozens of futures. Like every good story, the plot lines branch out. If you change one character's relationship with another character, the outcome is very different. In our deliverables, we explore these alternate realities living today only as possibilities. Once they choose which future they want to aim for, we then get quite prescriptive about what they need to do to get there. If, for example, we're looking at creating a remarkable guest pathway at a theme park, we might identify a half dozen archetypical characters who embody different attributes of their guest universe. We take each of those personas and ask, "What do they think? What do they feel? What do they smell? What's on their mind? What's the main thing they want?" From here, we develop a core story that defines the things you're required to give those characters if you want them to feel good. If it's about redesigning a motorcycle, then it needs to have this much horsepower and this kind of chrome. Or, if it's a theme park, it has to have six lands with these kinds of rides and experiences.

What's important about this process of fiction-making is it does have tangible links to reality. In almost every case, we tie all of that narrative material to market analytics. With the core story in one hand and the market realities in the other, we begin designing artwork and storyboards to visualize what is happening in this new future. Then, the architects, engineers, and marketing professionals have something truly tangible to inform every facet of their work.

The longevity of these kinds of insights and story-making often surprises us. One healthcare organization came to us seeking to create a remarkable patient experience and used our deliverables for years as a reference when designing training and other enculturation activities. Recently, we reconnected with a client at a large law enforcement training facility where we helped them envision how training should be developed and delivered in the twenty-first century. He sent us a picture of a dog-eared, coffee-stained, beaten-up version of the story bible we created for them years ago, saying he takes it to every single meeting when they're making decisions on training design. This ensures everybody is staying "on story."

Here's the most crucial lesson from StoryJam when it comes to envisioning the future. Plenty of diverse voices in the room will create a better picture of tomorrow, essential in making up your prospective story. Even have naysayers at the table. Over the many years facilitating StoryJams, we discovered twenty-five people is optimal for the process. The power of these many differing points of view becomes rich fodder for creating a robust, durable story that's likely to succeed.

Look Around—The Future Is Staring You in the Face

There's an old saying: the future is already here, it's just spotty in the way it's showing up. A few people in every field of life are pioneers, innovating new approaches to all kinds of things and solving problems vexing large swathes of society. Often, they labor away quietly in obscurity, but all too often, their work is in plain sight, if only we took the time to look.

From the world of positive deviance, there's a recognition these people can teach us a great deal about how to solve what appear to be intractable issues.

This idea got its start when Jerry and Monique Sternin, who worked with Save the Children, were sent to Vietnam to tackle malnutrition in children under age five.[24] They weren't the first nongovernmental group attempting to address this chronic issue. Upon arrival, they were summarily called into the Ministry of Health and told they had six months to come up with a solution, or they would be put back on a plane to the United States. The Vietnamese government had grown weary of outsiders coming in to tell them how to improve their population's health with no demonstrable results.

Where to start, given such a short window of time? They decided to define a small region of the country and collect as much information as possible by interviewing mothers, weighing their young children, and gathering data on what and when they were feeding them. Something remarkable emerged. Those mothers whose children were malnourished, the vast majority surveyed, provided their children the same foods adults ate—a relatively low-protein diet relying on rice. Moreover, the young children were fed just twice a day like the adults, served at the same table, and had to compete with the older children and adults for their share of the meal.

But a minority of children were not malnourished. When Jerry and Monique looked at their data, an entirely different picture surfaced. Mothers of these kids went into the rice paddies and collected small freshwater shrimp and various vegetable greens, then mixed them into the rice mixture. Plus, they fed their children three times a day, not twice, and did so away from the large table where the adults ate, so their children didn't have to compete for food. These moms were the positive deviants, and no doubt probably learned these practices from their mothers, as their mothers had learned from their mothers. This simple difference in practice seemed to be at the heart of the elusive solution. It had been there all along, but no one looked for it.

The next big question was, how could they change the practices of the 80 percent of women who were feeding their children in the traditional manner? The answer proved relatively straightforward. Who would have more credibility with mothers in a village, their neighbors or an outside government official? The obvious answer was their neighbors, so the researchers created a program whereby the positive deviant mothers invited other mothers in their village to their home to teach them their secret. It worked. Within a short time, they eliminated childhood malnourishment.

Since this experiment, people have been using this principle to tackle all kinds of stubborn problems. For example, in hospitals struggling with MRSA bacterial infections, often there are floors where they're not having any issue with this kind of contagion. Sure enough, people on those floors have quietly experimented and found ways to prevent the spread of the disease. All that's needed is for them to teach other teams in the hospital what they have learned.

Whatever problem you're facing begging for a different future, look around for places where others have already solved it. They're the positive deviants who have already been to the future and returned with knowledge and insight that can help you travel to your future at the speed of light.

How the Story of the Future Can Humanize Today

We all spend an excessive amount of time concerned about what may or may not happen tomorrow. This obsession can make us anxious. Alternately, it can fill us with excited anticipation. While so many Eastern religious traditions admonish us to "to be here now," it appears none of us can avoid peeking around the corner. Why? What would it mean to live without a future? In some ways, we'd be living without a story. We are, after all, when all is said and done, story creatures at heart. We all need an account of a future filled with optimism and possibility. The ability to imagine a brighter future imbues us with strength and courage, especially if we're presently experiencing pain or misery.

In contrast, if all we can imagine is a continuation of a gloomy desolation, we become hollow shells, lost. Moreover, when we don't know the story of people spanning their past, present, and future, it is much easier to treat them as less than human. Something about knowing another's hopes and dreams makes them more real for us, more multidimensional and deserving of our highest regard.

The story of Robert Desnos powerfully captures this idea. He was a French poet who dared to face down a Nazi death squad while imprisoned in Buchenwald. His story may lend inspiration to your journey with your future in your hands. This account was captured by Nicky González Yuen,[25] who had been told the tale by a Holocaust survivor who witnessed the event.

One morning, Desnos and dozens of other camp inmates were hustled onto a truck and driven into the nearby countryside. Wordlessly everyone on the transport knew that the Nazis were going to kill them. The guards motioned for them to stand in a line. Somberly, they waited for their gruesome fate. Unexpectedly, Desnos stepped out of line and took the palm of a young woman and enthusiastically asked if he could tell her fortune. Shocked, she barely nodded yes. He began weaving a tale where she would find romance, marry the man of her dreams, have many children, and live a long, prosperous life. This prediction, amidst the horror of the impending execution, brought a faint smile to her face as she imagined this future.

A man standing next to her thrust his hand forward. "Tell my fortune." Desnos wove a tale of remarkable accomplishments and a life fulfilled. Another person extended her hand, requesting the fortune teller to weave his magic. Then another. And another.

Each person endowed with Desnos' predictive power became exuberant, no longer prisoners of a horrible dead-end reality defined by their Nazi captors.

The young guards witnessing this transformation were themselves touched. Shooting lifeless shells was an act they had all participated in numerous times. But killing beings endowed with a future became something they simply couldn't stomach. They hustled the assembled crowd onto the truck and drove them back to the camp without a word. While there is no way to account for how many of these people who had their fortune told survived the Nazi death machine, some did. Their imagined future saved them. Without Desnos, the storyteller, they would have most surely been lost.

We each need the future. The future needs us. It's beckoning. Calling. Waiting. It's time we all create this story and fill it with optimistic possibilities. Our lives depend on it, as do the lives of future generations. Let's be sure we are envisioning a world where our children, their children, and their children can experience the wonder of being human. Let's create a living story worthy of the heroic tales of old.

Journey Deeper

What If . . .

How can we best leap from the present into a future that is only a glimmer in our eye? The two words "What if . . ." are a story-starter game that authors of fiction and oral storytellers have been playing for centuries. *What if* invites the imagination to journey out and explore the consequences of someone taking an unexpected step. Nothing is fixed. Everything is possible. The only limitation is the inventiveness of your imagination. This is how people innovate new products, forge transformative new directions in their lives, and discover new lands, either physically or metaphorically. So, look around and imagine what could be different if only . . .

Use Metaphors to Create Thought Experiments

When asked how he made significant scientific leaps, Albert Einstein attributed it to his ability to travel to the future in his imagination using a metaphor to embody the problem he was contemplating. These thought experiments revealed many of the secrets of the universe. For example, once he imagined himself riding on a train chasing a beam of light, which led him to his theory of relativity.

Instead of using your abstract and analytic thought processes to discern the future, imagine the future through the lens of a metaphor taking you to places you might not have conceived. Be a butterfly adrift in the winds of change, lighting only at highly attractive and conducive places. How might you see your future as such a creature? Or, consider being a hurricane sweeping in from the Gulf of Mexico. How would that change the obstacles you confront? Or, be a ferocious lion who is single-minded about catching its prey. What can you learn about creating a parallel future from these points of view? How could you travel through time by chasing a beam of light?

Imagine a Failed Future

Bob Allen's IDEAS team often invites StoryJam participants to imagine a failed future in its story-envisioning process. For those of you who believe only positive visions of the future are desirable, here's a contradictory idea. Seek to identify potentially adverse outcomes, befriending a future filled with failure. It can teach you a great deal about things you need to do today to avert such an unfavorable conclusion. Consider the faults in your best plans, then write about them. If it's helpful, imagine you're a reporter from a reputable business publication researching the failure. What led to the demise of your undertaking? This approach can illuminate the things you need to do today to shift the dynamics or issues causing this undesirable outcome. What did leaders do incorrectly? How did people underestimate certain factors? How did your team overestimate the degree to which customers would embrace what you offered them? Seeing the future through this lens can help you get better at everything you do today, which has a lot to do with what happens tomorrow.

See the Future through Others' Eyes

We tend to look ahead of us from only our unique point of view. It can be powerfully instructive to step out of our skin and figuratively inhabit the body of others who have distinctive perspectives about a particular policy, product, or service. For example, if you were designing a new customer experience for a hospital, how could you see the delivery of care through the unique eyes of different kinds of patients? This perspective would reveal things you'd never see as an administrator or a doctor. These insights can help you set the trajectory for a whole new approach to caring for people. The result may even be safer care, given research suggests there's a very high correlation between positive patient experience and patient safety. In one hospital system I worked with years ago, they developed stories written from the perspectives of a doctor, a nurse, a housekeeper, a food service worker, and patients with different needs and diagnoses. These aspirational stories gave their staff a tangible sense of what was needed to deliver quality care in the twenty-first century.

Books We Recommend

Our friend Arvind Singhal introduced us to the concept of positive deviance. Every blue moon a mind-blowing idea comes along that can change the world, and this is one. Here are two great primers on how you can use this idea in every facet of your work to produce lasting change:

The Power of Positive Deviance: How Unlikely Innovators Solve the World's Toughest Problems by Richard Pascale, Jerry Sternin, and Monique Sternin

Inspiring Change and Saving Lives: The Positive Deviance Way by Arvind Singhal, Prucia Buscell, and Curt Lindberg

There are some terrific resources being published today that can teach you how to expand your approach to innovation and design thinking. Here are a few of our favorites:

The Design Thinking Playbook: Mindful Digital Transformation of Teams, Products, Services, Businesses, and Ecosystems by Michael Lewrick, Patrick Link, and Larry Leifer

Sprint: How to Solve Big Problems and Test New Ideas in Just Five Days by Jake Knapp, John Zeratsky, and Braden Kowitz

New Thinking, New Future by Samuel R. Chand

EPILOGUE

The Power of Story to Elevate and Heal Our World

As we complete our story journey, we want to sew together the new perspective of Story Intelligence with a more fundamental idea. Story is an inescapable force akin to gravity that infuses every thought that enters our minds and every experience we have. To be human is to be a storyteller. When you tell a story, you are sharing your heart, your vision, and your hopes. You are also giving your listeners your invaluable energy, an energy that's rooted in the creation of the world. As Muriel Rukeyser so aptly describes our human reality, "The Universe is made of stories, not of atoms."[1]

Every cultural tradition we're aware of has honored this force in nature, building ritual containers to unleash its power in our communities and ignite the imaginations of younger generations. In one East African tradition that we admire, story played an essential role in helping people better understand their relationship to this world and the imagined and unseen worlds that existed eons before we inhabited this planet.

Imagine as the moon began to rise, the tribe gathering around a roaring fire. In the early hours of the evening, they'd share about the events that occurred that day. Someone might remark how he had witnessed a hawk swooping in to catch a field mouse. A mother would recount a funny incident in which a young baby dumped her food on her brother's head. An elder in the community might share how she discovered a small glade where a unique and valued herb grew.

As the evening progressed, the telling would turn to remembrances of treasured times as people reminisced about small, incidental things that, in retrospect, became infused with meaning and relevance. Now, imagine one of the older tribe members turning to a younger person and telling her of fond times he spent fishing or hunting with her grandfather, who is long since dead. This touching recollection would remind others of fond memories of the dearly departed, sparking more sharing that would bring tears to some, but most often laughter and joy.

As the moon rose higher in the sky, the telling would turn to stories about the ancestors going back many generations, perhaps as much as ten thousand years ago. These were not just mythical stories about bygone days. In traditional cultures like this one, people remembered the ancestors by their names and their legendary accomplishments that often bordered on the edge of supernatural powers.

As the flames died down with the coals still radiating heat and light, the storytelling would turn to the folktales about the ordinary people embodying insights about our human foibles and the challenges of living in a community. Then came the fables about the animal people, filled with fundamental truths. These tales embody the archetypal difficulties inherent in being human even though their protagonists were creatures like Anansi the Spider and Raven.

In the early-morning hours, as the fire faded to soft, glowing embers, the telling would seamlessly turn to how the world came into being. These stories reached back into time, imagining what was in our Creator's mind when he or she first decided to make the stars, the earth we inhabit, and the first humans. They even included stories about the creation of stories themselves.

Over a few hours, the people linked the experiences of their everyday lives with all those who preceded them to the beginning of time itself. In this tradition they call this journey through time "Climbing the Ladder to the Moon." Imagine if all of us had that sense of perspective and connection to our ancestors, to the stories of the beginning of human history, weaving together our personal stories with accounts of the origin of our cosmos. What if we could all see ourselves as made from "star stuff," as Carl Sagan so fittingly put it?[2] Even better, maybe now we are each discovering that we are essentially, in every fiber of our body, the stuff of stories. Like a force as compelling as gravity, it can weave us together into a people with a collective, shared history.

Story is indeed a universal force driving all of human culture. But it is up to us whether we use it for good or for evil. If misused, it can lead to tragic consequences, creating discord between peoples. It can even destroy lives. If used with integrity, it can lead to myriad opportunities to generate healing for ourselves and the world as a whole and deepen our understanding of "the other."

Two pertinent concepts come from the Jewish tradition, Tikkun Halev and Tikkun Olam, translated loosely as healing the heart and healing the world. These ideas have roots in a story that goes back to the beginning of time first described by Isaac Luria, a mystic who lived in the sixteenth century. Before the world came into being, the Creator fashioned vessels to hold Divine Light. But the Light was so powerful it shattered the vessels and scattered the shards across the cosmos, creating the diverse worlds that now populate our universe.

This creation story concludes with us. It's our task as humans to gather these scattered shards and reunite them to, in a sense, finish God's work. We must repair our broken and hardened hearts—Tikkun Halev—and stitch back together all that is damaged and fractured in our world—Tikkun Olam.

There is nothing in the universe better suited to this task than the Seven Powers of Story and nurturing your Story Intelligence. As you explore these powers in your own life, we encourage you to embrace them as invaluable resources to deepen your self-understanding. By becoming masterful in their use, you are collecting the shards of light that reflect your memories of the past, your experiences of the present, and your hopes for the future. By understanding the ethical and existential implications of every story you tell, you can heal all that is broken within you and in the world around you. Let the light illuminate all that you cherish about the past. Shine it as a beacon to brighten your path forward as you work to address the many issues begging for repair in your community and the world at large. In this way, you can become a powerful vessel for humanity's light, bequeathing this vision to those around you and to the children who will become tomorrow's storytellers. They will become part of a grand tradition of giving birth to new, hopeful, and wondrous tales to sustain this beautiful planet.

Acknowledgments

Between us, we have close to eighty years of working with story, which in the parlance of Hollywood, that's how you become an overnight success. Along the way, a lot of people have contributed to our learning and have opened many doors. Sam Keen and Donald Davis have been significant teachers for both of us. Richard met Paula Underwood serendipitously at a Native American storytelling conference in the early '90s, and her wisdom still echoes loudly in his life and this book. Some guides and mentors we never met in person, but their writings have profoundly influenced our life directions, like Joseph Campbell.

Taking *Story Intelligence* from concept to completed manuscript has been a journey spanning nearly three years. Along the way, many have lent us a hand. We especially want to thank Kären Blumenthal for her editorial comments and direction. James Roose-Evans provided invaluable insight on how to better communicate the central themes of the book.

If you're one of Richard's friends, you no doubt lent your voice to the discussion of the book's title, and we appreciate your input. Each of our wives has played an instrumental supporting role. Richard's wife, Elizabeth Cohen, graciously read earlier drafts and provided invaluable feedback. Scott's wife, Michelle Livengood, has been an inspiration, sounding board, and supporter of the book and our StoryWork endeavor.

We so appreciate all of our colleagues who weighed in and reviewed the book. It's hard to know what you've got when you've been laboring so long, and your comments and encouragement have been affirming.

Finally, we want to acknowledge you, the reader. We hope that when you conclude *Story Intelligence* it's just a first step on an exciting journey that can change the way you see your life and the possibility to create a better future.

Endnotes

Introduction

[1] Emily Esfahani Smith, *The Power of Meaning: Crafting a Life That Matters* (Crown, 2017).
[2] Steven Sieden, *A Fuller View: Buckminster Fuller's Vision of Hope and Abundance for All* (Divine Arts Media, 2011).
[3] Daniel Goleman, *Emotional Intelligence* (Bantam, 2005).
[4] Joel Davitz and Michael Beldoch, *The Communication of Emotional Meaning* (McGraw-Hill, 1964).
[5] Howard Gardner, *Frames of Mind: The Theory of Multiple Intelligences* (Basic Books, 1983).
[6] Joseph Campbell, *The Power of Myth* (Anchor, 1991).
[7] Ezra Klein, *Why We're Polarized* (Avid Reader Press / Simon & Schuster, 2020).

Chapter 1

[1] Yuval Noah Harari, *Sapiens: A Brief History of Humankind* (Harper Perennial, 2018).
[2] Plato, *Phaedrus* (Hackett Publishing Company, 1995).
[3] Ibid.
[4] Kevin McSpadden, "You Now Have a Shorter Attention Span Than a Goldfish," *Time* (May 2015), time.com/3858309/attention-spans-goldfish/.
[5] Samuel Merritt University, "5 Ways Technology is Altering our Brains," Samuel Merritt University (March 2017), www.samuelmerritt.edu/news/5-ways-technology-altering-our-brains.

6 Chris Weller, "Silicon Valley parents are raising their kids tech-free — and it should be a red flag," *Business Insider* (February 18, 2018), www.businessinsider.com/silicon-valley-parents-raising-their-kids-tech-free-red-flag-2018-2.

7 Jerome Bruner, "The Narrative Construction of Reality," *Critical Inquiry* (1991).

8 Norman Holland, *Literature and the Brain* (The PsyArt Foundation, 2009).

9 Gregory S. Berns, Kristina Blaine, Michael J. Prietula, and Brandon E. Pye, "Short- and Long-Term Effects of a Novel on Connectivity in the Brain," *Brain Connectivity*, vol. 3, no. 6 (December 9, 2013), doi.org/10.1089/brain.2013.0166.

10 Ye Yuan, Judy Major-Girardin, and Steven Brown, "Storytelling Is Intrinsically Mentalistic: A Functional Magnetic Resonance Imaging Study of Narrative Production across Modalities," July 31, 2018, www.mitpressjournals.org/doi/abs/10.1162/jocn_a_01294.

11 Danielle N. Gunraj, Sri Siddhi, N. Upadhyay, Kenneth J. Houghton, Deanne L. Westerman and Celia M. Klin, "Simulating a story character's thoughts: Evidence from the directed forgetting task," *Journal of Memory and Language*, vol. 96 (October 2017).

12 Cristel Antonia Russell and Hope Jensen Schau, "When Narrative Brands End: The Impact of Narrative Closure and Consumption Sociality on Loss Accommodation," *Journal of Consumer Research*, vol. 40, no. 6 (April 2014), doi.org/10.1086/673959.

13 Pamela McClintock, "2019 global Box Office Revenue Hit Record $42.5B Despite 4 Percent Dip in U.S.," *Hollywood Reporter*, January 10, 2020, www.hollywoodreporter.com/news/2019-global-box-office-hit-record-425b-4-percent-plunge-us-1268600.

14 Branka Vuleta, "How Much Data Is Created Every Day?" SeedScientific, January 30, 2020, www.seedscientific.com/how-much-data-is-created-every-day/.

15 Paige Cooper, "23 YouTube Statistics that Matter to Marketers in 2020," Hootsuite Blog, December 17, 2019, www.blog.hootsuite.com/youtube-stats-marketers/.

16 Jim Milliot, "Print Sales Up Again in 2017," *Publishers Weekly*, January 5, 2018, www.publishersweekly.com/pw/by-topic/industry-news/bookselling/article/75760-print-sales-up-again-in-2017.html.

17 *Video Game Market Size, Share & Trends Analysis Report By Device, By Type, By Region, And Segment Forecasts, 2020–2027* (San Francisco: Grand View Research, 2020), www.grandviewresearch.com/industry-analysis/video-game-market.

18 Statista, "Value of the global entertainment and media market from 2011 to 2024," www.statista.com/statistics/237749/value-of-the-global-entertainment-and-media-market/.

19 Robert Fagan and Johanna Fagan, "Juvenile survival and benefits of play behavior in brown bears," *Ursus arctos, Evolutionary Ecology Research* (2004).

20 Stuart Brown, *Play: How it Shapes the Brain, Opens the Imagination, and Invigorates the Soul* (Avery, 2009).

21 Sergio M. Pellis, Vivien C. Pellis, and Brett T. Himmler, "How Play Makes for a More Adaptable Brain," *American Journal of Play* (Fall 2014).

22 Donald Winnicott, *Playing and Reality* (Routledge, 2005).

23 Henry B. Wonham, *Mark Twain and the Art of the Tall Tale* (Oxford University Press, 1993).

24 Isaac Weld, *Travels through the States of North America, and the Provinces of Upper and Lower Canada, during the Years 1795, 1796, and 1797* (J. Stockdale, 1800).

25 Mark Twain, *The Celebrated Jumping Frog of Calaveras County and Other Sketches* (Oxford University Press, 1996).

Chapter 2

1 Nikhil Swaminathan, "Gender Jabber: Do Women Talk More than Men? In a word: No. But then, how did the rumor get started?" *Scientific American* (July 6, 2007), www.scientificamerican.com/article/women-talk-more-than-men/.

2 Paul Reber, "What Is the Memory Capacity of the Human Brain?" *Scientific American Mind* (May 1, 2010), www.scientificamerican.com/article/what-is-the-memory-capacity/.

3 D. O. Hebb, *The Organization of Behavior* (Wiley, 1949).

4 Uri Hasson, "What Happens in the Brain When We Hear Stories," *TedBlog* (February 18, 2016), blog.ted.com/what-happens-in-the-brain-when-we-hear-stories-uri-hasson-at-ted2016/.

5 Tiffany Field, "Attachment as psychobiological attunement; being on the same wavelength," *The Psychobiology of Attachment and Separation* (Academic Press, 1985).

6 Angeles Arrien, "Four Questions," www.youtube.com/watch?v=HUJQlVeGZzY.

7 Robert Krulwich, "Mirror Neurons," *NOVA Science Now*, PBS (January 25, 2005).

8 Raymond A. Mar, Keith Oatley, and Jordan B. Peterson, "Exploring the link between reading fiction and empathy: Ruling out individual differences and examining outcomes," *Communications* (2009).

9 Ibid., 421.

10 Ibid., 422.

11 R. A. Mar, K. Oatley, M. Djikic, and Mullin, "Emotion and narrative fiction: Interactive influences before, during, and after reading," *Journal of Cognitive Emotion* (August 25, 2011).

12 Yuan, Major-Girardin, and Brown, "Storytelling Is Intrinsically Mentalistic."

13 Doriana De Marco, Elisa De Stefani, Diego Bernini, and Maurizio Gentilucci, "The effect of motor context on semantic processing," *Neuropsychologia* (May 2018).

14 Melanie C. Green and Timothy C. Brock, "The Role of Transportation in the Persuasiveness of Public Narratives," *Journal of Personality and Social Psychology* 79, no. 5 (2000), 701–721.

15 Ibid., 704.

16 Ibid., 707.

17 Ibid.

18 Russell Fazio and Mark Zanna, "Direct Experience and Attitude-Behavior Consistency," in *Advances in Experimental Social Psychology* (Elsevier, 1981).

19 Green and Brock, "The Role of Transportation in the Persuasiveness of Public Narratives," 702.

20 William Shakespeare, *Hamlet* (Simon & Schuster, 1992).

21 M. A. Bezdek, R. J. Gerrig, W. G. Wenzel, J. Shin, K. Pirog Revill, and E. H. Schumacher, "Neural evidence that suspense narrows attentional focus," *Neuroscience* (September 2015).

22 A. de Graaf and L. Hustinx, "The effect of story structure on emotion, transportation, and persuasion," *Information Design Journal* (2011).

23 Paul J. Zak, "Why Inspiring Stories Make Us React," Cerebrum (2015).

24 J. A. Barraza and P. J. Zak, "Empathy toward strangers triggers oxytocin release and subsequent generosity," *NY Academy of Science* (June 2009).

25 P. Y. Lin, N. S. Grewal, C. Morin, W. D. Johnson, and P. J. Zak, "Oxytocin increases the influence of public service advertisements," *PLoS One* (2013).

26 *Mind, Society, and Behavior*, International Bank for Reconstruction and Development (2015), www.worldbank.org/content/dam/Worldbank/Publications/WDR/WDR%202015/WDR-2015-Full-Report.pdf.

27 Daniel Kahneman, *Thinking, Fast and Slow* (Farrar, Straus and Giroux, 2011).

28 Dave Gold, "'Data-Driven' Campaigns Are Killing the Democratic Party," *Politico Magazine* (February 9, 2017).

29 Lauren Griffin and Anne Neimand, "Persuasion in a 'Post-Truth' World by Troy Campbell," *Stanford Social Intervention Review* (January 15, 2017).

30 Ibid.

31 Miranda Kennedy, "After Scandals, Ireland Is No Longer 'Most Catholic Country in the World,'" NPR, August 26, 2015, www.npr.org/2015/08/26/434821443/after-scandals-ireland-is-no-longer-the-most-catholic-country-in-the-world.

32 Troy Campbell, Lauren Griffin, and Annie Nieman, *Stanford Social Innovation Review*, "Persuasion in a "Post Truth" World," January 25, 2017, ssir.org/articles/entry/persuasion_in_a_post_truth_world.

33 J. Martin and M. Powers, "Organizational Stories: More Vivid and Persuasive than Quantitative Data," in *Psychological Foundations of Organizational Behavior*, B. Staw (ed.) (Scott, Foresman 1983).

34 Statista Research Department, "The Syrian Civil War – Statistics & facts," Statista, February 7, 2020, www.statista.com/topics/4216/the-syrian-civil-war/.

35 Paul Slovic, "Numbed by Numbers," *Foreign Policy* (March 2007).

36 Berkeley Media Studies Group, www.bmsg.org/.

37 Lawrence Wallack, *News for a Change: An Advocate's Guide to Working with the Media* (Sage Publications, 1999).

[38] "Mr. Fred Rogers: Senate Statement on PBS Funding," delivered May 1, 1969, video, 6:35, American Rhetoric Online Speech Bank, www.americanrhetoric.com/speeches/fredrogerssenatetestimonypbs.ht m.

[39] Frederick W. Mayer, *Narrative Politics: Stories and Collective Action* (Oxford University Press, 2014).

[40] Francesca Polletta, *It Was Like a Fever: Storytelling in Politics and Policy* (University of Chicago Press, 2006).

[41] Ibid.

[42] Arthur Frank, *Letting Stories Breathe: A Socio-Narratology* (University of Chicago Press, 2012).

[43] Mayer, *Narrative Politics*.

[44] Robert Shiller, *Narrative Economics: How Stories Go Viral and Drive Major Economic Events* (Princeton University Press, 2019).

[45] Robert J. Shiller, "Narrative Economics," Cowles Foundation Discussion Paper No. 2069 (January 2017), cowles.yale.edu/sites/default/files/files/pub/d20/d2069.pdf.

[46] Roosevelt Fireside Chat No. 1, March 12, 1933, www.youtube.com/watch?v=r6nYKRLOFWg.

[47] David Armstrong, *Managing by Storying Around* (Currency Books, 1992).

[48] "Top Box Office Logline Examples," Film Daily, accessed November 13, 2020, www.filmdaily.tv/logline/top-box-office-logline-examples.

Chapter 3

[1] Jerome Bruner, *Actual Minds, Possible Worlds* (Harvard University Press, 1986).

[2] Thirty Million Words, Center for Research Informatics, cri.uchicago.edu/portfolio/thirty-million-words/.

[3] Nanopdf.com, "Language Registers," nanopdf.com/download/language-registers-oeyc_pdf.

[4] R. Payne, "A Framework for Understanding Poverty (aha! Process, 1996).

[5] Ruby K. Payne, Philip E. DeVol, and Terie Dreussi Smith, *Bridges Out of Poverty: Strategies for Professionals and Communities* (Bantam Books, 2001).

[6] Begin to Read Staff, "Literacy Statistics," WriteExpress Corporation, accessed November 17, 2020, www.begintoread.com/research/literacystatistics.html.

[7] Christopher Zoukis, "Basic Literacy: A Crucial Tool to Stem School to Prison Pipeline," *Huffington Post*, May 12, 2017.

[8] Ruby K. Payne, "How the Environment of Poverty (Having Fewer Resources) Impacts Cognition and Learning," www.ahaprocess.com/wp-content/uploads/2013/08/Understanding-Poverty-How-Poverty-Impacts-Cognition-Learning.pdf.

[9] Michaeleen Doucleff and Jean Greenhalgh, "The Other Side of Anger: How Inuit Parents Teach Kids to Control Their Anger," NPR (March 13, 2019), www.npr.org/series/688838187/the-other-side-of-anger.

[10] Ibid.

[11] K. Lee, V. Talwar, A. McCarthy, I. Ross, A. Evans, and C. Arruda, "Can Classic Moral Stories Promote Honesty in Children?" *Psychological Science* (2014).

[12] C. E. Smith and M. T. Rizzo, "Children's confession- and lying-related emotion expectancies: Developmental differences and connections to parent-reported confession behavior," *Journal of Experimental Child Psychology* (2017).

[13] Paula Underwood, *Who Speaks for Wolf: A Native American Learning Story* (A Tribe of Two Press, 1983).

[14] Translated by A. Charles Muller, *The Analects of Confucius*, www.acmuller.net/con-dao/analects.html.

[15] Aristotle, *Nicomachean Ethics* (Harvard University Press 1934)

[16] John Dewey, *How We Think* (BN Publishing, 2009).

[17] Peter Pappas, "Taxonomy of Reflection," Copy/Paste (2010), www.peterpappas.com/2010/01/taxonomy-reflection-critical-thinking-students-teachers-principals-.html.

[18] Janie McDrury and Maxine Alterio, *Learning Through Storytelling in Higher Education: Using Reflection and Experience to Improve Learning* (Kogan Page, 2003).

[19] Giada Di Stefano, Francesca Gino, Gary Pisano, and Bradley Staats, "Making Experience Count: The Role of Reflection in Individual Learning," *Harvard Business School NOM Unit Working Paper No. 14-093, Harvard Business School Technology & Operations Mgt. Unit Working Paper No. 14-093, HEC Paris Research Paper No. SPE-2016-1181* (2014).

20 The Leapfrog Group, "Hospital Errors Are the Third Leading Cause of Death in U.S., and New Hospital Safety Scores Show Improvements Are Too Slow," Leapfrog Hospital Safety Grade, October 23, 2013, www.hospitalsafetygrade.org/newsroom/display/hospitalerrors-thirdleading-causeofdeathinus-improvementstooslow.
21 N. Hatton and D. Smith, "Reflection in Teacher Education: Towards Definition and Implementation," *Teaching & Teacher Education* 11, no. 1 (1995).

Chapter 4

1 Plato (translated by Benjamin Jowett), *Apology* in *Five Dialogues* (Digireads.com Publishing, 2015).
2 "Psychological factors and mortality in the Japan Collaborative Cohort Study for Evaluation of Cancer" (JACC), *Asian Pacific Journal of Cancer Prevention* (January 2007).
3 Jerry Mander, *In the Absence of the Sacred: The Failure of Technology and the Survival of the Indian* Nations (Sierra Club Books, 1992).
4 Alan Parry and Robert E. Doan, *Story Re-Visions: Narrative Therapy in the Postmodern World* (Guilford Press, 1994).
5 E. Klinger, "The search for meaning in evolutionary goal-theory perspective and its clinical implications," in P. T. P. Wong (ed.); *The Human Quest for Meaning: Theories, Research, and Applications* (Routledge, 2012).
6 F. Heider and M. Simmel, "An experimental study of apparent behavior," *American Journal of Psychology* 57 (1944).
7 Aaron Antonovsky, *Health, Stress, and Coping* (Jossey-Bass, 1979).
8 James Hillman, *The Soul's Code: In Search of Character and Calling* (Ballantine Books, 2017).
9 Robyn Fivush, Catherine A. Haden, and Elaine Reese, "Elaborating on Elaborations: Role of Maternal Reminiscing Style in Cognitive and Socioemotional Development," *Child Development* 77, no. 6 (November/December 2006).
10 Jennifer G. Bohanek, Kelly A. Marin, Robyn Fivush, and Marshall P. Duke, "Family Narrative Interaction and Children's Sense of Self," *Family Process* 5 (2006).

[11] Robyn Fivush, "Maternal Reminiscing Style and Children's Developing Understanding of Self and Emotion," *Journal of Clinical Social Work* 35 (2007).

[12] A. Bird, E. Reese, and G. Tripp, "Parent–child talk about past emotional events: Associations with child temperament and goodness-of-fit," *Journal of Cognition and Development* 7, no. 2 (2006).

[13] Tilmann Habermas and Susan Bluck, "Getting a life: The emergence of the life story in adolescence," *Psychological Bulletin* 126, no. 5 (2000).

[14] Ibid.

[15] Ernst Bohlmeijer, Marte Roemer, Pim Cuijpers, and Filip Smit, "The effects of reminiscence on psychological well-being in older adults: A meta-analysis," *Aging & Mental Health* (May 2007).

[16] Bruce Rybarcyzk and Albert Bellg, *Listening to Life Stories: A New Approach to Stress Intervention in Health Care* (Sloan Press, 2017).

[17] Encanación Satores, Paz Viguer, and Jaun Carlos Mélendez, "Effectiveness of instrumental reminiscence intervention on improving coping in healthy older adults," *Stress and Health: Journal of the International Society for the investigation of Stress* (2018).

[18] J. C. Meléndez, F. B. Fortuna, A. Sales, and T. Mayordomo, "The effects of instrumental reminiscence on resilience and coping in elderly," *Archives of Gerontology and Geriatrics* (March/April 2015).

[19] About ADAA, "Facts & Statistics," Anxiety and Depression Association of America, accessed November 17, 2020, www.adaa.org/about-adaa/press-room/facts-statistics.

[20] Antonio Machado, "Last Night as I Was Sleeping," Translation Robert Bly, *Times Alone: Selected Poems of Antonio Machado* (Wesleyan University Press, 1983).

[21] H. Karimi, B. Dolatshahee, K. Momeni, A. Khodabakhshi, M. Rezaei, and A. A. Kamrani, "Effectiveness of integrative and instrumental reminiscence therapies on depression symptoms reduction in institutionalized older adults: an empirical study," *Aging Mental Health* (September 2010).

[22] L. M. Watt and P. Cappeliez, "Integrative and instrumental reminiscence therapies for depression in older adults: intervention strategies and treatment effectiveness," *Aging & Mental Health* 4, no. 2 (2000).

[23] S. D. Hollon and J. Garber, "Cognitive therapy for depression: A social cognitive perspective," *Personality and Social Psychology Bulletin* 16 (1990).

[24] Sonja Lyubomirsky, Lorie Sousa, and Rene Dickerhoof, "The Costs and Benefits of Writing, Talking, and Thinking About Life's Triumphs and Defeats," *Journal of Personality and Social Psychology* 90, no. 4 (2006).

[25] Martin Buber, *Tales of the Hasidim* (Schocken, 1991).

[26] Parker J. Palmer, "Are You Listening to Your Life? It can take a long time to become yourself," *O, The Oprah Magazine* (January 2001).

[27] Thomas Curran, Andrew P. Hill, Paul R. Appleton, Robert J. Vallerand, and Martyn Standage, "The psychology of passion: A meta-analytical review of a decade of research on intrapersonal outcomes," *Motivation and Emotion* 39, no. 5 (October 2015).

[28] Richard Leider, The Inventure Company, richardleider.com/calling-cards/.

[29] Michele W. Gazica and Paul E. Spector, "A comparison of individuals with unanswered callings to those with no calling at all," *Journal of Vocational Behavior* 91 (December 2015).

Chapter 5

[1] Jennifer Lin, "Chinese Folk Tales: The Lost Horse (A Blessing in Disguise)," The Daily China, April 16, 2018, www.thedailychina.org/chinese-folk-tales-the-lost-horse-a-blessing-in-disguise-%E5%A1%9E%E7%BF%81%E5%A4%B1%E9%A6%AC/.

[2] Bob and Lisa Gfeller, personal interview with Richard Stone, August 2018.

[3] J.R.R. Tolkien, "On Fairy-Stories," initially written (and entitled simply "Fairy Stories") for presentation by Tolkien as the Andrew Lang lecture at the University of St. Andrews, Scotland (March 8, 1939).

[4] Igor Grossman and Ethan Kross, "Exploring Solomon's Paradox: Self Distancing Eliminates the Self-Other Asymmetry in Wise Reasoning About Close Relationships in Younger and Older Adults," *Psychological Science* (2014).

[5] E. Kross and O. Ayduk, "Self-Distancing: Theory, Research, and Current Directions," *Advances in Experimental Social Psychology* (2016).

[6] A. T. Beck, "Cognitive therapy: Nature and relation to behavior therapy," *Behavior Therapy* 1, no. 2 (1970).

[7] E. Kross and O. Ayduk, "Facilitating adaptive emotional analysis: Distinguishing distanced-analysis of depressive experiences from immersed-analysis and distraction," *Personality and Social Psychology Bulletin* 34, no. 7 (2008).

[8] B. E. Wisco, B. P. Marx, D. M. Sloan, K. R. Gorman, A. L. Kulish, and S. L. Pineles, "Self-distancing from trauma memories reduces physiological but not subjective emotional reactivity among Veterans with posttraumatic stress disorder," *Clinical Psychological Science* 3, no. 6 (2015), 956–963.

[9] E. Kross, M. Davidson, J. Weber, J., and K. Ochsner, "Coping with emotions past: The neural bases of regulating affect associated with negative autobiographical memories," *Biological Psychiatry* 65, no. 5 (2009).

[10] Viktor Frankl, *Man's Search for Meaning* (Beacon Press, 2017).

[11] Sam Keen, *Your Mythic Journey: Finding Meaning in Your Life Through Writing and Storytelling* (TarcherPerigree, 1989).

[12] Donald Davis, "How the story transforms the teller," TEDxCharlottesville, www.youtube.com/watch?v=wgeh4xhSA2Q.

[13] Michael White, *Narrative Therapy Classics* (Dulwich Centre Publications, 2016).

[14] Adam Grant and Jane Dutton, "Beneficiary or Benefactor: Are People More Prosocial When They Reflect on Receiving or Giving?" *Psychological Science* 23, no. 9 (2012).

[15] Timothy Wilson, *Redirect: Changing the Stories We Live By* (Back Bay Books, 2015).

[16] Ibid., 16.

[17] Steve Denning, personal interview with Richard Stone, 1995 and 2020.

[18] USC - The Tamale Lesson: Narrative Education on Cervical Cancer, www.youtube.com/watch?v=Lyhv9KmLroc.

[19] Arvind Singhal and Rafael Obregon, "Reconstructing the story of Simplemente Maria, the most popular telenovela in Latin America of all time," *International Communication Gazette* (August 1995).

[20] Paul and Anne Ehrlich, *The Population Bomb* (Buccaneer Books, 1995).

²¹ Danielle Arigo and Joshua M. Smyth, "The benefits of expressive writing on sleep difficulty and appearance concerns for college women," *Psychology & Health* 27, no. 2 (January 2011).

²² H. E. Koschwanez, N. Kerse, M. Darragh, P. Jarrett, R. J. Booth, and E. Broadbent, "Expressive writing and wound healing in older adults: A randomized controlled trial," *Psychosomatic Medicine* 75, no. 6 (2013).

²³ Mark Lumley, James Leisen, Ty Partridge, Tina Meyer, Alison Radcliffe, Debra Macklem, Linda Naoum, Jay Cohen, Lydia Lasichak, Michael Lubetsky, Angelia Mosley-Williams, and Jose Granda, "Does emotional disclosure about stress improve health in rheumatoid arthritis? Randomized, controlled trials of written and spoken disclosure," *Pain* 152, no. 4 (April 2011).

²⁴ M. A. Lumley and K. M. Provenzano, "Stress management through emotional disclosure improves academic performance among college students with physical symptoms," *Journal of Educational Psychology* 95 (2002).

²⁵ K. M. McGuire, M. A. Greenberg, and R. Gevirtz, "Autonomic effects of expressive writing in individuals with elevated blood pressure," *Journal of Health Psychology* 10, no. 2 (2005).

²⁶ Carl de Moor, Janet Sterner, Martica H. Hall, and Carla L. Warneke, "A pilot study of the effects of expressive writing in a phase II trial of vaccine therapy for metastatic renal cell carcinoma," *Health Psychology* 21, no. 6 (December 2002).

²⁷ James W. Pennebaker and John F. Evans, *Expressive Writing: Words that Heal* (Idyll Arbor, 2014).

²⁸ Ibid.

²⁹ Stephen Denning, *The Springboard: How Storytelling Ignites Action in Knowledge-Era Organizations* (KMCI Press, 2000).

Chapter 6

¹ Pat Speight, Storyteller in Residence to Cork County Council, Ireland.

² About *Mankind Quarterly*, accessed November 13, 2020, www.mankindquarterly.org/about.

³ George Lakoff, *Don't Think of an Elephant!: Know Your Values and Frame the Debate* (Chelsea Green Publishing, 2014).

⁴ Ibid.

[5] Rabbi Jonathan Sacks, "C&C Family Edition: Loving the Stranger" (Mishpatim 5779), rabbisacks.org/cc-family-edition-mishpatim-5779/.

[6] Stephen Carter, *Civility* (Harper Perennial, 1998).

[7] Ibid.

[8] Charles G. Lord, Mark R. Lepper, and Elizabeth Preston, "Considering the Opposite: A Corrective Strategy for Social Judgment," *Journal of Personality and Social Psychology* 47 (1984).

[9] Molly Andrews, *Narrative Imagination and Everyday Life* (Oxford University Press, 2014).

[10] Katharine Hayhoe, "I'm a Climate Scientist Who Believes in God. Hear Me Out," *New York Times* (October 31, 2019).

[11] Antonya M. Gonzalez, Jennifer R. Steele, and Andrew S. Baron, "Reducing Children's Implicit Racial Bias Through Exposure to Positive Out-Group Exemplars," *Child Development* (2016).

[12] N. Dasgupta and A. G. Greenwald, "On the malleability of automatic attitudes: Combating automatic prejudice with images of admired and disliked individuals," *Journal of Personality and Social Psychology* 81 (2001).

[13] Dan R. Johnson, Brandie L. Huffman, and Danny M. Jasper, "Changing Race Boundary Perception by Reading Narrative Fiction," *Basic and Applied Social Psychology* 36, no. 1 (2014).

[14] *International Criminal Tribunal for Rwanda – UNICTR*, International Organizations (2012), archived website, www.loc.gov/item/lcwaN0010101/.

[15] Hollie Nyseth Brehm and Laura C. Frizzell, "They Committed Genocide. Their Neighbors Welcomed Them Home," *New York Times* (April 24, 2019).

[16] Combatants for Peace, cfpeace.org.

[17] Ibid.

[18] Combatants for Peace, cfpeace.org/personal-stories/maia-hascal/.

[19] Ibid.

[20] Ibid.

[21] Paul Costello, personal interview with Richard Stone, 2019.

[22] Michael White, *Maps of Narrative Practice* (W. W. Norton & Company, 2007).

[23] Costello, interview with Stone.

[24] Storywise – The Center for Narrative Studies, "Notes on Listening," storywise.com/index.php/2017/12/18/notes-on-listening/.
[25] Martin Buber, *I and Thou* (Touchstone, 1971).
[26] Rabbi Jonathan Sacks, "The Home We Build Together," rabbisacks.org/rabbi-sacks-home-build-together/.
[27] Ibid.

Chapter 7

[1] Andrews, *Narrative Imagination and Everyday Life.*
[2] Lori Ansbach Eckert, "The Effects of Mental Imagery on Free Throw Performance," Kinesiology, Sport Studies, and Physical Education Master's Theses (1989), digitalcommons.brockport.edu/pes_theses/3.
[3] L. V. Clark, "Effect of mental practice on the development of certain motor skills," *Research Quarterly* (1960).
[4] E. Ryan and J. Simons, "Efficiency of mental imagery in enhancing mental rehearsal of motor skills," *Journal of Sports Psychology* 4, no. 1 (1982).
[5] Daniel T. Gilbert and Timothy D. Wilson, "Prospection: Experiencing the Future," *SCIENCE* 317 (September 7, 2007).
[6] Karl K. Szpunar and Daniel L. Schacter, "Get real: Effects of repeated simulation and emotion on the perceived plausibility of future experiences," *Journal of Experimental Psychology: General* 142 (2013).
[7] F.C.M. Dassen, A. Jansen, C. Nederkoorn, and K. Houben, "Focus on the future: episodic future thinking reduces discount rate and snacking," *Appetite* (2016).
[8] J. O'Neill, T. O. Daniel, and L. H. Epstein, "Episodic future thinking reduces eating in a food court," *Eating Behaviors* (2016).
[9] H. G. Jing, K. P. Madore, and D. L. Schacter, "Worrying about the future: an episodic specificity induction impacts problem solving, reappraisal, and well-being," *Journal of Experimental Psychology: General* (2016).
[10] M. Altgassen, P. G. Rendell, A. Bernhard, J. D. Henry, P. E. Bailey, L. H. Phillips, and M. Kliegel, "Future thinking improves prospective memory performance and plan enactment in older adults," *Quarterly Journal of Experimental Psychology* (2015).

[11] A.E.G.F. Arnold, G. Iaria, and A. D. Ekstrom, "Mental simulation of routes during navigation involves adaptive temporal compression," *Cognition* (2016).

[12] D. Morisano, J. B. Hirsh, J. B.Peterson, B. Shore, and R. O. Pihl, "Personal goal setting, reflection, and elaboration improves academic performance in university students," *Journal of Applied Psychology* (2010).

[13] Priyali Rajagopal and Nicole Votolato Montgomery, "I Imagine, I Experience, I Like: The False Experience Effect," *Journal of Consumer Research* 38, no. 3 (2011).

[14] L. A. King, "The health benefits of writing about life goals," *Personality and Social Psychology Bulletin* 27, no. 7 (2001).

[15] Gilbert and Wilson, "Prospection: Experiencing the Future."

[16] S. Schubert, L. Caviola, and N. S. Faber, "The Psychology of Existential Risk: Moral Judgments about Human Extinction," *Scientific Reports* 9 (2019).

[17] Jared Diamond, *Collapse* (Penguin Books, 2011).

[18] Sabine Pahl, Stephen Sheppard, Christine Boomsma, and Christopher Groves, "Perceptions of time in relation to climate change," *Wires Climate Change* 5, no. 3 (May/June 2014).

[19] B. Tonn, A. Hemrick, and F. Conrad, "Cognitive representations of the future: survey results," *Futures* (2006).

[20] Energy Policy Institute at the University of Chicago, "New Poll: Nearly Half Of Americans Are More Convinced Than They Were Five Years Ago That Climate Change Is Happening, With Extreme Weather Driving Their Views," epic.uchicago.edu/news/new-poll-nearly-half-of-americans-are-more-convinced-than-they-were-five-years-ago-that-climate-change-is-happening-with-extreme-weather-driving-their-views/.

[21] Gordon Shaw, Robert Brown, and Philip Bromiley, "Strategic Stories: How 3M Is Rewriting Business Planning," *Harvard Business Review* (May–June 1998).

[22] Ibid.

[23] IDEAS Orlando, ideasorlando.com/.

[24] Richard Pascale, Jerry Sternin, and Monique Sternin, *The Power of Positive Deviance: How Unlikely Innovators Solve the World's Toughest Problems* (Harvard Business Press, 2010).

[25] Nicky González Yuen, *The Politics of Liberation: An American Studies Primer* (Kendall Hunt Publishing, 2003).

Epilogue

[1] Muriel Rukeyser, *The Speed of Darkness* (Vintage, 1971).
[2] Carl Sagan, *Cosmos* (Random House, 1983).

About the Authors

Richard Stone

For the past thirty years, Richard has been assisting organizations across the country to tell their story better. As CEO of StoryWork International, he has been pioneering new approaches to bringing the practical applications of storytelling into all facets of business, healthcare, education, and society. In the healthcare sector, he's the co-creator of StoryCare, a web-based product to help healthcare organizations improve patient safety and help educators better prepare nurses and doctors. Richard also created the LivingStories program for Novant Health, which facilitates patients' telling their life stories to improve their health outcomes. He codeveloped the award-winning board game Pitch-A-Story and is a recognized national speaker in addition to authoring numerous books. When Richard is not writing or telling stories, he is an accomplished visual artist, and you can see some of his work at www.richardstoneart.com. He earned a MS in clinical psychology from Peabody College at Vanderbilt University.

Scott Livengood

Scott has devoted the lion's share of his working career to leading major organizations, first as CEO of Krispy Kreme Doughnuts. Currently, he's an owner and executive director of Dewey's Bakery, a national purveyor of premium, Southern-inspired cookies and crackers headquartered in Winston-Salem, North

Carolina. But his real work has always been about story, both defining and executing the brand story of the companies he has led, and through his lifelong exploration of how to use story to impact every facet of his own personal and professional journey. As Chairman of StoryWork International, Scott provides the strategic guidance to the company's direction as he and Richard have developed the MasterStory Experience—a transformational program designed to assist a company and its leaders discover their deeper purpose and how to live it. Scott earned his BS from the University of North Carolina, and he and his wife, Michelle, are active in the community, both through Dewey's and the Livengood Family Foundation.

StoryWork International

If you don't know the trees, you may be lost in the forest,
but if you don't know the stories, you may be lost in life.

—Siberian elder

We created StoryWork International (SWI) to advance and promote a world where people, communities, organizations, institutions, and countries constructively employ the universal language of story to foster cooperative relationships. SWI is also working to develop employment and organizational models that emanate from a commitment to mutual value creation and fully engage people's gifts, talents, and callings. In healthcare, we endeavor to enhance healing environments. In education, we want to elevate the desire and potential for learning. Most importantly, we wish to gain insights and pathways for building inclusivity and unity that expand our understanding of the multifaceted potential of the human spirit when it is awakened, aware, and inspired.

Our mission is to align people and communities with the narratives that elevate their possibilities and potential and bring them to life. We are also committed to supporting and nurturing applied research into the power of story, storytelling, and story sharing. In the years ahead, we endeavor to expand the understanding of story through:

- **Convening:** Bringing together thought leaders from the world of applied storytelling as well as experts from a range of disciplines to brainstorm, innovate, and imagine ways story can enhance and elevate work in their field, including education, business, government, conflict resolution, healthcare, economic justice, journalism, and law enforcement.

- **Public Conferences:** Hosting educational conferences open to the broader public to explore the applications of story, storytelling, and story sharing to address local and global challenges and opportunities.
- **Research:** Supporting cutting-edge research that can demonstrate the efficacy of story, storytelling, and story sharing in various fields.
- **Demonstration Projects:** Nurturing concepts and ideas that we can then translate into real-world applications.
- **Media:** Just as the seminal Bill Moyers' interviews of Joseph Campbell socialized his work with a broader community, SWI endeavors to do the same with current thinkers. These interviews will be made available through social media channels and broadcast through more conventional media outlets.
- **Publishing:** Supporting the work of thought leaders to write and publish new books that focus on the power of Story Intelligence.
- **Workshops:** Providing the public, corporations, and government entities high-level training to expand the Story Intelligence of their teams and the individuals whom they serve.
- **Speaking:** Sharing the wealth of what we are learning about the power of Story Intelligence with audiences everywhere.

Other Books by Richard Stone

Stories: The Family Legacy

The Healing Art of Storytelling

The Kingdom of Nowt

The Patient Survival Handbook